UNCERTAIN FUTURES

Foster Youth in Transition to Adulthood

by Edmund V. Mech, PhD
University of Illinois at Urbana-Champaign

With contributions from

Hewitt B. Clark, PhD

Carrie C. Fung, MSW, JD

Betsy Krebs, JD

Mark Kroner, MSW

Elizabeth L. Leonard, MSW

Janet Legler Luft, LMSW-AP

Dagmar Moravec, MSC

Michael Olenick, PhD

Paul Pitcoff, JD

Lora Schmid-Dolan, MSW

CWLA PRESS
Washington, DC

CWLA Press is an imprint of the Child Welfare League of America. The Child Welfare League of America is the nation's oldest and largest membership-based child welfare organization. We are committed to engaging people everywhere in promoting the well-being of children, youth, and their families, and protecting every child from harm.

CHILD WELFARE LEAGUE OF AMERICA, INC.
HEADQUARTERS
440 First Street, NW, Third Floor, Washington, DC 20001-2085
E-mail: books@cwla.org

CURRENT PRINTING (last digit)
10 9 8 7 6 5 4 3 2 1

Cover design by Michael Rae and text design by Jennifer R. Geanakos
Edited by Julie Gwin

Printed in the United States of America

ISBN # 0–87868-869-2

Library of Congress Cataloging-in-Publication Data
Mech, Edmund V.
    Uncertain futures : foster youth in transition to adulthood / by
Edmund V. Mech ; foreword, John D. Rockefeller IV ; with contributions
    from Hewitt B. "Rusty" Clark ... [et al.].
        p. cm.
    Includes bibliographical references.
    ISBN 0-87868-869-2 (alk. paper)
    1. Youth—Services for—United States. 2. Foster children—
        Deinstitutionalization—United States. I. Clark, Hewitt B.
    II. Child Welfare League of America. III. Title.
HV1431 .M37 2003
362.73'3'0973—dc21   2002152824

Contents

Chapter 5

Chapter 6

Chapter 7

Chapter 8

Chapter 9

Chapter 10

Chapter 11

Chapter 12

Chapter 13

Chapter 14

Chapter 15

Community College Opportunities for Older Foster Youth: The California Profile 221

Chapter 16

Personal Responsibility: A Goal for Adolescents in Foster Care 231

Chapter 17

Wraparound Services: Facilitating the Transition from Foster Care to Young Adulthood 243

Chapter 18

Assessment: An Interpretive Summary 253

Appendix 1

Foster Care Independence Act of 1999 273

Appendix 2

Transition to Adulthood:
  A Foster Youth Resource Inventory 279

Appendix 3

National Youth-in-Transition Database 285

Tables

Foreword

For many years, I have worked in the Senate to improve our child welfare system, including the independent living program, which is intended to help teens in foster care make a successful transition to adulthood. Such teens need and deserve support and understanding. *Uncertain Futures* provides information and insight into the needs of such teenagers, as well as a summary of the public policies that affect them.

Although I have worked on child welfare issues for many years, my specific interest in the independent living program began in 1999. At the request of Senator John Chafee, I helped host a meeting of young people who had aged out of foster care. They were a remarkable group and were willing to share their own tragic stories in the hope of improving the foster care system for others. Each young person had struggled in the system, and some had endured homelessness. But each person overcame obstacles and each person was eager to give back to their community and help other teens. It was a moving meeting. The stories of those teens and others inspired the Senate to enact reforms of the independent living program, which was later named in honor of Senator Chafee. Throughout his distinguished career, Senator Chafee was a leader in child welfare, health care, and a wide range of other social policy issues.

The Chafee Independent Living Act is an important start in the ongoing effort to help teenagers move from foster care into adulthood. To achieve these bold goals, however, many people need to understand the issues facing such teenagers and work together to create programs to provide the support that such teens need in communities across our country. This book can help achieve this important goal by increasing the understanding of officials, caseworkers, and caring adults about the challenges facing teens in foster care. Learning more about foster care and the children in the system is crucial to developing public support to change the distressing statistics about many children in foster care, especially teens as they age out of the system.

—*Senator John D. Rockefeller, IV*

Comment

Enactment of the John H. Chafee Foster Care Independence Act of 1999 was one of my late father's most rewarding achievements as a senator. He understood that expanding the assistance available to foster youth is a valuable investment, because graduates of our nation's foster care system have tremendous potential to contribute to society. Dr. Edmund Mech's book, *Uncertain Futures*, helps draw attention to the great outcomes that can be achieved when foster youth are given the tools they need to live productive and fulfilling lives as adults. Dr. Mech draws on years of valuable experience in the areas of child welfare and foster youth, and this book will be a valuable resource for those who work in this field.

—*Lincoln Chafee, U.S. Senator (RI), son of the late John H. Chafee*

Preface

Uncertain Futures is about foster youth in transition to adulthood. Thousands of young wards age out of state care without the knowledge, skills, or preparation to be able to compete in a technological society. Nearly 500,000 children and youth are currently in out-of-home placement. Of this number, 30% to 35% are adolescents. Each year, 25,000 to 30,000 young people approximately 18 years old emancipate from care. Once emancipated, the majority struggle for economic survival. Many transfer from one dependency system to another, including public aid, food stamps, housing subsidies, and other societal supports. Studies are consistent in documenting low educational attainment, unemployment, early parenting, and high rates of homelessness. The inescapable conclusion is that their potential for self-sufficiency and independence is low. Experts are concerned that a foster-care underclass is evolving. The dismal results cited in research have captured the attention of child welfare administrators, youth advocates, citizen groups, and state and federal lawmakers. Emphasis in this volume is on the best practices to prepare foster youths for independent living. This text is evidence based, in that its content reflects state-of-the-art ideas from practice and research with the aim of improving transitional programs for young people leaving placement. The book includes information about transitional issues in moving from adolescence to adulthood, school-to-work expectations, legislative requirements contained in the Foster Care Independence Act of 1999, analysis of state-level programs for independent-living, use of subsidies as aging-out supports for older wards, the experiences of graduates of the foster care system, the role of scattered-site apartments in promoting independent behavior in foster wards, effective practices in facilitating career preparation, comparative profiles of "successful" and "unsuccessful" graduates of foster care, and a blueprint for the improvement of independent-living services.

There is a need for a text in this area. Many articles are written on independent living, but no single work exists that integrates and interprets the knowledge base relative to preparing foster wards for independence. Independent-living preparation is now a permanent aspect of child welfare practice. The essential theme of this book is that society has a major social and financial investment in foster care. Most wards who age out have spent five or more years in care, have experienced "progressive insertion" into placements rated as highly restrictive, have gone through multiple placements, have changed schools many times, and on leaving state care, are ill prepared to make it on their own. The cost to the community in the postdischarge period is considerable, and it is manifested in periodic homelessness, reliance on public aid, and impaired capacity to become productive citizens and self-supporting members of their community. The assumption that underlies this book is the necessity to build opportunity structures that permit young wards to more easily make a transition to self-sufficiency.

Federal legislation authorizing expenditures for foster youth independent-living services is a major step forward. The contributions of legislative pioneers such as Senator Daniel Patrick Moynihan, Senator John Chafee (Rhode Island), Senator John Rockefeller (West Virginia), and Representatives Robert Matsui (California), Nancy Johnson (Connecticut), and Ben Cardin (Maryland), plus numerous other congressional leaders, attests to the importance of the independent-living initiatives. Introduced in the U.S. House of Representatives in May 1999 by Representatives Nancy Johnson and Ben Cardin, the proposed Foster Care Independence bill provided extended support for youth aging out of foster care. A companion bill, S. 1327, was introduced in the U.S. Senate by Senator John Chafee and cosponsored by Senator John D. Rockefeller IV. The Foster Care Independence Act of 1999 represents a miniature G.I. Bill for youth in placement. Hopes are high that state child welfare agencies can build an independent-living services infrastructure that makes it possible for youth in placement to achieve successful transitions to adulthood.

There are multiple audiences for this book. They include independent-living specialists, state agency coordinators, public and private agency staff, youth advocacy groups, foster parents, child care workers in residential settings, organizations with interest and expertise in family law, juvenile court judges, and legislative staff for state and federal lawmakers. Workshops, seminars, and training modules in child welfare services sponsored by schools of social work can benefit by incorporating content on preparing foster wards for independence. Preparing young people for effective adult living is an issue that transcends national boundaries. The text includes material from countries other than the United States. Australia, Canada, Germany, Great Britain, and Norway are examples of countries with a vested interest in preparing youth in care for self-sufficiency and productive citizenship.

The volume is divided into five parts. Part 1 describes the evolution of program, policy, and legislation in the United States toward building a youth transition system that enhances independence and self-sufficiency. Part 2 analyzes the status of independent-living programs with respect to preparing foster wards for self-sufficiency. Part 3 discusses program and service interventions that are likely to make a difference in helping foster wards transition to self-sufficiency. Working within an evidence-based framework, topics covered include: subsidies—including educational assistance and tuition waivers—mentors for adolescents in placement, transitional apartments with emphasis on scattered-site arrangements, use of natural systems resources in developing and implementing wraparound plans, and increased use of specialized foster homes in preparing foster wards for independence.

Part 4 contains contributions from program specialists and master practitioners in various areas of independent-living services. Contributors are: Janet Luft, who describes trends in emancipation services in the state of Texas; Mark Kroner, Lighthouse Services in Cincinnati, Ohio, who discusses apartment options as preparation for independence; Dr. Michael Olenick, Division Chief for Emancipation Services, Los Angeles County Department of Children and Family Services, who describes opportunities for foster wards in California to access postsecondary education; Betsy Krebs and Paul Pitcoff from the Youth Advocacy Center in New York City, who discuss independent-living services from a legal perspective; and Dagmar Moravec, a wraparound service practitioner in Lansing, Michigan, and Dr. Hewitt B. "Rusty" Clark from the University of South Florida in Tampa, who discuss the applications of the wraparound process to preparing foster wards for independence.

Part 5 provides an assessment and interpretive summary of trends in emancipation services. Emphasis is on: (a) developing transitional structures that provide opportunities for youths to prepare for independence, (b) the importance of state agencies and service providers to implement programs and services in accordance with state plans, and (c) increased emphasis on knowledge building and program experimentation. Providing services that are evidence based depends on continued analysis and testing of program and practice concepts. The ultimate arbiters and referees of what works and what does not are the service providers and foster youth who are the recipients of services.

—*Edmund V. Mech, PhD*
Chartwell On-the-Bay
Bellingham, WA

Acknowledgments

FOR ELIZABETH LINDEMAN LEONARD—
PARTNER, FRIEND, AND COLLEAGUE

A book such as *Uncertain Futures* requires contributions from many sources. It is a pleasure to acknowledge support received from Lilly Endowment, Inc., for preparation of this book (Grant No. 1997 1387-000). Mr. Willis K. Bright, Jr., Director, Youth Programs at Lilly Endowment, served as project officer for this work. His support, encouragement, and guidance are acknowledged with gratitude. Willis Bright has never wavered in his belief in the achievement potential of the thousands of young people in foster care or in their ability to become productive citizens. It is our hope that this volume contributes in some measure to the improvement of independent-living services for youth in placement. In addition to Lilly Endowment support over the past decade for our research and dissemination efforts, we acknowledge with appreciation grant support received from the William T. Grant Foundation in New York City, and the U.S. Department of Health and Human Services, Administration on Children, Youth and Families, Children's Bureau, Washington, D.C. The combined Lilly Endowment–William T. Grant Awards made it possible to conduct a major prospective aging-out study of foster youths in Illinois, Indiana, and Ohio. The Foster Youth Project, conducted under the auspices of the University of Illinois at Urbana-Champaign, was able to collect information about youths leaving care at ages 18, 21, and 28. Nearly

1,000 interviews were completed in the follow-up periods. A research award from the Administration on Children, Youth and Families, Children's Bureau, made possible a national study of mentors for adolescents in foster care. The researchers studied 29 programs across 15 states. We collected information on several hundred mentor-mentee matches. Our concept of an evidence-based text was to draw on empirical data sources whenever possible and to supplement quantitative information with qualitative case–style vignettes. It is a pleasure to acknowledge an outstanding University of Illinois research team, who, over a 10-year period, conducted field work, assisted with data analysis, contributed to report preparation, and participated in the dissemination and publication of data. Data collection for the Foster Youth Follow-up project was coordinated by Elizabeth Leonard, MSW, Research Associate. Julie Pryde, MSW, Research Associate, supervised data collection for the National Foster Youth Mentor Project. I convey my personal thanks to the indispensable "A" team, who worked long hours, spending time away from family, friends, and colleagues to conduct interviews that required travel from Maine to Florida, Illinois to California, and points in between. Members of this special unit are listed in alphabetical order: Carrie Che-Man Fung, MSW, JD; Frances Hulseman, MSW; Christine Ludy-Dobson, MSW, PhD; Lisa Merkel, MSW; Julie A. Pryde, MSW; and Lora Schmid-Dolan, MSW.

It was a pleasure to conduct this project under the auspices of the University of Illinois at Urbana-Champaign. The resources and support available in a major research university made our task easier. As Principal Investigator for the Foster Youth Research program, it was comforting to learn that the case files, original interviews, and all raw data for the mentor project and foster youth follow-up are now housed in the University of Illinois Archives, where they are available to graduate students, faculty, and research investigators for review and further analysis.

The decision of the Child Welfare League of America (CWLA) to publish *Uncertain Futures* is appreciated. CWLA is in a unique position to reach hundreds of agencies and their staffs, not only in the United States but also in Canada, the United Kingdom, Western Europe, and Australia, where much emphasis is placed on preparing young people in care for self-sufficiency. I want to acknowledge with appreciation the contributions of an outstanding manuscript team for helping prepare this book for publication. With gratitude to:

- Debra Sams, for typing draft chapters of the manuscript;

- Jeannie Gilbert, for meticulous attention to detail in verifying sources and content, and for providing invaluable assistance in finalizing the manuscript; and

- Julie Gwin, CWLA, whose editorial queries, comments, and decisions were vital in helping move this book across the finish line.

Finally, thanks to all persons and organizations, named and unnamed, who have contributed or are contributing to the advancement of independent-living services as a movement and as a field of practice that can make a difference in the futures of foster youth.

—Edmund V. Mech, PhD
Chartwell On-the-Bay
Bellingham, WA

Transition Systems for Youth

Edmund V. Mech

*Every society must somehow solve the
problem of transforming children into adults,
for its very survival depends on that solution.*

—President's Science Advisory Committee,
Panel on Youth (1974, p. 1)

Societies, communities, and families have a major stake in preparing young people for responsible adulthood. Making the transition from adolescent to adult is a critical task in the process of life-course development. All youth must make this journey. For some, the path is made easier by support, resources, and the presence of enablers and people who help the youth. For others, the transition from adolescence to adulthood is difficult and devoid of support, assistance, or encouragement.

Transitional periods are characterized by uncertainties that individuals face in learning to respond to a series of new and unfamiliar developmental challenges. Leaving adolescence and moving into adulthood is a critical transition. Relationships with family, peers, churches, and community institutions are redefined or terminated. Matters associated with progressing toward self-sufficiency, such as making career decisions, assuming responsibility for decisionmaking, and acquiring the knowledge and skills for adult living must be confronted. At some point, all young people in out-of-home care must leave the jurisdiction of the child welfare system and enter the world of adult living.

For youth who grow up at the margins of society, as is the case with thousands of adolescents who each year emancipate from foster care, the road ahead is risky and problematic. Young people in transition to adulthood are a heterogeneous and diverse population. Many factors influence transitional progress, including socioeconomic position, race and gender, family characteristics in terms of composition and resources, individual orientation toward achieving self-sufficiency, and the extent to which community resources are available and accessible to the youth in transition.

Transitional Expectations for Adulthood

Transitions are changes that occur within certain time frames and/or developmental periods. Transitional stages are usually age related and concerned with normative expectations for a particular age group or stage of human development. With respect to the transition from adolescence to adulthood, the expectation is that young people will move from dependency toward independence, self-sufficiency, and responsible citizenship. Society has established a series of normative targets or expectations for young people preparing for adult living. Human development theorists refer to these expectations as developmental tasks. A *developmental task* is defined as

> *a task which arises at or about a certain period in the life of an individual, successful achievement of which leads to his happiness and to success with later tasks, while failure leads to unhappiness in the individual, disapproval by the society, and difficulty with later tasks. (Havighurst, 1953)*

The developmental tasks of early adulthood span a decade, beginning at age 18 and continuing until about age 30. The United States is a pragmatic nation, and the tasks of early adulthood reflect a utilitarian philosophy. The essential expectations include five elements:

1. **Family Formation**—Selecting a partner, starting a family, and raising children.

2. **Adequate Housing**—Issues of affordable housing and home ownership are paramount, as are the routines of managing a home. Responsible home management means paying bills, managing money, living within a budget, and maintaining one's house and property in good condition.

3. **Completion of Education**—The high school diploma is considered as a minimal educational standard for transitioning to adulthood. Proficiency in reading, writing, and computational skills are viewed as essential for adult living.

4. **World-of-Work Connections**—It is expected that youth in transition will begin an occupation—preferably one that offers career-ladder opportunities—or prepare for entering a recognized profession.

5. **Social, Community, and Civic Involvement**—Finding a compatible social group, developing friendships, getting connected with a neighborhood organization, becoming active in a religious group, or becoming affiliated with a political and/or social action movement can contribute to the quality of life in one's community. Although participation in significant elements of community life is difficult in the early stages of transitioning to adulthood, the mature adult will seek to establish community connections at some point in the transitional process.

Assessment of Transitional Systems for Youth

The structure, scope, and effectiveness of transitional systems for the nation's youth are receiving close scrutiny. So far, the report card is pessimistic. In theory, the major transitional systems—families, schools, employment and training programs, community youth and recreational organizations, religious groups, labor unions, and businesses and industries—should operate in concert to facilitate the movement of young people to adulthood. In reality, transitional systems for young people in America are characterized by fragmentation, discontinuity, and structural deficiencies. Assessments by the President's Science Advisory Committee, Panel on Youth (1974), and the National Commission on Youth (1980) document numerous shortcomings in the nation's transition-to-adulthood strategy. The assessment profile prepared by the National Commission on Youth highlights the following concerns:

- **Traditional Systems Are Breaking Down.** Many of the traditional systems that help prepare youth for adulthood are breaking down. The declining role of family units is cited as a weakness. Schools are criticized for failure to teach marketable skills to pupils. The commission expressed concern that although many students complete school and are awarded a diploma, large numbers lack practical knowledge to compete in the marketplace.

- **Overemphasis on a School-Based Transitional Strategy.** The commission expressed concern that the public school has emerged as the main vehicle for socializing, educating, and preparing young people for transitioning to adulthood. A school-based strategy is now the dominant transitional mechanism. Schools have replaced and/or diminished the family, workplace, church, and community as settings that help prepare youth for adulthood.

- **Schools Lack Transitional Reality.** Separation of traditional school-based education from actual work and real-life situations tends to delay the transition to adulthood. Influenced by the Progressive Education movement, the proposed solution was for schools to provide pupils with experiences that simulate real-life situations. Several decades of experience with attempts to bring real-world situations into the school have received mixed reviews. The President's Science Advisory Committee, Panel on Youth (1974), offered the observation that school learning is not perceived by students as the real world. School assignments lack the discipline of production goals that are established by marketplace standards. In real-world situations, employees can be fired from jobs for shoddy performance, poor attitudes and work habits, or lack of punctuality. Conversely, it is not possible to fire a student from school. Compulsory education statutes require school attendance. Also, use of grades as rewards probably act as intrinsic motivators for a relatively small number of students.

- **Age Segregation of Youth.** Social historians, educators, and theorists, including anthropologists, sociologists, and psychologists, are consistent in noting that contemporary society increases the transitional difficulties of adolescents by the common practice of age segregation in schools. One viewpoint is that placing adolescents in same-age educational settings tends to slow down and/or interfere with the transitional process. Anthropologists Schlegel and Barry (1991) concluded that "the transformation of the adolescent social setting from one of apprentice to a parent or other adult to one composed primarily of peers has marked effects" (p. 179). The essential point is that the practice of segregating youth by age reduces the chances of meaningful contact with adults in work-related settings, other than with family members or schoolteachers.

    A by-product of age segregation is the emergence of a youth culture in which adolescents view themselves as outsiders, who are often at odds with the system. The age-segregation phenomenon has an insulating effect that tends to isolate youth from mainstream adult society. One outcome is a delay in the transitional process and a perception on the part of youth that they have no meaningful role to play in the community. The President's Science Advisory Committee, Panel on Youth (1974), concluded that "a major means by which skills, culture, ideas, and information is transmitted is vanishing as direct contacts between youth and adults...decline" (p. 132).

- **Transition from School to Work.** The United States keeps its young people in school longer than any other country. The assumption that underlies the strategy of extended education is that schools can prepare young people for adult living, including employment, citizenship, and social responsibility. The problem for youth-in-transition programs is that universal secondary education is geared to prepare students for subsequent schooling and favors students who are headed for colleges and university study, including graduate-level work. The Princeton Manpower Symposium (1968) on transitions from school to work expressed concern that public schools tend to ignore the needs of the "other half," the approximately 50% of students who do not continue in some postsecondary or higher education. Consensus is growing that although school settings are valid environments for transmitting cognitive information and knowledge, schools are not proficient in teaching lifeskills considered vital in the transition to adulthood. Decisionmaking, learning how to work, learning how to take responsibility for one's life, and acquiring marketable skills are transitional tasks that schools attempt to simulate with minimal success. The William T. Grant Foundation Commission on Work, Family and Citizenship (1988) in its report, *The Forgotten Half*, concluded that

  more and more of the non–college bound now fall between the cracks when they are in school, drop out, or graduate inadequately prepared for the requirements of society and the workplace....There is a sharp disparity between what Americans do for college-bound youth and what they do for the Forgotten Half. (p. 3)

Separation of educational activity from job training poses a challenge for advocates of a clear-cut school-to-work continuum. Grubb (1996) discussed the potential of the School-to-Work Opportunities Act as a possible link to job-training programs. One of Grubb's recommendations is that occupational/ vocational skills be integrated with academic content, and the two combined within a single class. One model calls for team teaching, with a minimum of two instructors per class. In essence, school-to-work transition practices reflect the view that specific job skills will be acquired after leaving school. Mortimer (1996) concluded that links between schools and employers are unstructured and that "there is a notable absence of transition supports of any kind for 75% of youths" (p. 39). The U.S. system as it now operates is insufficient with respect to providing work preparation support for youth leaving school. The population most affected are the 50% of youth (the other half) classified as non-college bound. In this category are many highly vulnerable young people, including thousands of foster wards who emancipate from placement on or about age 18.

U.S. General Accounting Office (GAO) testimony to the Congressional Committee on Education and Labor supports the goal of providing meaningful workplace experiences for all students (Morra, 1993). In terms of implementing the provisions of the School-to-Work Opportunities Act of 1993, compliance has been uneven, and progress slow.

Cross-National Comparisons

Cross-national studies on educational preparation and economic competitiveness suggest that America trails many of the industrial nations in preparing youth to transition from school to work. Countries such as Japan, Germany, England, and Sweden have national policies that target the preparation of youth for the workplace. In Japan, secondary-school graduates obtain employment mainly through school-employer contacts, and employers base hiring decisions on school recommendations. In the United States, employers pay little attention to a student's high school academic performance or to requesting workplace-relevant information from school officials.

Many school-to-work transitional experts in the United States are enthusiastic about apprenticeship models. In the apprenticeship area, Germany is a recognized leader, with nearly two-thirds of all youth participating in some type of apprenticeship (Moray, 1993). An *apprenticeship* refers to people who are learning a trade or occupation. The German apprenticeship system has attracted worldwide attention. It is estimated that apprenticeship training is offered in about 375 occupations (Glover, 1996). Apprenticeships are reputed to produce high skill levels, and in the German system, they confer recognition to hundreds of occupations not requiring college or university enrollment. Studies of transitional policies in Japan and Germany suggest a number of lessons. Glover (1996) highlighted three elements:

1. Achievement in school is required to qualify for high-quality training and employment positions after high school.

2. Preparation of adolescents for the workplace is the joint responsibility of schools and employers. Early connections are made, with hiring starting in the teenage years.

3. Employers are expected to provide assurances that on-the-job experiential systems are in place. Business, industry, and labor organizations accept responsibility for the assessment and certification of youths' skills.

In the German model, emphasis is on using state-of-the art equipment and ensuring that training takes place under real-life conditions. The German apprenticeship model is difficult to replicate, particularly in countries that lack institutional structures that include: (a) subsidies for apprenticeships, (b) strong links between schools and postschool training, and (c) the influence of local chambers of commerce on the number and type of apprenticeships offered. Based on an analysis of West Germany's system of preparing noncollege youth for adult careers, Hamilton (1990) concluded, "The success of the German system suggests that some kind of apprenticeship might improve the transition of U.S. youths from school to work" (p. 4).

With respect to transitional employment training strategies in England, in the 1960s, industrial training boards were created to promote skill development in the workforce. Structures were developed for apprenticeship programs. However, in the Thatcher era, training boards and governmental subsidies for apprenticeships were discontinued. The argument was made that programs terminated by the Thatcher government were in fact "relatively unsuccessful in training school leavers" (Blanchflower & Lynch, 1992, p. 2). As a consequence, the number of employer-supported apprenticeships in England have been in sharp decline. Issues of postsecondary school training for non–university graduates persists in England, as it does in the United States. Apprenticeships in England were replaced by government-sponsored youth training programs (YT). YT programs are administered at a local level by training and enterprise councils. Training and enterprise councils are voluntary organizations that depend on employer contributions. Local councils are not industry-based and receive limited government support (Blanchflower & Lynch, 1992).

Heinz (1996) pointed out that striking differences exist in how various countries respond to the issue of transitioning from school to work. In Austria and Switzerland, as well as in Germany, vocational networks are organized around the apprenticeship model, which has significant labor-force status. In France, vocational training occurs in the school, but in the context of a "highly stratified and selective educational system" (Heinz, 1996, pp. 7-8). In Canada, as in the United States, youth in transition are more likely to aspire to postsecondary education and to rely on classroom learning prior to completing high school and college rather than seek vocational type experiences.

Investment in Human Potential

In his volume entitled *The Third Way*, Giddens (1998) emphasized the importance of cultivating human potential. The political strategy espoused is one of inclusion. In a comprehensive sense, *inclusion* refers to citizenship obligations, civil and political rights, as well as access to education and work-related opportunities. Giddens raised a critical issue with respect to the inclusion/exclusion dichotomy, namely the trend toward societal practices that are exclusionary in nature. Reference is made to exclusion of "those at the bottom, cut off from the mainstream of opportunities" (p. 103) in society. To what extent are successive cohorts of thousands of foster wards, who each year emancipate or age out of state care, likely to experience inclusionary or exclusionary practices in their transition to adulthood?

Many child welfare practitioners report that foster wards tend to experience exclusionary care, which results in undesirable separation from mainstream opportunity structures. In the foster care population, the probable outcome of exclusion is weak preparation for independence and limited readiness for adult living. Society makes a substantial investment in the placement system. However, little attention is paid to the magnitude of the investment or to placement outcomes. On average, youth with a permanency plan of independent living spend about five years in placement prior to emancipation. Each year, nearly 25,000 young people age out of placement. Based on this estimate, over the past decade, nearly 250,000 youth have left state care and moved into community life. Cumulative pre-emancipation dollar costs for these cohorts is $2.5 billion (25,000 youth in placement, each for five years, at a cost of $100,000 each). Over the past decade, federal-state expenditures directed at preparing foster wards for independent living have approached $2.5 billion. This amount constitutes a major investment in the future of young people. Once emancipated from the child welfare system, how do young people progress with respect to becoming self-supporting, self-sufficient, self-reliant, and independent? How many transfer from one dependency system to another? What about relations with family, relatives, and peers? How many have stable housing? These and other questions remain to be answered. It is highly unlikely that financial markets would ignore the status of a $2.5 billion business investment. Why then should federal and state agencies not inquire about the status of an annual $2.5 billion investment in the future of foster wards? Investment in human potential is usually referred to as human capital development. It is to our advantage to consider the importance of governmental expenditures in human services programs. Hershberg (1996) wrote, "Highly developed human capital will be the source of comparative advantage in the twenty-first century global economy" (p. 43). Human capital development refers to helping individuals acquire the knowledge, skills, and problem-solving abilities needed for productivity in the changing economy and technological society that is forecast for the next century. To what extent are foster wards being prepared for transitioning into a society where most new jobs will require high skill levels? All youth in foster care are candidates for human capital development, particularly those who spend a majority of their adolescent years in placement. The human capital concept is based on the notion that skills and knowledge increase productivity, are beneficial to society, and justify the costs in acquiring them. Expenditures on improving capabilities are referred to as social investments (Salamon, 1991, p. 3).

Risk Factors Associated with Foster Placement

Raising children and youth carries with it significant risk. The National Research Council (1993) via its Panel on High-Risk Youth, concluded that "adolescents who pass through the child welfare system are at high risk of educational failure, unemployment, emotional disturbance, and other negative outcomes." The panel concluded that "studies show that adolescents released from foster care fare far worse than either low-income youths or a cross section of the general adolescent population" (p. 4).

In general, young people who are in out-of-home placement experience discontinuity in parenting and are typically without the protection, affection, encouragement, and day-to-day intimate contact that is associated with normal family life. Children who enter the foster care system do so under difficult circumstances. Neglect, abuse, exploitation, abandonment, running away from home, and inability and/or unwillingness on the part of parents to care for their children are some of the reasons that placement is necessary. The constellation of special risk factors include the following:

1. Separating from families and experiencing the discontinuities associated with out-of-home care. When placed with nonrelatives, placement is a new and often strange experience. Typically, young people experience multiple placements, and the replacement pattern is often one of progressive insertion into more restrictive settings.

2. Out-of-home placement usually means growing up in a system in which parenting responsibilities are divided. Some responsibility is assumed by the state agency, some by foster parents and/or other caregivers, and some may be assumed by the birthparents. Caseworker turnover is a chronic problem, as is inconsistency in terms of having a stable case advocate.

3. Out-of-home placement tends to isolate children from their community and to separate them from normalizing community resources (i.e., YMCA, YWCA, Boys & Girls Clubs, Junior Achievement, numerous other youth development organizations, as well as special teachers and tutors). In short, the foster care experience often means that young people miss out on many enrichment experiences.

4. Foster youth are likely to experience delays, obstacles, and barriers to maintaining normal educational progress. Education is a passport to career employment and vocational opportunities. Growing up in care and spending significant amounts of time in placement carries with it the risk that living environments become custodial rather than developmental. Following rules and regulations are a priority, and receiving treatment as second-class citizens is not unusual. If caregivers do not value and/or encourage educational accomplish-

ments and aspirations that are achievement oriented in the substitute home, young wards are placed at a substantial disadvantage.

5. Regrettably, out-of-home placement does not guarantee protection from physical and emotional abuse, neglect, or sexual predators. Numerous instances of the sexual maltreatment of young wards have been documented.

6. Young people with disabilities—mental, emotional, and physical— are represented in the foster care population. Many with a disability classification do not remain in kinship or relative homes on a long-term basis. Placement settings are often group and residential facilities that put a premium on discipline, control, and adherence to a regimen of rules and regulations.

7. The ultimate risk factor is age related and is associated with the "ready or not" syndrome, whereby young wards on or about age 18 are discharged from state care without resources or a feasible transitional plan.

Transitional Case Profiles: Ruth, George, and Carol

Consider the following profiles. Each depicts the transitional status of former foster wards at age 20, nearly two years after system discharge. Assume that you are a case manager, supervisor, line worker, or substitute parent: How would you gauge the progress of Ruth, George, and Carol with respect to achieving self-sufficiency?

Ruth

Ruth was placed in foster care at age 2, where she remained for 17 years. In her words, she came into care because: "Mom was poor and something happened." She was placed in a series of foster homes with a plan for adoption, "but the caseworker didn't finish the paperwork, so I didn't get adopted."

At age 4, she was evaluated at a mental health clinic, and a judgment was made that she would not be able to bond with a foster parent. Ruth was then placed in an institutional setting and was virtually unnoticed for 15 years. Her recollection of former foster homes was of being beaten by the foster parents and then placed again when she was 4 years old.

She attended school at the institution rather than in the community. During her school years, she attended a vocational program where she learned some baking and typing skills. She does not know why she was held back one year in school, because her grades were average or better. Ruth completed a diploma at age 19.

During her many years in care, Ruth did not receive training in independent living skills, was never encouraged to look for a job, and had no opportunity to shop, cook, or do minimal tasks. Most important, she had never had a job, even a babysitting job.

Peer group acquaintances had all left the institution. Ruth never had an opportunity to make friends in a neighborhood school or to be active in a church, club, or organization. Her family expressed little interest in her, and she had few, if any, visitors while in placement. When asked who she considered to be family, she replied "No one!" Her career goal for the future was to learn how to decorate a cake, and perhaps get a job in a bakery.

At age 20, an interview was held with Ruth, who then was living in a foster home, still under state care. The home was located in a rural area. She was not at all happy with this arrangement, feeling as isolated in the country as she had been in the institution. There were few neighbors, no friends, and no educational, vocational or independent living skill opportunities available.

George

George was placed in a foster family home when he was 9 years old. Based on the case record, "he couldn't get along with his mother," who "wanted nothing to do with him." He stated that he had really liked this foster home and considered his foster parents "his family." However, he had not had contact with this family in more than a year, because "when I became older my foster parents told me that I needed to learn to live on my own and sent me to the Children's Services Board." In a very matter-of-fact way, George explained to his worker that he had to leave this home "because the foster parents were not getting any money anymore, and they needed room for more kids." According to the worker, he acted as if that was to be expected and that people should not feel sorry for him.

After several years in group/residential placements, when discharged at age 18, George had nowhere to go except a homeless shelter. Since emancipation, he has lived in several shelters. He is afraid of going back into a homeless shelter environment, saying, "Shelters have too many rules, and too many scary people."

When the aftercare worker learned that George, now age 20, had moved and was currently living in an undesirable and unsafe living arrangement in another city, she set out to locate him. She found George living in a rented room in a very rundown section of the city. The front of the building had a large, crumbling porch crowded with worn, rain-soaked furniture intended for the interior of the building. The porch was occupied by several people who appeared to be in their late 50s or early 60s, who were drinking. George described the occupants of the apartment as "a bunch of old alcoholics." He said they often defecated in the halls because they were "so out of it." George said he drank beer and/or wine every day, a habit that started when he moved to this address.

The apartment building had 58 rooms on three floors. The first two floors had new carpeting and seemed freshly painted. The third floor where George lived was dingy and in need of repairs. The floor was covered in filthy, peeling, black and white linoleum. The room next to his was a bathroom with a nonfunctioning bathtub. Only the toilet and sink worked. George reported that each floor had two bathrooms that were shared by everyone on each floor. George's room, for which he paid $120 a month (utilities included), was furnished with a twin bed, a padlocked three-drawer dresser, an apartment-sized stove and refrigerator, and a utility sink. There was also a small table with two torn vinyl chairs, and a badly worn, severely stained rocker recliner, which smelled of urine. Although the room was desperately in need of repair and cleaning, it looked as if George made an attempt to keep it tidy. His bed was made, his dresser neatly arranged, and his kitchen table cleaned off, and there were only a few dishes in the sink. There was one window with a view of a small grocery store, which, according to George, also doubled as a frequently raided crackhouse. He pointed to several houses in the neighborhood used for selling drugs that were frequently raided by police. He made it clear that he does not feel safe in this neighborhood. He fears for his safety because "people think I owe them money."

Threatened with eviction and having no money, he has no real hope of keeping this rented room for another month. He had moved in with only his clothes and personal possessions, which included a blanket, two half-used bottles of cologne, a Little League photo taken when he was 6 years old, a wrestling photo taken when he was in junior high school, and an expandable file folder containing his discharge documents and medical records. He didn't know where his birth certificate was.

Since emancipation, George has had difficulty in finding and keeping a job. He had worked at a variety of food service and retail jobs. He said he had trouble taking orders from managers who shout or "ride his back." At this point, he was desperately searching for a job to pay his rent. He would like to go to a community college for truck driver training.

The aftercare worker's assessment was that George is a young survivor who is knowledgeable about community resources. In George's view, survival was a skill acquired since emancipation. He told the worker that he gets what he needs "even if I have to lie and manipulate to get it," a fact which appeared to embarrass him. The worker was not aware of his situation prior to emancipation, but believed that his current situation was exposing him not only to immediate personal harm from people in his neighborhood, but also to possible situational harm caused by poor nutrition, stress, and exposure to drugs and alcohol.

Carol

When Carol was 2 years old, she was removed from home because her mother was put in prison, accused of strangling Carol's younger sister, Marcella. Carol was placed in a foster home and then returned to her mother on her release from prison.

Over the next 10 years, Carol's mother physically abused her. Carol tried running away from home to get attention from the authorities to stop the abuse, but nothing ever happened. She tried shoplifting so they would remove her from the home, but this didn't work either. As last resort, she ran to the police, who took pictures of her injuries and hospitalized her. The hospital called the children's protective services, and she was put into a group home. She recalls being in two group homes and two institutions before ending up in a group home she really liked, which had an apartment program for older teens and an independent living skills training program.

Carol believed her mother abused her because she, herself, had been physically and sexually abused as a child.

Carol sees her mother at irregular intervals. Her father is not interested in visits. After discharge from care, Carol enlisted in the U.S. Navy. In reflecting on her foster care experience, she is quite critical of the foster care system, saying she was raped twice while in a foster home (once by the foster father and once by an in-boarder). Also, Carol insists that the foster parents kept the money the state gave them for the children's allowance instead of giving it to the children.

Carol reported that for her, group homes were not good places for young people to learn to acquire independence skills. Speaking of her future, Carol was uncertain about staying in the Navy as a career. However, the Navy has helped her in many ways. Her contact with older adults in the service helped her to see she needs more education. Through them, she has become interested in studying for one of the professions, possibly law.

Analysis of Transitional Case Profiles

The transitional profiles of Ruth, George, and Carol suggest a five-stage, placement-related domino effect. The process begins in Stage 1 with events within families that precipitate placement. Risk factors present in case profiles include poverty, neglect, and abuse. Family breakdown and separation is followed by Stage 2, out-of-home placement under state custody. First placements usually are in foster family settings, which reflects the principle of starting with the least restrictive setting. As time in placement lengthens, and weeks and months turn into years, the odds increase of re-placement and exposure to more restrictive arrangements. Following placement in a foster home, Ruth spent nearly 15 years in residential/institutional care. George started out in a foster family setting, then experienced a series of group home placements. Carol's placement profile also follows the pattern of moving from foster family care to a series of group/institutional settings. Stage 2 of the placement domino effect is characterized by progressive insertion into more restrictive settings. It is our conclusion that restrictive placements are less likely to expose wards to the knowledge, skills, and attitudes needed for adult living.

In Stage 3, the third phase of the placement domino effect occurs when young wards are on the threshold of emancipation, or aging out of the child welfare system, on or about age 18. After spending many years in state care, to what extent are Ruth, George, and Carol prepared to make it on their own? Ruth is poorly prepared for economic self-sufficiency, at least in the near future. At age 20, she lacks job skills, stable housing, and a support system necessary for satisfactory transition. George is living at the margins of society. His is a hand-to-mouth existence. Since leaving care, George's transitional experience has been marked by a series of shelter arrangements. His current housing consists of a rented room in an undesirable neighborhood. He has few, if any, immediate prospects for gainful employment. With respect to the transitional trajectories of Ruth and George, it is difficult to characterize them as anything other than problematic.

A more favorable transition pattern may be unfolding for Carol. One of her group home placements included an apartment experience, supplemented by a skills training program. In conjunction with the benefits of her experience in the U.S. Navy, Carol's self-sufficiency path looks promising. Her plan for the future includes more education with the possibility of applying for law school. In Carol's situation, military service was a positive element. Colleagues in the Navy were a source of support and encouraged her to develop a career track. Overall, Stage 3 of the placement domino effect—the emancipation phase—represents an accumulation of the weaknesses of antecedent stages. The emancipation stage is characterized by premature discharge from state care and the likelihood of insufficient preparation and support resources for transitioning to adulthood.

Stage 4, the postemancipation phase, constitutes the period from ages 18 to 21. In this critical segment, foster wards struggle to make it on their own. Many trade one dependency system (child welfare) for another (public assistance, corrections, etc.).

Stage 5, the transition to young adulthood phase, extends through age 25 and comprises a continuation of the postemancipation transition challenge. Of the three profiles cited, Carol appears most likely to progress toward meeting societal expectations for young adulthood. Ruth has to overcome the disadvantages of 15 years in an institution. The future for George is cloudy. He is drifting and lacks a transitional plan. Overall, the case profiles cited are representative of the thousands of foster wards who each year emancipate from state care. Empirical documentation supports the conclusion that the overwhelming majority are poorly prepared to make the transition to adulthood. In the years following discharge from care, many continue to be a cost to the community. It is clear that the postemancipation phase—the period from age 18 to 25—is a time when former wards must play an active role in the transition and take responsibility for their futures. Society can create an opportunity structure and provide assistance, support, and resources. In the final analysis, it is up to foster wards to make optimal use of the resources and opportunities that are available.

Toward Community Transitional Systems

One of the issues that face child welfare agencies and youth development organizations is the need to establish networks that can help young people transition to adulthood. In the case profiles discussed, Ruth and George were without a transitional plan or resources necessary to implement a plan. Carol was more fortunate, in that her postemancipation experience provided an adult support structure within a military organization.

As a nation, the United States is composed of thousands of urban, suburban, and rural communities. Cities, towns, villages, and neighborhoods are characterized by diversity—racial, ethnic, socioeconomic, religious, political, and so forth. Community resources are vital in the task of creating transition systems for young people. The dilemma is that no agency, institution, or organization is designated to coordinate a transition system. There is no overall czar to plan, direct, and oversee the development of youth transitional systems. Prospects for strengthening existing community-based transitional systems for youth are diminished, primarily because of a "progressive decline of the family, the church, and the school" (Ianni, 1989, p. 261). Ianni (1989) referred to the fragmentation of institutions traditionally charged with socializing youth as "community-level dissonance." As a consequence, networks of cooperating and supportive institutions are slow to materialize. Youth workers refer to the situation as lack of a caring community. With respect to foster wards, little has been written on transitional structures for youth who emancipate from placement. Efforts are under way in state child welfare systems, in partnership with private sector organizations, to establish opportunity structures for young people leaving care. At a minimum, youth leaving care should have an individualized but feasible plan that includes: (a) housing/living arrangements; (b) information and resources necessary to continue their education and/or vocational preparation; (c) agreements with community organizations and/or adults to serve as resource mentors for employment or other matters pertinent to transition; (d) a social support network, including family and friends; and (e) access to health, medical, and dental care.

Support mechanisms that connect adults with youth in formal as well as informal arrangements are important in any transitional structure. One type of link is via one-on-one transitional mentors for young people leaving care. Intergenerational links can normalize the transitional process. Adults who have achieved a measure of success can serve as role models and offer young people a reservoir of knowledge, skills, and experience. It is not our intention that transitional systems be imposed on young people. It is our hope that as community transitional structures evolve, young people will view these as opportunities that can work to their advantage.

Transition Systems for Youth: Interpretive Summary

One of the trends in the child welfare system is the influx of adolescents who "age into" placement at about 12 years old, remain for 5 or 6 years, and age out of care when they are about age 18. Table 1.1 summarizes the trend for adolescents ages 13 to 18 in out-of-home care for the 15-year period from 1982 to 1996. On average, the number of children in place-

TABLE 1.1

Adolescents in Out-of-Home Placement, Ages 13 to 18: 15-Year Trends: 1982–1996

YEARS	AVERAGE NUMBER OF CHILDREN	PERCENTAGE OF ADOLESCENTS	AVERAGE NUMBER OF ADOLESCENTS
1982–1984	269,000	47.9	128,850
1985–1987	285,000	42.8	121,900
1988–1990	374,000	33.4	124,946
1991–1993	428,000	31.5	135,030
1994–1996	484,000	29.6	143,264

NOTE: The cumulative number of youth ages 13 to 18 in out-of-home placement for the period 1982–1996 was 1,959,000 (nearly 2 million teens).

ment has increased from 269,000 (1982-1984) to 484,000 (1994-1996). Although the percentage of adolescents in placement has declined from 48% to approximately 30%, in absolute numbers the adolescent population has increased from approximately 122,000 to 143,000 per year.

In effect, child welfare is in large measure an adolescent welfare system. Nearly 40% of children and youth in placement are early, middle, or older adolescents. This trend has caught the attention of child welfare administrators, legislators, and youth development organizations. A GAO (1999) report prepared for the House Committee on Ways and Means highlights many of the difficulties that foster youth face in making the transition to living on their own. Problems cited include education deficiencies, insufficient employment preparation, inadequate housing, and lack of transitional assistance.

The transition period from youth to adult is much longer now than in the past. In his work entitled *Rites of Passage*, Kett (1977) discussed the process of growing up in pre–20th century America. With reference to the phenomenon of age segregation, Kett concluded, "If adolescence is defined as the period after puberty during which a younger person is institutionally segregated from…contacts with a broad range of adults, then it can scarcely be said to have existed at all" (p. 36). The American socioeconomic structure has become more complex, differentiated, and stratified than in past eras. Young people now spend considerably more time in age-segregated institutional settings such as school, which serve as a passport to future opportunities. Societal emphasis is increasingly on education that is oriented toward career development. If young people want to distance themselves from so-called dead-end jobs, then education and training is a necessity. The price to be paid for additional years in school and extended education is prolongation of dependency. Implications for foster wards, caregivers, and program specialists are numerous. For youth who grow up away from their families of origin, often living in nonstimulating, marginal environments, as do many foster wards, emancipation from placement is a critical event. Emancipation poses serious challenges for young wards. Youth must find answers to such questions as "What do I need to do to make it on my own?" "Who can I count on for help?" "What does the future hold?" Each year, thousands of young people emancipate from foster care. The majority are truly at the crossroads in terms of knowing where they are going or how to get there. Federal, state, and local governments have a stake in the progress of foster wards, as do the communities in which the wards live. Each year, millions of dollars are invested in cohorts of youth who are in placement. Expenditures and/or investments in foster care raise practical questions. What are the dividends and/or returns to society? To what extent are former wards on the road to self-sufficiency, independence, and productive citizenship? Young people who live away from their families of origin, in substitute care, under state supervision are usually in placement through no fault of their own. The state assumes the role of parent and thereby incurs a responsibility to create opportunity structures that can assist youth in the transition to adulthood. It is in the public interest to provide foster youth with preparation for independent living while in placement and assistance in the postemancipation transitional period. In a practical sense, foster wards should be viewed as a disadvantaged population. With respect to federal level policy, the U.S. Department of Labor has designated foster youth as a disadvantaged group eligible for employment services under the Job Training-Partnership Act.

The road to independence and self-sufficiency is not easy. Young people today grow up in a society characterized by family instability and uncertain futures. Nuclear families must work hard to stay together. Divorce rates remain high. Single-parent households are increasing. Millions of families experience economic hardship and live in poverty. What effect do these social trends have on how youth are prepared for adulthood? It is clear that young people who require out-of-home placement come from vulnerable families. Accordingly, focus in this volume is on evaluating the progress of foster youth toward achieving self-sufficiency, describing societal efforts to respond to the needs of foster wards, analyzing an evolving national-level opportunity structure for youth in placement, identifying best practices and promising interventions, as well as recommending policies, programs, and services for the 21st century.

References

Blanchflower, D., & Lynch, L. (1992). *Training at work: A comparison of U.S. & British youths* (Discussion paper No. 70). London: London School of Economics, Centre for Economic Performance.

Giddens, A. (1998). *The third way: The renewal of social democracy*. Cambridge, UK: Polity Press.

Glover, R. (1996, March). The German apprenticeship system: Lessons for Austin, Texas. *Annals, 544*, 83-94.

Grubb, W. (1996). *Learning to work. The case for reintegrating job training & education*. New York: Russell Sage Foundation.

Hamilton, S. (1990). *Apprenticeship for adulthood. Preparing youth for the future*. New York: Free Press.

Havighurst, R. (1953). *Human development and education*. New York: David McKay.

Heinz, W. (1996). Youth transitions in cross-cultural perspective: School-to-work in Germany. In B. Galaway & J. Hudson (Eds.), *Youth in transition* (pp. 2–13). Toronto, Canada: Thompson Educational.

Hershberg, T. (1996, March). Human capital development: America's greatest challenge. *Annals, 544*, 43-51.

Ianni, F. (1989). *The search for structure: A report on American youth today*. New York: Free Press.

Kett, J. (1977). *Rites of passage: Adolescence in America 1790 to the present*. New York: Basic Books.

Morra, L. G. (1993, September 29). Transition from school to work. Testimony before the Committee on Education and Labor, U.S. House of Representatives (GAO/T-HRD-93-31). Washington, DC: U.S. General Accounting Office.

Mortimer, J. T. (1996). U.S. research on the school-to-work transition. In B. Galaway & J. Hudson (Eds.), *Youth in transition. Perspective on research and policy* (pp. 32–45). Toronto, Canada: Thompson Educational.

National Commission on Youth. (1980). *The transition of youth to adulthood: A bridge too long*. Boulder, CO: Westview Press.

National Research Council Commission on Behavioral and Social Sciences and Education. (1993). *Losing generations: Adolescents in high-risk settings*. Washington, DC: National Academy Press.

President's Science Advisory Committee, Panel on Youth. (1974). *Youth transition to adulthood. Report of the Panel on Youth of the President's Science Advisory Committee*. Chicago: University of Chicago Press.

Princeton Manpower Symposium. (1968). *The transition from school to work*. Princeton, NJ: Woodrow Wilson School of Public & International Affairs.

Salamon, L. (1991). Overview: Why human capital? Why now? In D. Hornbeck & L. Salamon (Eds.), *Human capital and America's future* (pp. 1–39). Baltimore: John Hopkins Press.

Schlegel, A., & Barry, H. (1991). *Anthropological inquiry*. New York: Free Press.

U.S. General Accounting Office. (1999). *Statement of Cynthia Fagnoni. Foster care: Challenges in helping youths live independently* (GAO/T-HEHS-99-121). Washington, DC: Author.

William T. Grant Foundation, Commission on Work, Family and Citizenship. (1988). *The forgotten half: Pathways to success for America's youth & young families*. Washington, DC: Author.

Chapter 2

Potential for Independence

Edmund V. Mech

> *Virtually nothing is known about*
> *how such young adults fare in society.*
> *In view of so much criticism of*
> *the foster care system, it seemed important to try*
> *to understand what it ultimately produces.*
>
> —*Festinger (1983, p. xiv)*

Interest in the effects of growing up in foster care is long standing. The 1909 White House Conference on Dependent Children, convened under the leadership of President Theodore Roosevelt, called attention to the need for information about the social functioning of foster youth. A conference report urged agencies to take steps to determine "what sort of citizens they become" (Bremner, 1971, p. 367). Evidence on the status of foster wards after leaving care has been slow to emerge. Although much has been written about foster care and many studies have been conducted, serious attention has only been directed to questions of self-sufficiency and the potential for independence since 1980.

Early Perceptions of Foster Care Influence

One of the earliest investigations was by Sophia Van Senden Theis, who in 1924, reported on a follow-up study of older foster youth conducted under the auspices of the New York State Charities Aid Association (Theis, 1924). Based on interviews with more than 500 older foster wards and their caregivers, nearly 75% of the study group was rated as "capable"; the remaining 25% were classified as "incapable." Ratings were based on general criteria that included judgments about ability to manage one's life and whether or not young persons were law abiding and adhering to the moral standards of their community. More than a decade later, a study conducted by Baylor and Monachesi (1939) reported similar outcomes. The Baylor-Monachesi sample included 500 foster youth who ranged in age from 5 to older than 29. With respect to personal-social behavior, for those in the age 21 or older group, nearly three out of four were rated as "favorable." A subsequent follow-up study on the outcomes of foster care was reported by Meier (1965). Meier interviewed 66 former foster wards who ranged in age from 28 to 32. Each had been in placement for at least five years and emancipated from placement in the late 1940s. Outcome ratings were based on respondent reports of their well-being. The majority of the ratings were positive. Meier concluded that "with few exceptions these young men and women are self-supporting individuals, living in attractive homes, and taking good care of their children" (p. 196). Studies cited share several elements in common: (a) Each reported positive outcomes for youth growing up in placement, (b) each used global criteria in making judgments about outcomes, and (c) studies were not targeted on economic self-sufficiency or potential for independence.

Reappraisals of Foster Care

Following the end of World War II, new and more detailed information about foster care began to emerge. In the 1950s, Dr. John Bowlby wrote about the deleterious effects of separating children from families and placement in out-of-home care. Bowlby was convinced that separation from one's family resulted in emotional deprivation and that the effects were irreversible, particularly when children were placed in institutional settings. Bowlby's formulations had a profound effect on child welfare practice in the United States. Early age adoption was emphasized, and congregate-institutional placement discouraged (Bowlby, 1951). Bowlby's critique was followed by the landmark Maas-Engler survey, which documented high levels of foster care drift throughout the nation's child welfare system. Entitled *Children in Need of Parents*, the Maas-Engler report prompted considerable soul-searching in the child welfare field (Maas & Engler, 1959). In 1964, *The Annals of the American Academy of Political and Social Science* published a special issue on the topic "Child Welfare Services Today." This was followed in 1970 by a conference report cosponsored by the Child Welfare League of America (CWLA) and the National Association of Social Work (NASW), entitled *Foster Care in Question*.

Many voices called for change. Overhaul of the nation's child welfare system was on the horizon. A movement that began in the 1950s to improve and redesign the system to achieve a responsive child welfare system culminated nearly 30 years later in P.L. 96-272, the Adoption Assistance and Child Welfare Act of 1980. This new act emphasized family preservation in terms of keeping children and families together, adoption subsidies, placement in least restrictive environments when out-of-home care was deemed necessary, periodic case reviews, and parent-child visitations during placement as a means of facilitating reunification of families. Despite its importance in terms of establishing a national-level child welfare system, the Act devoted little attention to issues pertaining to older youth in care or to their preparation for independent living. Subsequent reports by the Citizens' Committee for Child of New York (1984) and Barth (1986) described in detail the need for emancipation services for adolescents in foster care.

The Festinger Report

Festinger (1983) conducted one of the groundbreaking investigations of the status of former foster youth. The study group consisted of youth discharged from foster care between the ages of 18 and 21 in the New York City area, who had been in placement for at least five years prior to emancipation. The group was 277 former wards who ranged in age from 22 to 25 at follow-up. The majority were discharged from foster homes. The remainder left care from group/institutional placements. One of the conclusions was that young adults in the follow-up group "were not what might be described as problem ridden when they were discharged, nor did they become so in subsequent years....There was no evidence of undue economic dependence on public support" (Festinger, 1983, p. 294). Although Festinger's interpretation of the foster care experiences of young people in the follow-up was optimistic, her study left little doubt as to the vulnerability of this population. The effects of group/institutional placements were linked with fewer years of education completed, combined with a poor sense of personal well-being. With respect to educational progress of young people in the study, irrespective of placement type, the overall trend was for wards to fall behind in school. Festinger expressed concern that child welfare services overemphasize the emotional status of youth and neglect the educational dimension. Festinger stated, "Unless additional weight is attached to education, foster care cannot approach the goal of developing each individual's full potential" (Festinger, 1983, p. 268). The Festinger report was instrumental in drawing attention to the difficulties that older youth face in leaving placement to live on their own. Findings from this investigation highlighted the risks associated with the period following discharge from care, particularly for youth who emancipated from group/residential facilities. Festinger concluded her analysis by urging states to review policies on discharge age and recommended that consideration be given to extending placement up to age 21 for young people who need extra time to prepare for independent living. Kermit Wiltse, a professor at the University of California, Berkeley, was one of the first in the child welfare field to call attention to the need for independent-living services. Wiltse (1978) noted that "the frequency of emancipation as an outcome of foster care suggests that it deserves study in its own right" (p. 83). A subsequent article by Barth (1986) described in detail the need for emancipation services for adolescents in foster care.

The WESTAT National Survey

By the mid-1980s, a new movement was emerging in the area of services to children, youth, and families. Preparing foster adolescents for self-support was becoming recognized as an important goal for youth who were likely to age out of placement. Focus on self-sufficiency as a desired outcome has considerable precedent in U.S. social policy. That self-support is one of the cardinal aims of public aid programs is illustrated best by reference to the Aid to Families with Dependent Children program (AFDC), currently designated as Temporary Aid to Needy Families (TANF).

On September 8, 1983, the U.S. Department of Health and Human Services (DHHS) issued a request for proposal (RFP) to "study the adaptation of adolescents in foster care to independence and community life" (pp. 1–23). At the time the request was circulated, DHHS estimated that 41,000 adolescents were in placement who could neither return home to their families nor be placed in an adoptive family. The contractor for the survey was WESTAT, Inc., in Rockville, Maryland. More than 800 youth were interviewed approximately 2.5 to 4 years after discharge from foster placement. The average age at follow-up was 21 years. The essential findings were:

- 51% had completed a high school diploma.

- 60% had given birth to at least one child.

- 30% were classified as public assistance recipients.

- Approximately 50% were employed at follow-up. Annual income was about $10,000.

- With respect to employment stability, only 40% of youth classified as employed were able to maintain a job for at least one year.

- Female wards with children were more likely to use public assistance in the postemancipation period. Nearly 61% were classified as a cost to the community, compared with 22% without children. With respect to risk factors related to dependency on public aid, female wards with children were less likely to complete high school or to obtain employment than female wards without children.

- Housing was a problem for most foster wards. About one-third reported having moved five or more times. An estimated 25% experienced at least one night without shelter.

The findings of the federally funded, multistate WESTAT project were widely disseminated (Cook, 1997; Cook, Fleishman, & Grimes, 1991). With respect to postdischarge outcomes, policy analysts concur that the results are disappointing. As a group, former youth in the WESTAT follow-up demonstrated limited potential for independence. Gender proved to be an important risk factor, primarily because of the high rate of pregnancy and early childbearing among female wards.

San Francisco Bay Area Survey

A survey by Barth (1990) analyzed the experiences of youth after leaving foster care. The study group consisted of 55 foster youth in the San Francisco area, who were at least 16 years old when discharged. Each participant had been emancipated for at least one year. Information was collected on education, employment, housing, income, and contact with law enforcement. With respect to educational progress, more than 50% left foster care without completing a high school diploma. Other findings were the following:

- 47% received some form of public aid.

- 35% were homeless or moved frequently.

- 40% of the females reported a pregnancy.

- 35% had been arrested or spent time in jail or prison.

Foster Youth-in-Transition Project—University of Illinois

An important element in the Foster Youth-in-Transition project at the University of Illinois was the emphasis on evaluating adolescent wards with respect to potential for independence. A multistage, prospective data collection format was used. In Phase 1, information was collected from adolescent wards on or about age 18 and prior to emancipation from state care. Phase 1 instruments included a series of paper and pencil measures of life-skills knowledge. One reason for starting at age 18 was to establish the nucleus of a study group for subsequent follow-up contact.

Phase 2 information was collected when former wards were 20 to 21 years old. The main results of the Phase 2 follow-up interview are presented here (Mech & Fung, 1998). The Phase 1 sample consisted of 534 foster wards in Illinois, Indiana, and Ohio. The permanency plan for each ward was independent living. In Phase 2, it was possible to conduct in-person interviews with approximately 80% (410 youth) of the original sample. An incentive payment of $35 was offered for participating in the follow-up. Questions covered included: (a) What is the highest grade level that you have completed? (b) Are you currently employed? If so, provide the hours worked per week, type of job, earnings and wages, and number of different jobs since leaving care. (c) What was your total income last year? What are the main sources of your income? (d) What is your current housing/living arrangement? (e) Do you have children? If so, how many? Information cited is based on several hundred youth who were no longer in state care at the time of the follow-up interview. The salient trends were:

Education

Table 2.1 summarizes the educational status of emancipated foster wards at the age 20 to 21 follow-up.

Approximately 30% lacked a high school diploma or had not completed a general·equivalency diploma (GED). About 40% completed a high school diploma or a GED. Fewer than one in three (29.6%) were enrolled in a postsecondary education program. With respect to race/gender differences, nonwhite males and white females were least likely to enroll in a postsecondary educational program. Only 50% of the nonwhite male subgroup had completed a high school certificate at the point of follow-up.

Employment

Table 2.2 summarizes the employment status of a sample of emancipated foster youth at the age 20 to 21 follow-up.

Employment patterns were highly variable. Fewer than one in three youth reported full-time employment (30 or more hours per week). The majority (51%) were unemployed at the point of follow-up. Results with respect to having and holding a job were disappointing, particularly in view of the thriving economy in the mid-1990s.

TABLE 2.1

Educational Status of Emancipated Foster Youth (in percentages)

RACE/GENDER	LESS THAN HIGH SCHOOL	GENERAL EQUIVALENCY DIPLOMA	HIGH SCHOOL DIPLOMA	POSTSECONDARY EDUCATION	N
White Male	29.0	8.7	30.4	31.9	69
Nonwhite Male	48.5	15.2	18.2	18.2	33
White Female	24.8	13.6	34.4	27.2	125
Nonwhite Female	32.9	8.6	21.4	37.1	70
Overall	30.3	11.4	28.6	29.6	297

TABLE 2.2

Employment Status of Emancipated Foster Youth (in percentages)

RACE/GENDER	FULL-TIME	PART-TIME	NOT EMPLOYED	N
White Male	47.8	14.5	37.7	69
Nonwhite Male	15.2	12.1	72.7	33
White Female	30.4	22.4	47.2	125
Nonwhite Female	21.4	17.1	61.4	70
Overall	30.6	18.2	51.2	297

TABLE 2.3

Yearly Income of Emancipated Foster Youth (in percentages)

RACE/GENDER	$0	$1–$5,000	$5,000–10,000	$10,000–15,000	$15,000+	N
White Male	7.5	58.2	20.9	9.0	4.5	67
Nonwhite Male	19.4	54.8	25.8	0.0	0.0	31
White Female	13.1	59.8	20.5	4.9	1.6	122
Nonwhite Female	10.6	66.7	15.2	4.5	3.0	66
Overall	11.9	60.5	19.9	5.2	2.4	286

Income

Table 2.3 summarizes information with respect to earnings and income for emancipated foster wards.

Income and earnings data cited in Table 2.3 were based on 1994-1995 information. The average income was estimated at $4,100 per year. Nearly 70% reported an annual income of less than $5,000. With respect to income level, fewer than 1 in 10 wards were able to earn more than $10,000 per year.

Means-Tested Programs

Use of public aid as a source of income represents a useful measure of dependency on societal resources. Information used to determine reliance on means-tested programs included: AFDC (TANF), food stamps, Medicaid, subsidized housing, and cumulative use of means-tested programs.

AFDC and Women, Infants, and Children (WIC)

Table 2.4 summarizes use of public assistance by female wards in the form of AFDC and WIC programs.

Table 2.4 illustrates a clear trend; large percentages of emancipated female wards rely on public aid for survival. With respect to AFDC, nearly 40% of women in the 20- to 21-year-old follow-up group used this program. Use of WIC was somewhat higher, with more than one in two former wards using this program. Although nonwhite women were the highest users in either program, as a group, female wards are vulnerable with respect to achieving economic self-sufficiency. In the age 20 to 21 follow-up group, nearly 56% of emancipated females were either pregnant or parenting one or more children.

Food Stamps

Table 2.5 summarizes the food stamp use pattern among emancipated foster wards. Overall, about 45% reported food stamp use. Use rates varied by gender. High percentages of users were female wards. More than one in two relied on food stamps. With respect to male wards, the rate dropped to one in four.

Thus far, the self-sufficiency profile for emancipated wards suggests problematic futures, at least in the short term. Public aid, food stamps, and other societal resources appear to be indispensable to the transitional survival of foster wards as they struggle for self-sufficiency.

Use of Medicaid

Table 2.6 illustrates the widespread use of Medicaid among emancipated foster wards. Nearly two out of three former wards relied on Medicaid for health care services. Gender was a major factor in utilization rates. Females were the high users; the percentages ranged from 77% to 84% for white and nonwhite females. Medicaid use for emancipated male wards was considerably less, dropping to more than 40%.

One factor in the differential female-male Medicaid use pattern is the high rate of parenting among female wards. In the absence of Medicaid— the "poor people's" health program—most foster young adults and their

TABLE 2.4

Use of Public Aid by Female Wards (in percentages)

RACE/GENDER	N	AID TO FAMILIES WITH DEPENDENT CHILDREN (AFDC)		WOMEN, INFANTS, AND CHILDREN (WIC)	
		Yes	No	Yes	No
White	125	35	65	46	54
Nonwhite	70	57	43	63	37
Overall Use of AFDC and WIC	195	43	57	52	48

TABLE 2.5

Utilization Rates for Food Stamps (in percentages)

RACE/GENDER	YES	NO	N
White Male	24.6	75.4	69
Nonwhite Male	30.3	69.7	33
White Female	50.4	49.6	125
Nonwhite Female	62.9	37.1	70
Overall	45.1	54.9	297

TABLE 2.6

Use of Medicaid (in percentages)

RACE/GENDER	YES	NO	N
White Male	44.9	55.1	69
Nonwhite Male	42.4	57.6	33
White Female	76.8	23.2	125
Nonwhite Female	84.3	15.7	70
Overall	67.3	32.7	297

families were without health insurance and unable to afford health or medical services.

Housing/Living Arrangements

With respect to postemancipation housing and living arrangements, a range of options were reported. Table 2.7 summarizes the distribution of living arrangements.

Fewer than one out of five lived by themselves, usually in an apartment or mobile home unit. The highest percentage resided with a signifi-

TABLE 2.7

Living Arrangements of Emancipated Foster Youth

LIVING ARRANGEMENT	%
Self	17
Significant Other	27
Birthparents	16
Relative Home	14
Friends	14
Foster Family	6
Jail	5
Shelter	1
Total	100

cant other, usually a boyfriend or girlfriend. In this group, a few were married. A small percentage were living with their parents or with a relative. The remaining options included living with friends, a foster family, in jail, or in a shelter arrangement. Affordable housing is a critical need for youth in transition. Overall, approximately 20% of emancipated foster wards used housing subsidies. The highest rate of subsidy use was by women. Nearly 40% of nonwhite women and 16% of white women required a subsidy. Among male wards, use of housing subsidies was negligible and ranged from 3% to 5%.

Cumulative Use of Means-Tested Programs

Overall, nearly 80% of emancipated wards used one or more means-tested public assistance programs. Table 2.8 summarizes these data.

The main trend was that nearly one out of four female wards used five or more means-tested programs. The main programs were AFDC, WIC, food stamps, Medicaid, and subsidized housing vouchers. The need for a social safety net is evident, particularly for female wards parenting young children.

Foster Youth Transitions to Adulthood— University of Wisconsin Follow-up Study

The Wisconsin project tracked the progress of foster youth after discharge from placement. Based on 113 interviews, the results 12 to 18 months after leaving care were as follows:

With respect to educational status, more than one-third had not yet completed high school; 55% had completed a high school diploma; and 9% were reported enrolled in college. Nearly one in three reported being

TABLE 2.8

Use of One or More Means-Tested Programs (in percentages)

GENDER	NUMBER OF PROGRAMS USED					
	0	1	2	3	4	5+
Male	34.3	37.3	11.8	12.7	4.0	0.0
Female	13.8	12.3	14.9	17.9	17.4	23.6
Overall	20.9	20.9	13.8	16.2	12.8	15.5

poorly prepared to live on their own. Only one out of four former wards expressed confidence in being "very prepared" to live on their own. With respect to use of means-tested programs, nearly one in three received some form of public aid. Of this group, nearly 40% were women. Health, medical, and dental services were identified as a continuing need. The investigators concluded, "There should be little doubt that, at least in Wisconsin, a significant proportion of foster youth have a very difficult time in making the transition to self-sufficiency" (Courtney, Piliavin, Grogan-Kaylor, & Nesmith, 1998, p. 12).

Key elements in the assessment of the progress of emancipated foster wards in Wisconsin were: (a) Only 40% of the study group was employed at the 12- to 18-month postdischarge follow-up; (b) those who were employed earned less, on average, than "a full-time worker paid the minimum wage" (Courtney et al., 1998, p. 12); and (c) many youth encountered housing instability and homelessness and were victims of violence.

Older Wards Study—State of Illinois

The Illinois Department of Children and Family Services conducted a review of the status of more than 400 older youth in state custody. Information was provided by caseworkers for a sample of wards who were 17 years of age or older. Wards were still in state custody, but all were on the threshold of aging out of placement. Data from caseworkers were collected in the following areas: (a) educational status, (b) employment status, (c) impediments to self-sufficiency, and (d) caseworker predictions as to the probable future success of wards to live independently. Findings were as follows (Leathers & Testa, 1999):

Education

Of wards age 18 and older, 45% completed a high school diploma; 7% completed a GED or vocational certificate. In the 17-year-old group, 22% completed diplomas or a GED. Approximately 25% enrolled in a special education program or nontraditional program or school. About 20% of older wards were not attending a school program and classified as drop-outs.

Employment Status

About one-half of the sample was classified as employed, 31% part-time and 13% full-time. Job holding was reported as a significant problem. With respect to income, nearly two out of three employed youth were earning less than the minimum wage.

Impediments to Self-Sufficiency

Approximately one in three wards were identified as having one or more conditions that were probable impediments to achieving self-sufficiency. Barriers cited included mental health concerns, pregnancy and parenting, substance abuse, and related developmental disabilities. With respect to the risk factor of early parenting, 34% of female wards had one or more children or were pregnant at the time of the survey.

Caseworker Predictions

Caseworkers rated educational achievement as a pivotal element in the road to self-sufficiency. The probability of achieving self-sufficiency was inversely related to educational achievement. Estimated odds for success were as follows:

- *Postsecondary Education* provided a greater than 80% chance of achieving self-sufficiency.

- *High School Diploma* provided a 30% to 40% chance of achieving self-sufficiency.

- *Having Less than a High School Diploma* provided a 15% to 20% chance of achieving self-sufficiency.

Overall, postsecondary education was estimated to double or triple the chances of success in achieving economic self-sufficiency. Educational achievement in terms of a credential beyond high school was viewed by caseworkers as an element that increased the odds of success in dramatic fashion.

Cross-National Comparisons

Cross-national data on outcomes for older foster wards are consistent with the trends cited for youth in the United States. Research from Canada, England, Ireland, Australia, and Western Europe reports patterns similar to those obtained in the United States. In Canada, Martin (1996) analyzed the effects of leaving provincial wardship in Toronto at age 18. She concluded that "they were poor, under-employed, and under-educated...they had little or no support from their families, many had experienced the justice system" (p. 105). Martin asked, "How then can the state justify requiring children in care to leave at age 18" (p. 105)? In his analysis of the leaving-care situation in Nova Scotia, Fitzgerald (1995) concluded that "a critical gap exists in the child welfare system concerning...provision for older adolescents between the ages of 16 and 19" (pp. 728–729). In the United Kingdom, a study sponsored by the National Children's Bureau in London (Garnett, 1992), evidence cited by Pinkerton and McCrea from Northern Ireland (1999), and a report by Smit (1995) from the Netherlands provide a basis for concluding that the uncertain futures of youth leaving out-of-home care is a phenomenon of international concern.

Groundbreaking studies on leaving care in Britain were conducted by Biehal, Clayden, Stein, and Wade (1994). With respect to the qualifications required for success in a technologically driven society, few youth had acquired the educational preparation needed to compete in a career-oriented job market by the time they left care. Many young people in Biehal et al.'s cohort cited factors such as placement changes and related disruptions, as well as system disinterest in their education and employment, as barriers to achieving independence. In a report by Stein and Carey (1986), no less than 80% of the study group were unemployed two years after leaving care. Also, numerous surveys confirm that former wards are overrepresented among homeless groups. Analysis of homeless youth who used the Centrepoint Hostel in London revealed that 40% had previously been in out-of-home care. The National Children's Bureau Leaving Care project found that fewer than one in four youth departed from care with any formal education qualifications. At discharge, only 40% were in full- or part-time work or enrolled in an employment training program (Garnett, 1992). Similar results were reported by the Young People Leaving Care project in Northern Ireland. Pinkerton and McCrea (1999) noted that "reflecting their lack of employment or involvement in full time education, 75% of the care leavers received their income from social security or training allowances" (p. 61). The Northern Ireland project concludes on a pessimistic note: (a) Six months after leaving care, only 50% of youth were judged to possess the tools needed to achieve self-sufficiency; (b) about one in three were enrolled in a government-subsidized youth training project; and (c) although a small number were working, nearly one in four was classified as unemployed.

Potential for Self-Sufficiency: An Interpretive Summary

The main issue posed in Chapter 2 is the extent to which foster wards are prepared to achieve self-sufficiency. Based on the evidence cited, the inescapable conclusion is that potential for independence is low. Information collected over a span of decades on hundreds of emancipated foster wards in the United States, Canada, and the United Kingdom, including Northern Ireland, confirms numerous barriers to self-sufficiency. The likelihood of continued dependency not only characterizes the futures of many emancipated foster youth, but applies to other youth groups classified as disadvantaged as well. As a case in point, consider the thousands of young people who grow up in a public assistance household (AFDC), typically headed by a single parent. With respect to potential for independence, studies published in 1952 and 1963 under the auspices of the American Public Welfare Association (APWA) reported the following:

Nearly 70% of former AFDC children left school prior to age 18. The net result was that at age 20, nearly two out of three young people raised in public aid families were without a high school diploma. Upward mobility in terms of occupation and income was associated with education level. Of those classified as unskilled workers, 83% left school prior to age 18 (Blackwell & Gould, 1952).

In the APWA report entitled *An American Dependency Challenge* (Burgess & Price, 1963), little progress was noted in education since the 1952 survey. The educational progress of children and youth in public assistance households had dropped "far behind that of the school-age population for the country as a whole" (Burgess & Price, 1963, p. 185). Less than 25% of the youth 18 years old and older completed a high school diploma. Compared with the general population, the educational retardation rate was estimated as "more than twice as high for AFDC children." In the 1963 report, only 2% in the public assistance sample were enrolled in postsecondary education or vocational training, as compared with nearly 20% of youth age 18 to 24 in the general population.

An American Dependency Challenge ends on a pessimistic note. The essential conclusion was that "AFDC families faced as they are with lack of work experience or marketable skills, poor health, emotional instability...do not present an optimistic picture in terms of potential for independence" (Burgess & Price, 1963, p. 186).

Numerically, foster youth comprise a relatively small but highly significant segment of the population targeted as disadvantaged. Youth who grow up in public assistance households also qualify as an economically disadvantaged segment. Foster wards and welfare youth share a common experience, namely spending time in dependency environments. With respect to the prospects for achieving self-sufficiency, the prognosis is usually "low potential for independence." For the past 50 years, the intervention strategy for welfare-dependent families has been to bypass the children and youth and target household heads for rehabilitation. Young people in welfare-dependent families are usually ignored. The single-track intervention strategy is illustrated in an evaluation report by Friedlander and Burtless (1995) entitled *Five Years Later—The Long-Term Effects of Welfare to Work Programs*. In the sites evaluated, target participants were typically age 30 or older, fewer than one in two completed a high school diploma or GED, and approximately 50% of program participants had more than one child. Absent from the Friedlander-Burtless evaluation is information on the ages of children or data on their progress in school and/or community situations. With respect to public assistance, exploratory studies suggest that targeting adolescents and young adults in public aid households is more likely to produce beneficial results than is a head of household–only strategy (Mech, 1979).

It is important to collect information on self-sufficiency prospects for the next generation. For welfare families, the consequences of dependency often extend to the children. A study conducted in Baltimore, entitled *Adolescent Mothers in Later Life* (Furstenberg, Brooks-Gunn, & Morgan, 1987), illustrates the importance of documenting the progress of children and youth who live in welfare households. Based on a long-term longitudinal study, the Baltimore project calculated the influence of educational deficits on the likelihood of the children of welfare mothers continuing the cycle of dependency. The high school careers of the children of public aid parents was described as a "massive failure." Half of the youth sample repeated at least one grade, and 40% had been suspended or expelled from school.

In a synthesis of studies on the effects of foster care, McDonald, Allen, Westerfelt, and Piliavin (1996) concluded "that the level of educational attainment of persons who had been in care is below the average attainment of those citizens of comparable age" (p. 64); "that in the Casey Family Project one-third of the youth were behind grade level when placed, and the same proportion were behind grade level at discharge" (p. 65); and

that somewhere between 15% and 56% formerly placed in out-of-home care as children did not complete high school or earn a GED, a rate which is higher than that found among individuals who were not in care as children. (p. 120)

A survey of children in out-of-home care conducted for the Ohio Department of Human Services (1987) concluded the following:

- The overall educational progress of children in out-of-home care is dismal (p. 18). More than 50% are performing below grade level in reading and mathematics, with more than 75% of foster children receiving services from the Department of Mental Health. Those under jurisdiction of the juvenile court also perform below grade level in reading and math.

- Assistance in securing education services was provided to only 1 in 3 children, and remedial assistance to only 1 in 20 children.

- Of children in the care of the juvenile courts, 90% are performing below grade level, but less than 5% receive any sort of special educational assistance.

With respect to foster adolescents who emancipate from care, the odds of using means-tested resources are high, particularly so for female wards. An important distinction in comparative intervention strategies for disadvantaged youth is societal inclination to focus on foster wards as the target population, possibly because state wards usually live in out-of-home placements, whereas in welfare reform programs, because most youth live in an AFDC household, the tendency is to target family heads for rehabilitation and to bypass the task of preparing welfare youth for self-sufficiency.

In terms of self-sufficiency potential among foster wards, the evidence suggests problematic futures and difficulty ahead on the road to independence. Fortunately, the main deficits and barriers are known. In the aggregate, foster wards need to demonstrate higher levels of achievement in "bread and butter" areas such as education, employment, career preparation, and delay of pregnancy and parenting. Also vital in the intervention equation is the opportunity to target preparation for independence efforts directly to the needs of foster wards. In democratic societies, most citizens believe in the power of facilitative environments as avenues to positive change and in the concept of providing "second chance" opportunity structures for young people at the margins of community life. Although governments—federal, state, and local—can create opportunities for young people to succeed, results cannot be guaranteed. A critical element in an opportunity-based framework is the extent to which young people are motivated and willing to take advantage of the opportunities available. As a society, we are typically supportive of the underdog—the vulnerable person who can overcome formidable odds and achieve success. Opportunity structures are evolving that attempt to respond to the need to prepare young people leaving care for self-sufficiency and independent living.

References

Barth, R. (1986). Emancipation services for adolescents in foster care. *Social Work, 31*, 165-171.

Barth, R. (1990). On their own: The experiences of youth after foster care. *Child & Adolescent Social Work Journal, 7*, 419-440.

Baylor, E., & Monachesi, E. (1939). *The rehabilitation of children*. New York: Harper.

Biehal, N., Clayden, J., Stein, M., & Wade, J. (1994). Leaving care in England: A research perspective. *Children & Youth Services Review, 16*(3/4), 231-254.

Blackwell, G., & Gould, R. (1952). *Future citizens all*. Chicago: American Public Welfare Association.

Bowlby, J. (1951). *Maternal care and mental health*. Geneva, Switzerland: World Health Organization.

Bremner, R. (Ed.). (1971). *Children and youth in America. A documentary history* (Vol. 2). Cambridge, MA: Harvard University Press.

Burgess, E., & Price, D. (1963). *An American dependency challenge*. Chicago: American Public Welfare Association.

Citizens' Committee for Children of New York. (1984, September). *The foster care exit— Ready or not. An inquiry into how New York prepares children in foster care for discharge to independent living*. New York: Author.

Cook, R. (1997). Are we helping foster care youth prepare for their future? In J. Berrick, R. Barth, & N. Gilbert (Eds.), *Child welfare research review* (Vol. 2, pp. 201–218). New York: Columbia University Press.

Cook, R., Fleishman, E., & Grimes, V. (1991). *A national evaluation of Title IV-E foster care independent living programs for youth, Phase 2, final report* (Vol. 1). Rockville, MD: WESTAT, Inc.

Courtney, M., Piliavin, I., Grogan-Kaylor, A., & Nesmith, A. (1998). *Foster youth in transition to adulthood: Outcomes 12 to 18 months after leaving out-of-home care*. Madison: University of Wisconsin School of Social Work and Institute for Research on Poverty.

Festinger, T. (1983). *No one ever asked us...A postscript to foster care*. New York: Columbia University Press.

Fitzgerald, M. (1995). Homeless youths in the child welfare system: Implications for policy and service. *Child Welfare, 74*, 717-730.

Friedlander, D., & Burtless, G. (1995). *Five years later: The long-term effects of welfare-to-work programs*. New York: Russell Sage Foundation.

Furstenberg, F., Brooks-Gunn, J., & Morgan, P. (1987). *Adolescent mothers in later life*. New York: Cambridge University Press.

Garnett, L. (1992). *Leaving care and after*. London: National Children's Bureau.

Leathers, S., & Testa, M. (1999). *Older wards study: Caseworkers report on the status of DCFS wards aged seventeen and one-half years old and older*. Chicago: Illinois Department of Children and Family Services.

Maas, H., & Engler, R. (1959). *Children in need of parents*. New York: Columbia University Press.

Martin, F. (1996). Tales of transition: Leaving public care. In B. Galaway & J. Hudson (Eds.), *Youth in transition* (pp. 99–106). Toronto, Canada: Thompson Educational.

McDonald, T., Allen, R., Westerfelt, A., & Piliavin, I. (1996). *Assessing the long-term effects of foster care: A research synthesis*. Washington, DC: Child Welfare League of America.

Mech, E. (1979). *Preparing welfare youth for self-sufficiency*. Springfield: State of Illinois Commission to Revise the Public Aid Code.

Mech, E., & Fung, C. (1998, May). *Preparing foster adolescents for economic self-sufficiency*. Paper presented at the Independent Living National Conference, Pathways to Adulthood, Galveston, TX.

Meier, E. (1965). Current circumstances of former foster children. *Child Welfare, 44*, 196-206.

Ohio Department of Human Services. (1987). *Children in out-of-home care. Summary of findings*. Columbus, OH: Author.

Pinkerton, J., & McCrea, R. (1999). *Meeting the challenge? Young people leaving care in Northern Ireland*. Hants, UK: Ashgate.

Smit, M. (1995). Preparation for discharge from residential care: A report from the Netherlands. In E. Mech & J. Rycraft (Eds.), *Preparing foster youth for adult living* (pp. 37–41). Washington, DC: Child Welfare League of America.

Stein, M., & Carey, K. (1986). *Leaving care*. Oxford, UK: Blackwell.

Theis, S. (1924). *How foster children turn out*. New York: State Charities Aid Association.

U. S. Department of Health and Human Services, Office of Human Development Services. (1983, September 8). *Study of the adaptation of adolescents in foster care to independence and community life* (RFP #105-84-1811). Washington, DC: Author.

Wiltse, K. (1978). Current issues and new directions in foster care. In A. Kadushin (Ed.), *Child welfare strategy in the coming years* (pp. 51–89). Washington, DC: U.S. Department of Health, Education, and Welfare.

Chapter 3

Legislative Initiatives for Independent Living

Edmund V. Mech

> These young adults desperately need our help.
> Think of our own children turned loose in
> New York or Chicago at age 18 to find jobs and
> set up on their own.
>
> —Senator Daniel Patrick Moynihan (1988, p. 484)

Passage of the Adoption Assistance and Child Welfare Act in 1980 (P.L. 96-272) was a major step forward in foster care reform. Congressional intent was that P.L. 96-272 would solve recurring problems within the nation's child welfare system. Advocates for change were alarmed at the volume of out-of-home placements that were judged as unnecessary. Moreover, concern was expressed at the steady decline in adoptions, particularly for special needs children. Accordingly, the major components of the 1980 child welfare reform legislation included case plans, placement prevention, reunification services, and periodic court reviews. Allen, Golubock, and Olson (1983) reviewed the provisions of P.L. 96-272 as follows:

- **Case Plans.** Reform legislation required states to prepare written case plans for each child in placement. Emphasis was to be given to using the least restrictive living arrangement and to place children in locations that were in geographic proximity to the child's parental home.

- **Placement Prevention.** Legislative priority was on avoiding unnecessary placement, with the stipulation that if placement occurred, reasonable efforts were to be made to prevent removal of children from their homes.

- **Reunification Services.** When out-of-home placement occurred, the enabling legislation placed responsibility on the state agency to establish a family reunification plan. Congressional intent was that services sufficient to enable children to return home and to reunite with parents would be provided.

- **Periodic Court Review.** Administrative and judicial guidelines were established that required periodic oversight of case progress. A two-tiered review structure was set in motion, as follows: (1) There was to be a review at least every 6 months by the court or a duly constituted administrative entity, and (2) a dispositional hearing under court jurisdiction within 18 months following placement.

The purpose of the dispositional hearing is for a court to determine the probable future status of children and to influence progress toward achieving a permanent family arrangement for children. The 1980 child welfare reform legislation made three assumptions: (1) Large numbers of out-of-home placements would be prevented by virtue of providing comprehensive supportive services; (2) if placement was unavoidable, reunification planning and rehabilitation of families would be sufficient to return children to their own homes; and (3) procedures for streamlining termination of parental rights and freeing children for adoption, plus the availability of adoption subsides, would increase the likelihood of special needs children finding permanent homes with adoptive families.

During the implementation years following enactment of P.L. 96-272, it became apparent that the original legislation had overlooked an important population in need of system attention. Thousands of young wards were aging out of placement without the benefit of reunification with their families or adoptive placement in relative or nonrelative homes. The child welfare field moved rapidly toward recognizing that preparing foster adolescents for self-support must be accepted as a system goal. A movement in foster care was gaining momentum—one that many refer to as the independent-living movement. Events that followed culminated in a new legislative entitlement that provided independent-living preparation for older foster wards. The chronological highlights are as follows.

Early Advocacy Efforts

Concerns raised by citizens' groups, national youth organizations, child welfare agencies, foster parents, media reports, and former foster wards combined to draw attention to the risks associated with aging out of placement. Momentum for action was fueled by studies that documented high rates of homelessness among former foster wards. Homeless shelters surveyed in New York City, Chicago, and Minneapolis produced sobering results. Based on survey data, estimates of the percentages of homeless adults who were formerly in foster care ranged from less than 10% (Crystal, 1984), to 23% (Susser, Struening, & Conover, 1987), to a high of 39% (Sosin, Piliavin, & Westerfelt, 1990). A *New York Times* article (Barden, 1991) concluded that "a large and disproportionate number of the nation's homeless are young people who have come out of foster care programs" (p. 1). The point was made repeatedly that states may be hurting youth in placement by discharging them from care at age 18. In a 1980 report, *Redirecting Foster Care*, the New York City Mayor's Task Force on Foster Care concluded that there were gaps in services to youth leaving foster care that left the youth unprepared for living independently. Children's advocacy groups, such as the Citizens' Committee for Children of New York (1984), investigated how New York City prepares foster wards for self-sufficiency. The central question posed was, "Were these youngsters being helped to acquire the training and skills...to give them a chance to be responsible adults?" (p. ii).

Based on case record reviews, interviews with foster wards and caseworkers, and discussions with agency administrators, the main findings were:

- Approximately 40% of youth were in a special education curriculum or below the age-appropriate grade level in a regular class.

- Case records contained little or no information as to preparation in entry-level job skills or vocational training.

- The majority of foster wards had serious reading deficiencies as measured by standardized tests.

The committee report concluded that foster wards who were assigned the goal of independent living were largely ignored. However, the fact that nearly one in three adolescents in placement in New York City at the time of the survey had been assigned the goal of independent living placed a heavy burden on child welfare administrators to respond to the need. In testimony before the House Congressional Select Committee on Children, Youth, and Families, Ernesto Loperena, then President, North American Council on Adoptable Children, cited an example in New York City of an 18-year-old girl who had just been discharged from foster care. Loperena (1987) described the situation as follows:

*Four years ago one of our workers…encountered a con-
fused looking 18 year old riding the subways. She asked the
youngster what was troubling her. Apparently she had just
been discharged from a foster care institution with two sub-
way tokens and the address of an emergency welfare office.
(p. 164)*

Loperena continued by stating that the agency worker "who had been
shopping that evening, asked the youngster to come home with her and
told her they would deal with the problem the following day." On arriving
home, the worker told the young lady, "Go to the kitchen and help yourself to milk or soda while I put these packages away." Ten minutes later,
she saw the girl standing by the kitchen door. "Why didn't you have some
milk or soda?" Reflecting her experiences in foster care, the young lady
replied, "I'm not allowed to go into the kitchen." Loperena posed the following question: "Can we realistically expect an 18 year old aging-out of
foster care to seek employment, find an apartment, prepare meals, and
budget their expenses when they have been taught not to open a refrig-
erator door?" (Loperena, 1987, 164-165).

In reviewing gaps in the 1980 national child welfare reform legislation,
advocacy groups were consistent in identifying placement system deficiencies. The essential themes with respect to adolescent wards were:

1. Youth who are discharged to independent living are likely to have
   fewer familial, community, and social supports than are youth who
   emancipate from birthfamilies or adoptive families.

2. The child welfare agency may be the main resource open to youth
   who emancipate from placement. Advocates are convinced that
   postemancipation or aftercare services should be the responsibility of
   agencies that provide foster care services. The Citizens' Committee
   for Children of New York (1984) concluded that "agencies…carry the
   heavy responsibility to provide or arrange services and supports for
   these youngsters, as well as providing the youngsters with supportive
   adult relationships" (p. 72).

3. Regardless of the goal assigned (i.e., reunification, adoption, or independent living), all foster adolescents should receive services designed
   to prepare them for independence and self-sufficiency. Most experts
   recommend planning for independent living when adolescent wards
   are 14 or 15 years old, instead of waiting until they are 18.

4. Preparation of the foster adolescent for independence should contain the following elements: giving educational, prevocational, and vocational experience that is designed to prepare youth for self-support; gradually moving the foster ward from traditional placements to community-based settings, such as transitional congregate apartments or scattered-site apartments; providing extensive information with respect to the range of community services available, including linkage with community contacts, transitional mentors, and a "natural-systems" support team; and helping young wards to make decisions about educational choices, including postsecondary education, as well as employment and housing.

5. Postemancipation follow-up contact should occur for at least one year following discharge. Postemancipation contact is viewed by advocates as highly desirable, but remains a major weakness in the child welfare system. It is encouraging to note that research investigations in the United States, Canada, the United Kingdom, and Western Europe have demonstrated the feasibility of conducting follow-up contact with foster youth who have emancipated from state care. Follow-up contact with former foster wards can provide valuable information about their experiences in building a life after leaving placement.

Palmer v. Cuomo

A legal case in New York State was a pivotal event in the movement to extend child welfare legislation that would help thousands of adolescent wards prepare for independence. Plaintiffs in the *Palmer v. Cuomo* (1986) case claimed that both New York City and the State of New York had (a) "breached a statutory duty to prepare them for independent living outside of the foster care system" (p. 21) and (b) failed to supervise youth who were already discharged. Plaintiffs charged that the city not only failed to prepare them for independent living, but never contacted them following discharge. Plaintiffs were described as homeless and forced to seek shelter in "tenement buildings, subways, and public parks" (*Palmer v. Cuomo*, 1986, p. 21). Plaintiffs were "ten foster care youths between the ages of 17 and 21 years—seven of whom had been discharged, and three soon to be discharged from their placements to independent-living" (18 NYCRR 430-12 cf). Article 17 of the New York State constitution places responsibility on the state to provide aid to the needy. With respect to foster wards, there is a parens patriae burden on the state to meet that responsibility for children who require out-of-home placement. The city conceded that it did not provide adequate supervision to discharged youth. Although New York City had established a trial discharge period of 90 days, which could be extended to 6 months, there was no system in place for monitoring youth. The city argued that *supervision* means face-to-face contact, but that no regulations or administrative guidelines existed that required caseworker contacts until the discharged youth reached 21 years of age.

On August 30, 1985, the court granted a preliminary injunction that prevented New York State from discharging youth from placement until a number of conditions were satisfied. Key requirements were:

- A discharge plan must be prepared for plaintiffs in accordance with social services law (McKinney's Social Services Law).

- Plaintiffs are provided reasonable preparation for discharge, to include career counseling, training in a marketable skill or trade, and learning skills required for independent living.

- Supervision of plaintiffs until they reach 21 years of age, ensuring that during a transitional period, plaintiffs' basic needs are met, including appropriate housing, with the provision that such housing would exclude the New York City municipal shelter system. Moreover, plaintiffs charged that they were provided little or no opportunity to contest discharge from placement on the grounds of inadequate preparation for independent living. Their affidavits stated these inadequacies in readiness for independence led to their destitution.

The stage for a lawsuit was set by the following events (based on a report by Tobis, 1989, which summarizes the work of the litigation team).

One of the plaintiffs, Reggie Brown, was discharged from placement on his 18th birthday. He was given a transportation token with directions to a homeless shelter. According to the record, Reggie Brown spent 18 months being homeless, living in subways, and finding refuge in movie theaters, bus terminals, and shelters. Reggie had been in foster care for six years, but received no preparation for living on his own.

With assistance from the Legal Action Center for the Homeless and pro bono aid from the law firm of Sullivan and Cromwell, Reggie Brown joined nine other homeless youth in a class-action lawsuit, *Palmer v. Cuomo*. The plaintiffs charged New York City and New York State with failure to prepare foster wards for discharge and unwillingness to assist in the postdischarge transition to living on their own.

The case for the plaintiffs was based on convincing documentation. Testimony revealed that no program was in place to assist youth after discharge. The city's response for youth between ages 18 and 21 was a bed in one of the municipal shelters for the homeless. According to Tobis' (1989) description, "up to 1,000 men sleep in one room on beds three feet apart. Many of the older men are alcoholic, mentally disabled, or addicted to drugs; about half have been in jail" (p. 42). Once homeless, caught up in a deviant street culture, without job skills or employment experience, it was difficult to escape.

Before filing a lawsuit, the litigation team approached the city and state in an attempt to resolve program deficiencies without court action. The response from city and state was disappointing—both defended their programs as satisfactory. It was apparent that a class-action effort was needed to influence change.

In July 1985, approximately six months after the lawsuit was filed, the New York Supreme Court ruled in favor of the plaintiffs. A preliminary injunction was issued that ordered New York City and State to provide postdischarge services. Two years elapsed before New York State set in motion a satisfactory predischarge and postdischarge independent-living program. The postdischarge component contained three elements: (1) trial discharge with custody including aftercare, (2) relocation services due to loss of housing, and (3) supervision until 21 years of age.

Federal Independent-Living Initiatives

Advocacy efforts to improve foster care and adoption services culminated in a series of congressional hearings to amend aspects of P.L. 96-272. On June 19, 1985, the House Ways and Means Committee heard testimony related to H.R. 2810, a bill to amend Part E of Title IV of the Social Security Act. The objective of H.R. 2810 was "to more effectively meet the needs of children involved." The bill was entitled Foster Care, Adoption Assistance, and Child Welfare Amendments of 1985. Section 102 of the bill dealt with authorizing the Transitional Independent-Living Program for Older Foster Youth. The proposed independent-living initiatives legislation met with resistance from the Reagan administration.

In representing executive branch views with respect to congressional proposals to expand child welfare mandates, Dorcas R. Hardy (1985), then Assistant Secretary, Human Development Services, U.S. Department of

Health and Human Services), stated, "We oppose the provisions in H.R. 2810 which would greatly expand current law provisions or create new mandates for program elements" (p. 53). Hardy argued that new provisions "may now be provided at state option which can be funded under existing authorities" (p. 54). Hardy was clearly against establishing a new and separate aging-out entitlement program for older foster wards. Hardy stated that although foster wards "may have unique needs, in other ways they are not unlike the millions of young people who have not been in foster care, but must enter the world of work and independent-living at the age of eighteen" (p. 54). Administration testimony included the statement, "We must not overlook that many public school systems already provide independent-living training and that some states now require that residential care programs include self-sufficiency skills training in their service design" (p. 57). In particular, the Reagan administration opposed creating a foster youth "G.I. Bill of Rights" that would expand the period of support for older wards from 19 to 21 years. The administration's anti-independent-living theme was based on the concept that age 18 was the definitive criterion for adult status. Based on that view, Hardy commented, "I do not feel that we should have special programs for 18 to 20 year olds which could possibly just turn into an early welfare check" (p. 65). Despite the administration's objections, on April 7, 1986, Part E of Title IV–Social Security Act was amended by P.L. 99-272 to include Section 477, as follows:

> It shall be the objective of each program established under this section to help individuals participating in such program to prepare to live independently upon leaving foster care. Such programs may include programs to:
>
> - Enable participants to seek a high school diploma or its equivalent or to take part in appropriate vocational training.
>
> - Provide training in daily living skills, budgeting, locating and maintaining housing, and career planning.
>
> - Provide for individual and group counseling.
>
> - Integrate and coordinate services otherwise available to participants.
>
> - Provide for the establishment of outreach programs designed to attract individuals who are eligible to participate in the program.

- *Provide each participant a transitional independent-living plan which should be based on an assessment of need, and which shall be incorporated into his/her case plan.*

- *Provide participants with other services and assistance designed to improve their transition to independent living.*

Overall, the approach to the independent-living legislation was typically incremental. The annual entitlement amount of $45 million was authorized on a temporary basis, for 1987 and 1988. The original legislation in 1986 was limited to Title IV-E eligible children age 16 and older. Approximately one year later, in hearings convened by the House Select Committee on Children, Youth, and Families, Dodie Livingston (1987), Commissioner, Administration of Children, Youth, and Families, U.S. Department of Health and Human Services, stated that "our legislative proposal...requests repeal of the Independent-Living Initiative. We believe this new program is not necessary because states have existing authority to use...social services block grant funds" (p. 14). Although the legislation was not repealed, the administration demonstrated considerable reluctance to implement the budget provisions of 99-272 or to issue program instructions to states as to how to apply for independent-living funds. In the 1987 hearings, Linda Greenan (1987), representing the Child Welfare League of America, noted that the administration's agreement to finally move ahead to release funds and implement the program as authorized was

> *not because the administration has recognized the need for this program, and not because they have decided to follow the intent of Congress, but because of the potential threat of the Senate to withhold Dr. Jean Elder's confirmation as Assistant Secretary for Human Development Services, pending assurances that the independent-living funds would be released. (p. 97)*

Reauthorization hearings were held in March 1988 with respect to the independent-living initiative, which was scheduled to expire in September 1988. The Hon. Robert T. Matsui, Representative in Congress from California, provided testimony in support of extending this legislation. At one point in his testimony, Matsui (1988) said:

> *The abrupt termination of youth from foster care at age 18 or 19 serves neither the goals of foster care for the youth nor the community into which these young people are tossed.*

> *This abrupt termination better serves the goals of drug deal-*
> *ers and other criminals who can recruit these vulnerable*
> *youths." (p. 5)*

Representative Matsui also raised the possibility of extending independent-living eligibility to youth after they leave foster care. He proposed a
six-month extension. The extended services concept was based on the
increased complexity of life for young people and the need to examine
the intent of foster care, which is to prepare wards for successful lives.
Despite administration objections to reauthorizing the independent-
living legislation, testimony was obtained from numerous witnesses in
support of reauthorizing the legislation and extending its scope. Two elements were added: (1) To extend as a state option the federal foster care
subsidy up to age 21, and (2) to include in the legislation children who are
not in the Aid to Families with Dependent Children program in foster care.

Accordingly, in 1988, the program was expanded under P.L. 100-647,
which authorized states to (a) provide independent-living services to all foster youth ages 16 to 18, (b) provide follow-up services to youth up to six
months after discharge, and (3) if they wished, continue independent-living
services to youth to age 21. With respect to funding, the original amount of
$45 million was increased to $50 million for 1990, $60 million for 1991, and
$70 million for 1992. On August 10, 1993, nearly six years after the original
initiative, under P.L. 103-66, Congress extended permanent status to the
independent-living initiative with an allotment of $70 million.

Postemancipation Services

As a result of the 1988 amendments, states had the option of continuing
services to youth until they were age 21. In 1989, a survey was conducted
to ascertain how public child welfare programs responded to the needs of
foster wards after leaving placement. Welfare Research, Inc. (WRI), in conjunction with the Legal Action Center for the Homeless and the Metropolitan Studies Program at New York University, analyzed state laws, statutes, policies, and programs for wards after they leave foster care (Tobis et
al., 1989). Survey findings revealed the following:

- In only four states, Illinois, New York, Nevada, and Rhode Island,
  did state law require any type of postdischarge or aftercare services. As a result of the *Palmer v. Cuomo* case, New York State
  clearly required aftercare services. Rhode Island law also stipulates a mandatory age 21 extension, unless a youth does not want

assistance. Statutes in Illinois and Nevada are less clear, but appear to require aftercare services for emancipated wards.

- The law in most states is selective with respect to foster youth. Participation in a full-time educational or vocational program is one of the conditions for receiving support past age 18.

- Several states fail to provide postdischarge services or to allow an extension of the discharge age beyond 18. The philosophy in these "ready or not" states is that youth are "out the door" when they reach 18 years of age, regardless of preparation for self-sufficiency.

Recommendations of the survey groups were that federal law be revised to authorize reimbursement to states for postdischarge services to youth up to age 21 and that emancipated foster wards who are unable to make a successful transition to community life, or who have otherwise failed to adjust, should be able to return to foster care until age 21. Also, the survey group expressed concern at the preference given to youth older than age 18 who were in an educational program or to wards with a handicapping condition. The report recommended that a policy of legislative universalism replace the widespread practice of selectivity. Their conclusion was that "all youth who have been in foster care have a right to remain in care until a satisfactory transition to independent living is made" (Tobis, 1989, p. 7).

The Foster Care Independence Act of 1999

Efforts continued with respect to improving services to prepare foster youth for self-sufficiency. New legislative initiatives were aimed at extending assistance to older wards up to the age of 21. The objective was to reduce the odds of older foster wards trading one dependency system for another. In testimony before the U.S. House of Representatives Committee on Ways and Means, Dr. Carol W. Williams (1999), formerly Associate Commissioner, U.S. Children's Bureau, spoke in support of the White House proposal to expand the federal independent-living initiatives. The president's fiscal year 2000 budget contained the following elements:

- Increased funding for the independent-living program from $70 million to $105 million annually. The budget request was based on the growing number of foster youth 16 and older who were on an aging-out track. In 1992, approximately 62,000 youth age 16 and older were in placement. In 1998, that number rose to 77,000—an increase of 24%.

- Creation of a transitional support program for older youth. The intent was to conduct a series of demonstration programs that would provide economic subsidies to wards between the ages of 18 and 21 who were emancipating from the placement system. One stipulation was that foster youth must have a transition plan that includes participation in an educational or job training program.

- Health insurance for youth leaving care. The White House budget included a proposal that would allow states to extend medical coverage to foster youth until age 21.

Congressman Benjamin Cardin's bill, the Transition to Adulthood Program, proposed extending eligibility to age 21 for foster youth who have a specific case plan for achieving independence, are completing high school, are enrolled in a postsecondary program (or vocational training), or work a minimum of 20 hours a week. The Cardin proposal would authorize funds to place eligible youth in supervised transitional settings, including apartments that promote personal responsibility and self-sufficiency. In June 1999, the U.S. House of Representatives approved the Foster Care Independence Act of 1999 by a vote of 380 to 6. Responsibility for acting on the expanded independent-living legislation was now up to the U.S. Senate. Although Senate Bill §1327 was similar to the House version, it contained the proviso that youth may receive independent-living services concurrent with efforts to locate permanent homes, including adoptive family placements. Amendments to Section 477 of the Social Security Act stipulated that states provide support through mentors, and a "broad array of appropriate services including health care to former foster children between the ages of 18 and 21."

Cross-National Trends

In the past two decades, a number of countries have joined the United States in expressing concern about the deficits of young people in care moving into independence. England, Wales, Scotland, Ireland, Canada, Norway, Sweden, and the Netherlands have enacted legislation designed to improve the preparation of young people for leaving care. In England, in an analysis of the need for legislation with respect to leaving care, Biehl, Calyden, Stein, and Wade (1994) commented, "Young people spoke of 'not being prepared for leaving' and 'being kicked out of care'" (p. 232). Getting the attention of professionals and politicians "was a consequence of a number of actions—by young people in care, by researchers, by practitioners and managers in voluntary agencies,...and pressure groups" (Biehl et al., 1994, p. 13). In the United Kingdom, as in the United States, consciousness raising for politicians about the youth emancipation problem was a result of advocacy efforts over extended periods of time, brought about by organizations outside the political and bureaucratic structures of government.

In England and Wales, the legislative centerpiece in behalf of children and youth is the 1989 Children Act. Prior to enactment by Parliament, the provisions of the Act were debated for nearly six years. The Children Act of 1989 is described as "the most comprehensive and far reaching reform of child law which has come before parliament in living memory" (White, Carr, & Lowe, 1995, p. 1). Central to the act is the responsibility of local authority to respond to children who are "in-need." *In-need* is defined as a child who is "unlikely to achieve or maintain, or to have the opportunity of maintaining a reasonable standard of health or development without the provision for him of services by a local authority" (White et al., 1995, p. 147).

In the United Kingdom, the term *local authority* refers to the broad legal powers given to courts, counties, boroughs and city councils, and social services in matters of family and child law. With respect to sections of the Act pertaining to the welfare of youth, key elements in the legislation involve homeless adolescents and aftercare.

Homeless Adolescents
Section 6.37

> *A local authority has duties and powers relating to accommodation in respect of young persons found in their area who are between 16 and 21 years old. They are required to provide accommodation for 16 and 17 year olds in need, if they consider their welfare is likely to be seriously prejudiced if they are not provided with accommodation. (White et al., 1995, p. 155).*

Aftercare
Section 6.51

Local authorities have the power and duty "to prepare young people they are looking after for the time when they cease to be so looked after, and to provide after-care advice and assistance" (White et al., 1995, p. 159).

Section 6.52

"The powers and duties of local authorities cover all young people leaving a variety of forms of care when aged 16 or over. They continue until the person reaches the age of 21." (White et al., 1995, p. 158).

Section 6.53
Local authorities have the power

> to provide assistance in cash or in kind to any young person
> who qualifies for advice. Local authorities also have the
> power...to provide financial assistance connected with the
> young person's education, employment or training. Such
> grants may continue beyond the age of twenty-one to allow
> for completion of education or training. (Pinkerton &
> McCrea, 1999, p. 7)

Pinkerton and McCrea (1999), coinvestigators for the Northern Ireland Leaving Care Research Project at Queens University–Belfast, pointed out that the Children Order legislation for Northern Ireland was influenced by the "leaving care lobby that developed in England and Wales," and that the final version in 1995 "is almost word for word the same legislation found in the Children Act" (p. 8).

In Canada, organization and control of child welfare services is characterized by a tug-of-war between centralized provincial control and decentralized, local community control. In Alberta, province service delivery is described as being shortchanged by "a classic, bureaucratic, control-oriented, inflexible, highly centralized organizational model" (*Alberta Children's Advocate*, as cited in Rothery, Gallup, Tillman, & Allard, 1995, p. 594). On the other extreme, in Ontario, Canada's most heavily populated province, a decentralized child services system is in place. Referred to as the Children's Aid Society System, the Ontario model has been described as "successful over the years in minimizing the removal of children from their families, and in the development of innovative programming" (Rothery et al., 1995, p. 590). The move toward self-government with respect to child welfare services is especially strong among Native-Aboriginal communities in Canada. Apparently, the provinces of Manitoba and British Columbia were realizing success with decentralized services, until the local control model was "reversed by their respective governments" (Rothery et al., 1995, p. 591). Commenting specifically about the Maritime provinces (Nova Scotia, etc.), and in general about other provinces, Fitzgerald (1995) concluded, "Child welfare services in Canada offer little for youths age 16 to 19, and community resources are hard pressed to extend assistance to this challenged population" (p. 717). Canada clearly has numerous programs in place that are aimed at preparing young people for independence. Stone (1987) described innovative programs in Alberta,

Manitoba, and Ontario. Overall, the Dominion of Canada lacks child welfare legislation that is unified and consistent with across-the-board application in all provinces.

Interpretive Summary: Legislative Options for Self-Sufficiency

Recognition of the significance of the increasing numbers of adolescents in the child welfare system was slow to emerge. Oregon was one of the first states to advocate for preparing teen wards to take care of themselves when foster care support terminated on or about age 18. The Oregon plan, the Independent-Living Subsidy Program, began in 1973, more than a quarter-century ago. The subsidy plan was based on the theory that a subsidy program could promote maturity and independence among older adolescent wards. Obtaining support for the subsidy plan was difficult. State legislators were skeptical and expressed concern about "rewarding youngsters for failing in their foster home or institutional placements" (Simonitch & Anderson, 1979, p. 28). Ultimately, lawmakers authorized a two-year demonstration and later expanded the program statewide.

Prior to the subsidy proposal, caseworkers faced a familiar dilemma—older adolescents nearing emancipation who were not ready, with many system graduates already in the ranks of the homeless in Portland, Salem, and Eugene, Oregon. Most had experienced multiple placements, were untrained in social skills, rarely persisted in any task, and had difficulty in sustaining relationships for any length of time. In terms of the implementation of the plan, key elements were: (a) screening applicants, who were required to take responsibility for developing an independent-living plan; (b) the plan was to include a cost-of-living budget, as well as plans for education and employment; (c) controversially, participants were to live in apartments in their respective communities (roommates were discouraged); and (d) a written agreement was signed by youth and caseworker. Agreements and/or contracts typically delineated what youth were expected to do to meet the conditions of the subsidy (i.e., job, school attendance, paying bills on time, taking care of the apartment, shopping and food preparation, etc.). The maximum subsidy allowance was $265 a month (in 1975 dollars). Youth were required to supplement this subsidy with income-related employment. Subsidy payments extended over a two-year period, with a gradual decrease in the monthly amount, depending on the youth's income. At the end of the 24-month subsidy period, youth were expected to be self-supporting. An evaluation in 1978 of 30 wards who completed the subsidy program indicated that two out of three met their educational and employment goals and were on career tracks.

Momentum was building for a national legislative response to the issue of preparing older foster wards for self-sufficiency. Festinger's follow-up study of former foster wards, published in 1983, directed attention to adolescents in placement as a population in need of transitional assistance. Also in the mid-1980s, federal support, under the auspices of the U.S. Children's Bureau, provided a series of demonstration grants to test the effectiveness of independent-living services for adolescents in care. State demonstration projects were instrumental in setting the stage for congressional action. In 1986, Congress amended Title IV-E of the Social Security Act and established the federal independent-living initiatives (P.L. 99-272) under Section 477. This new independent-living entitlement program was opposed by the White House prior to enactment of the original legislation as well as in subsequent reauthorization hearings.

It was not until 1993, nearly six years after the original initiative, that Congress extended permanent status to the independent-living initiatives. At this point, a considerable body of empirical evidence had accumulated with respect to documenting the transitional difficulties faced by thousands of wards leaving placement. In 1992, the Congressional Committee on Ways and Means Green Book, in its analysis of the foster care independent-living program, estimated that 84,000 youth in placement were eligible for aging-out services. The largest state was California, with nearly 20,000 youth ages 16 to 18 classified as eligible. Other key states were New York (more than 6,000), Michigan (5,500), Pennsylvania (4,800), and Illinois (3,300).

Current estimates suggest that approximately 500,000 children and youth are in substitute care. It is not unreasonable to estimate that 75,000 to 100,000 wards ages 16 to 18 are on the aging-out track. Concern is mounting as to the ability of young wards to become self-sufficient. Among youth in the 18 to 25 age group, the risk for economic and social dependency is increasing. Based on current trends, it is likely that thousands of foster wards are in danger of becoming part of a permanent underclass in America. Understandably, much social legislation has a common objective, namely to prepare young adults for self-sufficiency. The Foster Care Independence Act of 1999 is a step in that direction. Other aspects of the legislative matrix designed to exert positive effects on self-sufficiency preparation include the School-to-Work Opportunities Act of 1994, the Job Corps, the Job Training Partnership Act, and a growing number of career academies that are prominent in California. Legislation alone cannot guarantee competence and efficiency in program implementation or effectiveness in producing positive outcomes. The stakes are high with respect to influencing the probable futures of thousands of foster wards. Legislative action via the Foster Care Independence Act of 1999 has now extended services and financial support to foster wards until age 21. Child welfare advocates have fought hard to arrive at this point. Legislative pioneers in Congress are to be commended for extending society's investment in foster youth. Although independent-living programs are relatively new, and state child welfare systems and their staffs are in the process of gaining experience in preparing wards for independence, it is in the public interest for advocates, legislative groups, and governmental entities to monitor the progress of new and emerging programs. It is of vital importance that states develop "opportunity structures" that are designed to assist youth who emancipate from care to achieve economic self-sufficiency.

References

Allen, M., Golubock, C., & Olson, L. (1983). A guide to the Adoption Assistance & Child Welfare Act of 1980. In M. Hardin (Ed.), *Foster children in the courts* (pp. 574-611). Boston: Butterworth Legal.

Barden, J. (1991, January 6). When foster care ends home is often the street. *New York Times*, pp. 1, 10.

Biehl, N., Calyden, J., Stein, M., & Wade, J. (1994). Leaving care in England: A research perspective. *Children and Youth Services Review, 16*, 231–254.

Citizens' Committee for Children of New York. (1984, September). *The foster care exit— Ready or not. An inquiry into how New York City prepares children in foster care for discharge to independent living*. New York: Author.

Crystal, S. (1984). Homeless men and homeless women. The gender gap. *Urban and Social Change Review, 17*, 2-6.

Fitzgerald, M. (1995, May/June). Homeless youths and the child welfare system. Implications for policy and service. *Child Welfare, 74*(3), 717–723.

Greenan, L. (1987, April 22). *Senior Policy Analyst, Child Welfare League of America. Statement regarding release of independent-living funds. House Select Committee on Children, Youth & Families*. Washington, DC: U.S. Government Printing Office.

Hardy, D. (1985, September 19). *Assistant Secretary, Human Development Services—Department of Health & Human Services. Testimony before U.S. Senate Committee on Finance, Subcommittee on Social Security & Income Maintenance Programs*. Washington, DC: U.S. Government Printing Office.

Livingston, D. (1987, April 22). *Commissioner, Administration for Children, Youth & Families. Testimony before Select Committee on Children, Youth & Families, House of Representatives*. Washington, DC: US Government Printing Office.

Loperena, E. (1987, April 22). *Testimony before the Congressional Select Committee on Children, Youth, & Families in continuing crisis in foster care*. Washington, DC: U.S. Government Printing Office.

Matsui, R. (1988, March 31). *Statement of Hon. Robert T. Matsui, Representative in Congress (California). Testimony before House Ways & Means Committee hearings on foster care independent-living initiatives* (Serial 100-66, pp. 4-6). Washington, DC: U.S. Government Printing Office.

Mayor's Task Force on Foster Care, New York City. (1980). *Redirecting foster care*. New York: Author.

Moynihan, D. P. (1988). Legislation for independent-living programs. *Child Welfare, 67,* 483–485.

Palmer v. Cuomo, 503 N.Y.S. 2d. 20 (1986).

Pinkerton, J., & McCrea, R. (1999). *Meeting the challenge? Young people leaving care in Northern Ireland*. Hants, UK: Ashgate.

Rothery, M., Gallup, J., Tillman, G., & Allard, H. (1995, May/June). Local governance of child welfare services in Alberta. *Child Welfare, 74*(3), 587-603.

Simonitch, B., & Anderson, J. (1979, September/October). On their own. An Oregon experiment. *Children Today, 8,* 28–31.

Sosin, M., Piliavin, I., & Westerfelt, H. (1990). Toward a longitudinal analysis of homelessness. *Journal of Social Issues, 46,* 157-174.

Stone, H. (1987). *Ready, set, go. An agency guide to independent living*. Washington, DC: Child Welfare League of America.

Susser, E., Struening, E., & Conover, S. (1987). Childhood experiences of homeless men. *American Journal of Psychiatry, 144,* 1589-1601.

Tobis, D. (1989). *Services to youth after leaving care, survey of state laws, regulations, and programs*. New York: New York University, Metropolitan Studies Program, Welfare Research, Inc., Legal Action Center for the Homeless.

White, R., Carr, P., & Lowe, N. (1995). *The Children Act in practice*. London: Butterworths.

Williams, C. (1999). *Testimony before Congressional Subcommittee on Foster Youth Independence Act of 1999*. Washington, DC: U.S. Government Printing Office.

chapter 4

Trends in Program Design

EDMUND V. MECH

It is hard...to design public policies and programs
that look good on paper...it is harder still to
formulate them in words...that resonate...in the
ears of political leaders...and it is excrutiatingly
hard to implement them.

—*Eugene Bardach (1977, p. 3)*

The original program to help foster youth become self-sufficient was
P.L. 99-272, authorized by Congress in 1985. The purpose of the initial
legislation was to provide federal funding to states to establish and implement services that could aid foster youth ages 16 and older in preparing
for adult living. In 1993, the federal independent-living legislation was re-
authorized and awarded permanent status as an entitlement to states.

Federal funding was increased from $45 million to $70 million per year.
The early legislation restricted participant eligibility to youth ages 16 and
older for whom foster care payments were made. The main legislative
target consisted of foster wards in the ages 16 to 18 category. Services to
youth age 18 and older were discretionary and at state option. Accordingly, the purpose of this chapter is to discuss program trends since enactment of the original federal independent-living initiative. The most recent
legislative action relative to preparing foster wards for aging out of state
care occurred in 1999, when the federal Foster Care Independence Act
was passed by Congress and signed into law by President Clinton.

Revised Independent-Living Legislation

Congressional intent with respect to the revised independent-living bill
was to extend services to foster wards and to emancipated foster youth
from ages 18 to 21. Numerous follow-up studies supplemented by practi-

tioner experience supported the wisdom of extending services until youth reach age 21. Key elements of the act include:

- Use of funds for room and board for youth ages 18 to 21 who leave state care.

- State option of extending Medicaid to youth ages 18 to 21 who emancipate from placement.

- Increase in the asset/savings limit from $1,000 to $10,000. The aim is to allow foster wards to save enough money for them to make an easier transition to community life.

Accordingly, Section 477 of the Social Security Act (42 U.S.C. 677) was amended to read as follows:

(a) Purpose. The purpose of Section 477 is to provide States with flexible funding that will enable programs to be designed and conducted to meet legislative goals, as follow:

(1) to identify children who are likely to remain in foster care until 18 years of age and to design programs that help these children make the transition to self-sufficiency by providing services such as assistance in obtaining a high school diploma, career exploration, vocational training, job placement and retention, training in daily living skills, training in budgeting and financial management skills, substance abuse prevention, and preventive health activities (including smoking avoidance, nutrition education, and pregnancy prevention);

(2) to help children who are likely to remain in foster care until 18 years of age receive the education, training, and services necessary to obtain employment,

(3) to help children who are likely to remain in foster care until 18 years of age prepare for and enter post-secondary training and education institutions;

(4) to provide personal and emotional support to children aging-out of foster care, through mentors and the promotion of interactions with dedicated adults; and

(5) to provide financial, housing, counseling, employment, education, and other appropriate support and services to

former foster care recipients between 18 and 21 years of age to complement their own efforts to achieve self-sufficiency and to assure that program participants recognize and accept their personal responsibility for preparing to make the transition to adulthood.

Federal requirements for states to receive funds include:

- Involvement of the public and private sectors in helping foster adolescents to achieve independence.

- Intent to cooperate in national evaluations of the effects of independent-living programs.

- Certification by states that assistance and services will be provided to former wards who have left foster care but who are not 21 years old yet.

- Certification by states that not more than 30% of the amounts paid to states for independent-living services will be expended for room or board for youth who have left foster care and have attained 18 years of age but not 21 years of age.

- Certification by states that training will be provided to foster parents, group home workers, and case managers to understand and respond to the issues that face adolescents preparing for independent living.

- Certification that state plans will include mechanisms that coordinate with other federal and state programs for youth, such as school-to-work programs, housing programs, and programs for disabled youth.

- Certification by states that foster adolescents will participate directly in designing their own program for independence with the expectation that wards accept personal responsibility for adhering to their part of the program.

- Coordination between the U.S. Department of Health and Human Services, state agencies, and local public officials responsible for administering independent-living programs with the objective of developing outcome measures that can be used to gauge the performance of states in operating independent-living programs.

Implementation Issues

Federal policy has broadened from emphasis on providing independent-living services to foster wards to include moving toward standardizing the measurement of outcomes.

Currently, the outcomes under review are practical, pragmatic, and measurable. Outcome markers include: (a) education, (b) employment, (c) housing, (d) financial stability, and (e) independence from means-tested welfare programs.

The rationale for the new extended services reform legislation is that compared with other adolescents and young adults their age, young people leaving state care are less likely to complete a basic high school education, are more often unemployed, tend to overuse means-tested welfare programs, have mental health problems, parent children too early, and experience high rates of homelessness. The revised federal framework for independent-living services, with additional monetary resources, permits states considerable discretion in planning and delivering services that will affect the futures of young adults who have left foster care, as well as wards who are on the aging-out track. The congressional policy of extending independent-living services until wards reach age 21 is a sound idea. A potential problem lies in the possibility that too much may be expected of the extended-services legislation. The problems and barriers that confront foster wards on the road to independence are formidable. The essential fact remains that program implementation and responsibility for producing outcomes resides with entities other than Congress or federal agencies. Entities that actually implement programs are at the state and local levels.

Legislators and units of the federal bureaucracy are not directly involved in translating legislative ideology into tangible, effective services. Federal units can interpret legislation, issue regulations, allocate resources, and monitor compliance, but implementation is carried out at state and local levels. It should be noted that service delivery personnel typically have little or no involvement in drafting legislation. It is not surprising that gaps exist between legislative intent and program reality. Moreover, a positive outcome depends on the extent to which services and program interventions are effective. Implementers rarely receive clear and unambiguous directions relative to program design. The policy process does not end when a bill becomes law. Implementers too often face the necessity of having to translate legislative ambiguity into operational action.

The difficulties associated with effective implementation are outlined in the Sabatier-Mazmanian framework. Three areas compose their analytical framework: (1) tractability of the problem, (2) ability of legislation to structure implementation, and (3) nonstatutory variables affecting legislation. Table 4.1 summarizes the main elements of the Sabatier-Mazmanian model.

Tractability of the Problem

Preparing large numbers of foster wards for self-sufficiency is highly difficult. Risk factors are numerous, particularly so for female wards. The risks include early parenting, child care issues, financial difficulty, limited educational progress, and little or no career-track preparation.

Causal Theory

The theoretical underpinning for independent-living preparation consists of an eclectic mix of common sense services and activities that are presumed to be effective in moving young wards toward self-sufficiency. The structure, duration, and intensity of independent-living services are uneven and vary from case-to-case and program to program. For best results, interventions for independent-living preparation should be operationalized, standardized, and field tested.

Nonstatutory Factors

Nonstatutory factors refers to the extent to which service delivery units are committed to attaining legislative objectives and the degree to which target youth are motivated to succeed and willing to take steps to capitalize on the opportunity structure authorized under the Foster Care Independence Act of 1999. It should be noted that Section 477 (Social Security Act) includes the necessity of program participants' accepting personal responsibility for preparing for the transition to adulthood. The extent to which the personal responsibility expectation for foster wards is implemented under field conditions requires documentation and analysis.

Standards for Improving Practice

The Council on Accreditation for Families and Children (COA) and the Child Welfare League of America (CWLA) have issued standards for independent-living services. Standards are viewed as goals for the improvement of practice. It is worthwhile to review some of the standards pertaining to preparing foster youth for independence. CWLA standards emphasize seven elements:

- Education—The acquisition of knowledge, skills, attitudes, and so forth are viewed as a lifelong task. Agencies should assist foster wards in gaining access to educational resources and encourage wards to capitalize on educational opportunities.

TABLE 4.1

Sabatier-Mazmanian Model for Analysis of Implementation Policy

ELEMENT	IMPLEMENTATION ISSUES
Tractability of Problem	*Tractability* refers to the ease with which a social problem can be controlled, solved, or ameliorated. Preparing foster wards for self-sufficiency is difficult. There are many risk factors, including limited education, marginal job skills, and limited computer competence.
Causal Theory	Validity of the causal theory behind the legislation is vital. Positive results depend on the extent to which the independent-living services provided are causally connected to influencing the progress of foster wards toward self-sufficiency.
Nonstatutory Factors	Nonstatutory factors that influence outcomes include the commitment of foster youth and service delivery agents to the achievement of legislative objectives. Factors such as the youth's motivation to succeed are critical but difficult to control.

SOURCE: Adapted from Mazmanian and Sabatier (1989).

- **Employment**—Employment success is closely connected to educational preparation, vocational skills, acquisition of effective world-of-work attitudes and behaviors, social skills necessary to job acquisition and job holding, and connections with public and private sector employees.

- **Health Services**—Youth should learn about healthy lifestyles and the importance of regular medical and dental check-ups. While in placement, wards require periodic health evaluations and should receive corrective treatment when needed. When leaving placement, CWLA standards state that wards "should be given their complete medical records and documentation" (CWLA, 1989, p. 14).

- **Housing**—Postemancipation progress toward independence is enhanced if wards can obtain housing that is affordable and safe. Youth require practical information and experience in topics such as tenants' rights, lease agreements and responsibilities to landlords, financial responsibilities, how to coexist with neighbors, and location of housing that is convenient to transportation, schools, and employment.

- **Legal**—Legal support is vital. Young wards are often without proper advocacy when their rights are violated or when difficulty occurs in handling situations involving possible violations of the law. Programs can provide training in how to obtain legal assistance in times of need.

- **Socialization**—Services are needed that help foster wards acquire "life skills and habits necessary for successful participation in small and large groups" (CWLA, 1989, p. 15). Socialization goals can be facilitated by interaction with positive adult role models (i.e., transitional mentors), participation in community service programs, and a variety of recreational and leisure time activities.

- **Aftercare**—Agency responsibility should not end when young people leave care. Most who age out of placement are not fully prepared for independence or self-sufficiency. A system of aftercare services is recommended. It should include financial aid, employment assistance, emergency shelter and housing assistance, and referral to various community support programs. COA recommends that aftercare services be made available to youth through age 21 and encourages agencies to maintain contact and provide support, either through an agency program or referral to a cooperating resource.

Independent-Living Plans: Selected State Profiles

Applications for federal funds under the Chafee Foster Care Independence Program (CFCIP) require states to provide information in a number of areas, including the following:

- **Lead Agency**—Applicants must identify the state agency that will administer, supervise, or oversee programs.

- **National Evaluation**—Applicants must stipulate that the designated state agency agrees to participate in national evaluations of program effectiveness.

- **Self-Sufficiency Framework**—Applicants must describe how a state intends to design and implement independent-living services to help target youth (a) achieve self-sufficiency; (b) receive the education and training necessary to obtain employment; (c) prepare for and access postsecondary education and training; (d) obtain emotional support through mentors and the promotion of positive contacts with adults; and (e) obtain financial, housing, employment, and related support in the transitional period following discharge from state care.

- **Differential Services for Independent Living**—Applicants are to describe how they will serve youth at various stages of achieving independence.

- **Community Involvement**—Applicants must describe plans to involve the public and private sectors in helping foster adolescents to achieve self-sufficiency.

- **Training**—Applicants must describe plans to train personnel to provide independent-living services to foster wards.

Summary Profiles for Selected States for Fiscal Years 2001-2004
Arizona

The Arizona Department of Economic Security is the agency responsible for administering the Independent Living Program authorized in Title IV-E of the Social Security Act. The Arizona program is state-administered, with services provided in communities throughout the state. Youth ages 16 and older with a permanency goal of independent living are referred to the Arizona Young Adult Program. The program encourages youth to take an active role in formulating their own transitional plan. Case plans for independent living summarize youth goals, resources, and responsibilities, as well as barriers to achieving self sufficiency. The youth must sign the plan.

Youth Participation

An excerpt from the Arizona CFCIP state plan for FYs 2001-2004 describes procedures for youth participation in program development. The following passage is from the application narrative:

> *The statewide Youth Advisory Board meets quarterly to discuss related issues and make program recommendations. The statewide youth conference, an annual event, has also proved to be a vehicle for gathering youth input. Regional youth ad-*

*visory groups meet throughout the year to discuss and prob-
lem solve issues pertinent in their area of the state. Mini-
youth conferences are held in different areas of the state as
well, providing youth with additional opportunities to formulate plans for increased involvement in the planning and
implementation of various components of the program, as
well as to discuss concerns. Area Program Administrators
are invited to attend these meetings to answer questions and
to be educated on current youth issues. (Arizona, 2001, p. 3)*

Native-American Youth
Another important element in the Arizona plan is coordinating with Native American tribes in the state:

*Native American youth who currently participate in ser-
vices under the Arizona Independent Living Program are
dependent wards in the custody of the department. Historically, youth who are likely to reach the age of majority while
in out-of-home care under tribal jurisdiction have not benefited from services through the Arizona Independent Living Program. With the new requirements of [CFCIP], the
department must make services available to Indian youth
on the same basis as to youth in the custody of the state.
The department has utilized their liaison with the Inter-Tribal
Council to facilitate communication and consultation with
tribal members with the goal being to coordinate programs,
benefits and services funded by the Chafee Independence
Program to eligible youth residing under the authority of the
Tribal Nations.... The tribal Nations have participated in both
a needs survey and in face to face meetings to gain input
into the state plan and to determine the number of youth,
within each Tribe, who are eligible for services under the
Chafee Program. Options and strategies as to the methods
by which services are made available to youth under Tribal
jurisdiction are being discussed and will require further discussion and planning toward fruition.... The agency is obtaining information on the number of eligible youth and is
moving forward in working with Tribes in identifying and
discussing the needs and recommendations of Tribal members. This is an ongoing process, which requires a consider-*

*able amount of time spent in meeting with Tribes on an indi-
vidual basis as well as in the larger group format, to ensure
the services available under the Chafee Program are appropriate and accessible. (Arizona, 2001, pp. 4–5)*

Medicaid

With respect to expansion of Medicaid eligibility, the Arizona plan
reports the following policy developments:

*In April, 2000, state statutes related to Medicaid eligible
persons in the state were amended to include as a new eligible group, those young adults who reached the age of 18
while in the custody of the Department in out-of-home care.
Eligibility was initially limited to those youth who meet the
basic Medicaid requirements and whose income is below
200% of the federal poverty level. Efforts continue to develop
a seamless enrollment process. (Arizona, 2001, p. 8)*

*All eligible youth are pre-enrolled in a Medicaid health plan
prior to turning 18. Medicaid coverage for eligible youth may
continue to the youth's 21st birthday. An amendment to this
statute was recently enacted which removes the income requirements. There are approximately 209 youth who have
completed applications for this health coverage to date. (Arizona, 2001, pp. 4–5)*

Self-Sufficiency

The key goals of the Arizona plan with respect to achieving self-sufficiency
are: providing access to education and training opportunities, providing
personal/emotional support, and providing financial, housing, employment,
and related support services. The plan ensures that youth who are viewed
as likely to age out of foster placement will have a transitional case plan.
The plan's emphasis is on skills training, re-establishing family relations,
building connections with community mentors and support persons,
obtaining medical coverage, and providing training and support services
for pregnant or parenting adolescent wards. The plan links youth with
school-to-work programs and allows them to receive assistance in developing job readiness skills, learn job interview procedures, and get individual
tutoring. Also, the program intends to provide training for caregivers and
service providers with respect to the issues that face foster adolescents in
preparing for independent living.

Florida

The Florida Department of Children and Families will administer CFCIP. Requisite services and program activities will be conducted directly by the state agency or under contractual agreements with private organizations. Florida subscribes to the key program elements outlined in the Chafee legislation, namely: (a) facilitate the transition to self-sufficiency, (b) help youth get the education and training needed to obtain employment, (c) help youth to prepare for and access postsecondary training or education, (e) provide emotional support through mentors and positive interactions with adults, and (f) provide financial, housing, and employment assistance, as well as other supportive aftercare services to former foster care recipients between the ages of 18 and 21.

Florida's aftercare program is described as follows:

> *Youth may continue to receive foster care services up to the age of 23 if s/he is enrolled full-time in a post-secondary educational institution. Currently youth who exit foster care at age 18 are able to attend independent living skills classes and conferences until s/he turns 21 years of age. Florida has assisted youth with bus passes, referrals to services, etc. in the past. Florida continues to develop its aftercare program. The program will be a voluntary, youth initiated program for former foster care recipients between the ages of 18 and 21. In order for youth to know about this service, a brochure about the aftercare program will be developed and inserted into the newly created aftercare packet which all youth leaving care at age 18 will receive. Program guidelines are being developed in order for the aftercare program to be uniform throughout the state.... Youth will be given an aftercare individual assessment and attend a staffing with the independent living coordinator. Housing assistance includes rent and mortgage payments and rental or utility deposits. Youth involved in the aftercare program will be eligible to receive a recommended lifetime maximum of $3,000.00 to assist in preventing homelessness. Until Florida's aftercare program comes to fruition, the independent living coordinators are providing youth in need with deposits for an apartment or paying the monthly rent, assisting in paying for vocational testing, and will continue to make appropriate referrals as*

necessary. Many independent living coordinators purchase
counseling services for youth who have exited foster care
and who are in need of this service. (Florida, 2001, p. 3)

One of the developments in the Florida plan refers to a legislative mandate to privatize child welfare services by the year 2003. The plan describes Florida as "gradually moving towards community based care, allowing individual communities to take responsibility for their youth through contracts with the department" (Florida, 2001, p. 5). Currently, five community-based independent-living programs are under contract with the Florida Department of Families and Children.

Kentucky

The Kentucky Cabinet for Families and Children, Department for Community Based Services, is responsible for administering CFCIP. Like Florida, Kentucky will develop programs directed helping youth transition to self-sufficiency and providing financial, housing, employment, and related support services to former foster wards age 18 and over who have not yet reached their 21st birthday. Key elements in Kentucky's strategy to facilitate self-sufficiency are: (a) training department staff and/or service providers, including foster parents, on issues faced by adolescents preparing for emancipation; (b) expanding partnerships that will enhance job readiness, placement, and retention; (c) legislating for scholarships for all youth based on grade point averages; (d) providing tuition waivers for postsecondary education for foster wards; (e) providing citizen-mentors for youth; (f) creating personal responsibility expectations for foster youth through with a mutually agreed on independent living plan; and (g) ensuring that housing resources will be available. Housing arrangements for former wards 18 through 20 years of age may include utilities, a security deposit, telephone, and ongoing rental assistance (Kentucky, 2001).

Michigan

The State of Michigan Family Independence Agency is the entity assigned responsibility for the administration and supervision of CFCIP. In the Michigan plan, foster youth are expected to play "an active role in designing their own program activities that prepare them for independent living and accepting person responsibility for achieving independence through the creation of a written plan" (Michigan, 2001, p. 1).

There are several elements of the Michigan plan. First is the possibility of establishing a standardized youth training curriculum that covers career exploration, job training, job placement, and job retention skills. The plan also provides youth who age out of placement with an aftercare brochure that describes services available and how to access these services and provides opportunities for foster parents to receive training about preparing eligible youth for independent living. The plan emphasizes educational training for employment through the Michigan Works! program. Michigan Works! includes unsubsidized jobs, basic and remedial education, on-the-job placement, work experience placement, job search assistance, and occupational information. The state hopes to conduct the Michigan Works! program on a year-round basis. Finally, the Tuition Incentive Program offers financial assistance to eligible youth who enroll in postsecondary education programs within the state.

Pennsylvania

The Pennsylvania Department of Public Welfare is the agency designated to administer and supervise CFCIP. The Pennsylvania program is a state-supervised, county-administered system that involves 67 county-based children and youth agencies. The state plan stipulates that the Pennsylvania Department of Public Welfare "is committed to ensuring that foster care youth are provided with the necessary skills and guidance to make the transition to self-sufficiency" (Pennsylvania, 2001). The programs and activities to be provided to achieve transition to self-sufficiency are as follows:

- Individualized assessments of the IL [independent-living] needs of eligible children (currently in foster care or who have "aged-out" of foster care);

- The development of IL case plans based on the results of the needs assessment, family and individual service plan goals and youth input;

- High school support and retention programs;

- Preparation for, and assistance in, obtaining a general equivalency diploma;

- Assistance in obtaining higher education and vocational training, including technical assistance, financial assistance and counseling;

- Job training, placement and retention in collaboration with local Workforce Investment Boards created through the Workforce Investment Act;

- Programs directed at improving self-esteem and self-confidence; e.g. retreats, youth conferences and workshops, group and individual counseling;

- Regionally established youth advisory boards that will focus on positive youth development and leaderships skills, co-facilitation at the annual youth retreat, and providing input into the design and implementation of Pennsylvania's [IL program];

- Programs that encourage pregnancy prevention, provide parent education and help teen parents make the transition from foster care;

- Preventive health instruction and personal health information for use after exiting substitute care;

- Optional funding for room and board costs for youth meeting the CFCIP requirements;

- Increased opportunities for youth to overcome current barriers of transportation issues;

- Stipends for participating IL youth that provide incentives, rewards and items youth may need after exiting foster care; and

- Mentoring and other supportive services to youth leaving foster care upon their 18th birthday and continuing these services throughout the youth's transition period. (Pennsylvania, 2001)

Special attention is devoted to issues relevant to room and board policy. Counties are advised that program funds for housing are limited and intended primarily to assist youth who "are most in need of assistance...and have exhausted other locally available housing programs or funding sources" (Pennsylvania, 2001, p. 4). Other solutions to containing room and board costs include the possibility of a "step-down approach where the youth and agency mutually agree on a process where funds directed at room and board costs are decreased over a period of time" (Pennsylvania, 2001, p. 4).

With respect to expanding Medicaid eligibility, the Pennsylvania plan (2001) notes that the state has "initiated the sequence of events necessary to expand Medicaid eligibility for youth transitioning from foster care" (p. 7). However, eligibility determination for a variety of related benefits and services may depend on a priority system established by the state. The plan cautions that "a prioritized system (of services) may be necessary for some county programs because of limited funding for IL programs" (Pennsylvania, 2001, p. 8). The federal government allocates funds to counties based on the "projection of eligible children in placement in each county" (Pennsylvania, 2001), county assessments of local needs, and the submission of a proposal acceptable to the State Department of Public Welfare.

Assessment

The Chafee Foster Care Independence legislation requires states to adhere to a systematic outline in applying for federal funds. The central aim of the application process is to focus state plans on providing services to prepare foster wards for self-sufficiency. States must describe plans to help foster youth obtain the education and training necessary for unsubsidized employment, access postsecondary education, and receive transitional support, including adult mentors, housing, financial assistance, and medical coverage.

Service provisions found in most plans are lifeskills training, educational and career planning, job skills training, community-resource connections, involvement of public and private sector organizations, subsidy assistance, youth advisory councils, youth advocacy organizations, tours of postsecondary institutions, tuition waiver policies, annual foster youth conferences, and workshops for caregivers.

The central issue facing state programs is that of implementation. Despite the philosophical soundness of state strategies, programs must contend with the prospect of encountering a risky implementation process. Administrators, supervisors, and line workers are aware of the difficulties in converting paper policies to behavioral reality. ILPs that serve older foster youth are no exception. Preparing foster teens for economic independence and self-sufficiency is a formidable task. It is highly difficult to prepare foster wards for economic self-sufficiency. A myriad of risk factors must be considered, including the limitations of short-range educational goals, marginal job skills, limited preparation for employment beyond meeting entry-level job requirements, variable literacy and computer proficiency, as well as difficult-to-control factors, such as the motivation of foster wards to make a successful transition to independence.

Although states are committed to achieving federal legislative goals with respect to preparing foster wards for independence, program implementation is likely to be uneven and inconsistent. In California, for example, decentralization prevails. Local advisory boards are responsible for providing oversight for ILPs conducted by more than 50 institutions within the state's community college system. In Ohio, lifeskills training for state wards is the responsibility of children's services agencies in each of its 88 counties. Likewise, Pennsylvania has a county-administered, state-supervised system of child welfare services. More than 60 agencies compose the Pennsylvania network. Michigan has 83 counties that are divided into zones. In the aggregate, implementation of ILPs across the United States is an unstandardized process. Koroloff, Lehman, and Lee (2000) noted potential deficiencies in the Foster Care Independence Act with respect to implementation. They concluded that "the lack of program mandates and funding contribute to poor monitoring and supervision of young people who are living in semi-independent settings" (p. 260). Monitoring on a sampling basis can be beneficial as a way of providing corrective feedback to programs. Moreover, monitoring efforts should include analysis of the extent to which foster wards are furthering their own preparation for self-sufficiency. Unless older wards take responsibility for a successful transition to independence, positive outcomes are unlikely.

References

Arizona CFCIP state plan for FY 2001-2004. (2001). Phoenix: Arizona Department of Economic Security.

Bardach, E. (1977). *The implementation game*. Cambridge, MA: MIT Press.

Child Welfare League of America. (1989). *Standards for independent living services* (pp. 1–51). Washington, DC: Author.

Florida, Chafee Foster Care Independence Program (CFCIP) FYs 2001-2004 application. (2001). Tallahassee: Florida Department of Children and Families.

Kentucky, John H. Chafee Foster Care Independence Program FY 2001-2004 application outline. (2001). Frankfort: Kentucky Cabinet for Families and Children.

Koroloff, N., Lehman, C., & Lee, M. (2000). Policies that facilitate the transition process In H. B. Clark & M. Davis (Eds.), *Transition to adulthood: A resource for assisting your people with emotional or behavioral difficulties* (pp. 245–263). Baltimore: Paul H. Brookes.

Mazmanian, D., & Sabatier, P. (1989). *Implementation and public policy*. Lanham, MD: University Press of America.

Michigan, John H. Chafee Foster Care Independence Program, Michigan FY 2001-2004 application outline. (2001). Lansing: Michigan Family Independence Agency.

Pennsylvania, John H. Chafee Foster Care Independence Program, federal fiscal year 2001-2004 application. (2001) Harrisburg: Pennsylvania Department of Public Welfare.

Chapter 5

Profiles of Emancipated Youth: 10-Year Outcomes

EDMUND V. MECH AND
LORA SCHMID-DOLAN

The societal assumption that young people in out-of-home placement can be self-supporting at age 18 is wishful thinking. Most youth in care experience multiple placements and frequent changes in living arrangements, schools, and neighborhood settings. Placement stability is a luxury. Instability is the more likely scenario. Older adolescents in care are also at increased risk of living in placements characterized as restrictive. Group homes, residential treatment centers, shelters, institutions, and hospitals are examples of restrictive placements. The essential characteristic of restrictive placements is that fewer opportunities exist for young wards to develop the attitudes, skills, and behaviors needed to succeed in mainstream community environments.

Accordingly, the aim of this chapter is to describe, analyze, and evaluate the postemancipation progress of former foster wards. The data cited derive from the University of Illinois Foster Youth Project, which tracked a group of emancipated youth over a 10-year period. Follow-up information was obtained at three points in time—age 18, age 21, and age 28. The eight case profiles that follow are illustrative of the myriad of transitional realities that face emancipated wards.

Wyatt

Caucasian Male Ages 18 to 21

Wyatt was placed in care at age 14 because of physical abuse by his mother's boyfriend. He spent four years in care with eight different placements, for a different placement, on average, every six months. Wyatt lived in a transitional apartment for about three months prior to his discharge from state care. He completed a high school diploma plus several semesters of college. Following discharge from care, Wyatt had some problems with the law. At age 19, he was incarcerated, charged with burglarizing garages. Wyatt served six months in county jail, followed by four years of probation with a 9 P.M. curfew. He also received several citations for reckless driving.

Wyatt's postsecondary education was attained close to home, where he lived with an uncle. His job experience included stock work at Wal-Mart, food handling at Burger King, summer jobs as a roofer's helper, a child care aide, and day care work through the Job Training Partnership Act. While enrolled in college, Wyatt received a monthly stipend from the state agency. He has used food stamps and reports his health as good, despite chronic asthma that requires an inhaler. He has no apparent problems with drugs or alcohol. His social support network consists of an uncle, a girlfriend, and a best friend. Wyatt has had no contact with his mother or a sister since he was in placement. At the age 21 follow-up, the prediction for Wyatt was that he would have great difficulty in becoming self-sufficient.

Age 28

Contact was made with Wyatt in February 2000, when he was 28 years old. He had moved from the Midwest to the West Coast. Although he completed two years of postsecondary, college-level courses prior to moving, when he was 26, he signed up for vocational training in welding and received a certificate of course completion. In terms of employment, at the point of follow-up Wyatt reported working full-time (40 hours per week) at an hourly rate of $23.86 (union scale). His estimated annual income is approximately $40,000. Fringe benefits include medical and dental coverage. Wyatt had a plan to obtain computer training and he wanted to upgrade and/or change jobs in the foreseeable future.

Commentary

If self-sufficiency at age 28 is gauged by tangible economic criteria such as income level, adequate housing, and availability of job-related health, dental, and medical insurance, Wyatt can be classified as self-sufficient.

However, evidence exists that suggests that Wyatt has not yet found a satisfactory career path. If taken at his word, he will obtain additional training, probably in a skill unrelated to welding. His encounter with the justice system appears to be past history. Program specialists in youth work are convinced that a relationship with a significant adult can make a difference in a child's life course. In Wyatt's case, his significant adult was a person he refers to as "Uncle John." Wyatt's uncle provided a safe haven for him in the transitional period following discharge from state care.

Also important is Wyatt's belief in his ability to succeed. When Wyatt was 20 years old, the prediction that he was unlikely to attain self-sufficiency was wide of the mark. Not to be overlooked are important supports received from the state child welfare system. These included an apartment-living experience prior to discharge and a financial subsidy to assist in getting postsecondary education. Overall, Wyatt has not yet settled on a career track, and in a very real sense, he is still in transition.

Jack
Caucasian Male Ages 18 to 21

Jack entered state care at age 5. By age 7, Jack's record indicates three different placements. Jack's cumulative placement/re-placement profile indicates an average of three placements per year. Despite an erratic placement history, Jack liked school and managed to complete a high school diploma. Geometry and mathematics are cited as his preferred subjects. His social supports appear reasonably good. Persons cited as important are a girlfriend, stepfather, a foster family, and grandparents. Jack prides himself on his sports orientation and "keeping in shape." He received educational loans and state financial help to enroll in a local community college. He expressed interest in specializing in math, but changed direction to general studies. The reason given was dissatisfaction with one of the math instructors. Jack exudes lots of confidence in his ability to make it on his own.

Age 28

Contact was made with Jack in February 2000, when he was 28 years old. He still lives in the Midwest. Jack graduated from high school in 1991 and continued postsecondary work at a local community college. He is several credits short of completing an associate of arts degree. In high school, Jack was in the general curriculum. Jack's postsecondary work was aided by a scholarship from his church, a Pell Grant, and money earned from part-time employment. At the point of follow-up, he was working full-time in a car wash. His job duties included picking up new cars from dealers, cleaning them, and returning them to the dealer. He has no medical or dental coverage, and his earnings are about $11,000 a year. The car wash job is temporary. Jack plans to finish an associate's degree at a community college. He hopes to upgrade or change jobs in the near future. Construction work is his preference. Jack rates as helpful the transitional living preparation he received after he entered a residential treatment center. He also describes his stepfather as an important person in helping him get connected to community living. Overall, he described the transitional living program as beneficial in terms of assisting with housing, a rent subsidy, and monitoring visits with his follow-up worker.

Commentary

At age 28, Jack continues to be in transition to self-sufficiency. Despite a high school diploma and nearly two years of community college enrollment, Jack has not yet identified a clear career perspective. Work in a car wash earning approximately $11,000 per year represents entry-level, dead-end employment. Although in terms of income Jack is technically above the poverty level, he lacks health, medical, and dental coverage and many other benefits associated with career-track workplace employment. Overall, it is difficult to classify Jack as making a successful transition to independence.

William
African American Male Ages 18 to 21

William came into care at age 13. His mother was declared unfit to care for her five children. William's first placement was a foster family home. Two subsequent placements were in group-residential facilities. William was discharged from state care at age 19. Shortly after discharge, he was expelled from high school. To complete a diploma and prepare for college, William planned to transfer to another school. At the age 21 follow-up, William was unemployed. He had recently quit a job at a fast-food restaurant. He said he was checking newspaper ads for another job. William's income for the year was less than $5,000.

With respect to encounters with law enforcement, William was cited for driving without a license, resisting arrest, and again for criminal trespass. He was sentenced to five days in jail and ordered to perform community service. In terms of a living/housing arrangement following discharge, he first moved in with his parents, two brothers, and a cousin. He is dissatisfied with this arrangement and plans to move again, this time to live with an older brother. William's support group appears quite strong, consisting primarily of family members. He reported having easy access to alcohol, drugs, and guns. William carries a gun, as do each of his friends. William's age 21 postplacement profile contains little evidence of a successful transition to independence. Insufficient education, episodes of unemployment, a court record, plus carrying a firearm and being involved with drugs increase his odds for a negative outcome.

Age 28

At age 28, William lacks a high school diploma or a general equivalency diploma (GED). The highest grade he completed is Grade 11. He indicated an interest in completing a GED and going on to college for a degree in social work. With respect to employment, William was not working at follow-up because of a car accident. For the past three years, William has worked as a temporary employee, primarily doing day factory work at $8 an hour. When asked about annual income, William was unable to provide a figure. In the past few years, William's mother was the key person in his life. William did not cite anyone from the placement system as helpful to him.

Commentary

At age 28, William reported low educational attainment but expressed a desire and intent to return to school. It is clear that, for William, the transition to independence is still unfolding. Based on the follow-up account cited, it is reasonable to conclude that William's case represents marginal self-sufficiency. Limited education, lack of technical/vocational skills, marginal work history, and difficulty in moving beyond entry-level employment does not signal an optimistic future for William.

Sergio
African American Male Ages 18 to 21

Sergio came into foster care at age 13 because he was physically abused by his aunt, who had adopted him. Sergio spent five years in three different foster homes. While in placement, he felt his caseworkers treated him poorly. His reasons included, "They never kept in contact," "They were hard to contact," and "I had to remind them of everything I needed." With respect to foster homes, Sergio rated his foster placements as helpful in preparing him for independence. Sergio's made C grades in high school. Sergio worked part-time in several fast-food restaurants. At age 19, just before leaving placement, Sergio rated himself as poorly prepared to live on his own without financial assistance from others. When emancipated, he moved in with his grandmother. Shortly after, he moved again, this time to live with an uncle and a cousin. At the age 21 follow-up, Sergio's income was estimated at less than $5,000 a year. Most was unearned and resulted from help he received while living with his uncle. Sergio's support system consisted mainly of relatives—his best friend is a cousin. At the age 21 contact, Sergio's plans were to continue to live with relatives, go to college, and qualify for employment in a management position. As we will learn from the age 28 contact, however, Sergio's plans for education and employment remain unrealized.

Age 28

In 1993, Sergio completed 11th grade, then dropped out. Several years later, in 1997, he received a GED. Prior to GED completion, Sergio was incarcerated for two years on a drug violation charge (i.e., selling cocaine). Sergio is an articulate young man who expresses a desire for further education. He refers to himself as lazy in terms of not moving ahead to obtain further schooling. At the age 28 interview, Sergio was employed at a dinner club as a dishwasher and banquet assistant. His pay was $7.35 per hour, with no health or medical benefits. He is moving to a new job at a firm that manufactures car and truck tire rims. The pay is $9 per hour, with a raise to $11 per hour after 60 days of satisfactory performance.

Significant people in Sergio's life are an uncle and a grandmother. Sergio vows, "Ten years from now I will be a model citizen." Overall, he reports receiving little formal preparation for independent living. In the correctional facility, Sergio assisted the public utility department in cleaning debris from power lines. Also while incarcerated, he spent about a year working in solid waste garbage disposal.

Commentary

At age 28, Sergio's effort to achieve self-sufficiency constitutes a work in progress. His stated goal of obtaining career-type education remains unrealized. Although Sergio cites an uncle and grandmother as important influences, it is not clear as to how each relative is contributing to his development. Sergio has issued himself a promissory note to "do better" in the next few years. Only additional or periodic follow-up contact can assess the extent to which Sergio achieves his educational/vocational goals. At this juncture, although a low level of economic self-sufficiency has been attained, Sergio's economic and social future remains uncertain.

Kathy

Caucasian Female Ages 18 to 21

Kathy came into care at age 14 because of physical and sexual abuse by the boyfriend of Kathy's babysitter. Her placement history is as follows: She ran away from home at age 14, was placed in a detention facility, then was transferred to the foster care system. At age 16, Kathy had a baby. During her 6 years in care Kathy lived in 11 different placements, distributed as follows: 2 foster homes, 5 group homes, 3 institutions, and 1 transitional apartment. Kathy completed a high school diploma. Her vocational goal at discharge was to become a medical doctor. At the age 21 follow-up, Kathy had been married and then divorced. She was employed in the area of telemarketing as a supervisor of surveys.

Her employment income at that time was about $25,000 a year. It should be noted that Kathy typically held down two or more jobs at the same time and was never unemployed. A major concern for Kathy was lack of health/medical coverage as an employment benefit. Her future plans as expressed at age 21 were "working on a college degree, having a house, a good paying job, and being able to raise my child."

Age 28

At the age 28 interview, Kathy had relocated from the Midwest to a southern state. In terms of additional education or vocational/technical training, Kathy enrolled in an advanced career training program for certification as a medical assistant.

In June 2000, Kathy completed a medical assistant program and received a license and national certification in this field. While in the medical assistant program, Kathy was in a work-study status earning $6 per hour. Her future plans call for additional education, with a goal of earning a bachelor's degree in nursing. She would like to work in emergency medicine or as a member of a surgical team. Kathy named her grandmother as a key source of emotional support and encouragement. With respect to what the placement system could have done better to prepare her for independence, Kathy's answer was, "Place more emphasis on the value of education and training along with financial assistance to meet educational goals."

Commentary

Kathy demonstrates considerable motivation to achieve her goal to have a career in the health/medical sciences. She had a child at age 16, married the father, and then was divorced. Currently remarried, her husband tends to support her career goals. Despite many barriers, including 11 placements while in care, Kathy managed to complete a GED, as well as postsecondary credits. It should be noted that her checkered placement history worked against completing a regular high school diploma. While in grades 10, 11, and 12, school transfers resulted in loss of credits applicable to graduation. She has a strong work ethic, as is attested to by her employment history, including completion of an advanced career certificate as a medical assistant. Kathy's educational agenda is incomplete and includes obtaining a bachelor's degree in nursing. Her interest in the medical field is undoubtedly related to her own multiple medical problems which include a pancreatic tumor, hypertension, diabetes, and asthma. If a postdischarge, transitional support system was available to Kathy, the elements of such a structure were not identified by her during follow-up contact.

Carol
Caucasian Female Ages 18 to 21
Carol came into care at age 15 as a result of sexual abuse by her birthfather and physical abuse by her stepmother. She remained in placement for about four years. The record indicates two placements—one foster home and one home of relative, with four caseworkers. Carol completed a high school diploma and then enrolled in community college to work toward an associate of arts (AA) degree. While in placement, Carol held a variety of part-time jobs including fast-food work at Hardees and stock work at K-Mart. She rates herself as a good worker. At one point, she enrolled in a federal job training program (through the Job Training Partnership Act) and worked with computers. At discharge, Carol shared an apartment with a friend. Her support system is strong and includes a roommate, a boyfriend, a brother, and foster family, as well as several relatives.

Age 28
At the age 28 contact, Carol reported taking community college courses, but has not yet completed the AA degree. Current classes include typing and computer applications. Carol talked about working toward a bachelor's degree in elementary education. She now works as temporary employee and receives job referrals from a private employment agency. In 1999, most of Carol's employment was related to doing temporary office work for private sector business firms. Based on an average of $7 hour and 40 hours a week, Carol's annual income was approximately $11,000. As a temporary employee, Carol is not entitled to medical or dental insurance.

Commentary
At age 28, Carol is still in transition to independence. Her short-term goal of an AA degree remains to be achieved. She is employed on a temporary basis and lacks a career-track perspective. Carol's long-term career goal is to complete a bachelor's degree, but she has taken no concrete steps toward fulfilling this goal. Even at age 28, Carol's transitional scenario is incomplete. She is still searching for a satisfactory career direction.

Michele
African American Female Ages 18 to 21

Michele came into care when her father died. She lived with relatives for a while. Michele spent a total of eight years in placement in two foster homes—one relative and one nonrelative. In high school, Michele was in the college preparatory track and graduated with honors. Her overall high school grade point average was 3.2. She attended an area community college with the intention of achieving a bachelor's degree. Michele received an educational scholarship from the state child welfare agency. At the age 21 follow-up, Michele was sharing an apartment with a friend and paid rent with financial assistance from the state. She is connected to a church but has no affiliation with other organizations or clubs. Her support circle consists of a former foster mother and father, a boyfriend, and the mother of a friend. Her part-time work experience is extensive, including jobs as a cashier in a parking system and general work in a clothing store.

Age 28

At the age 28 interview, Michele had completed 64 hours of community college credit and earned an AA degree with a nursing focus. However, Michele decided to take a job with the U.S. Postal Service. She has been a postal service employee for seven years. Job duties include working as a mail distribution clerk, sorting mail, and doing window duty. Her hourly rate of pay is about $16, and her annual income is approximately $32,500. Michele's fringe benefit package includes medical and dental coverage. She hopes to upgrade her position in the postal service and work in the money order division.

Commentary

Michele clearly meets the criteria for economic self-sufficiency. Her educational progress equals or surpasses that reported by other emancipated wards. She completed a two-year AA degree and has been employed with the U.S. Postal Service for seven years. Although Michele would prefer to earn a degree at a four-year college, she is likely to continue her job with the Postal Service. However, Michele still has aspirations of completing a bachelor's degree. The latest interview indicates that her vocational interests have turned away from nursing and are now directed toward computer programming. It is important to point out that state scholarship awards, coupled with work-study appointments and Pell Grant support, were vital in contributing to Michele's ability to achieve self-sufficiency. Other factors included encouragement and support from her husband, foster parents, and church members, as well as her commitment, determination, and motivation to achieve economic stability.

Ronna

African American Female Ages 18 to 21

Adopted early in life, Ronna had a relatively brief placement background. During her adolescent years, she became progressively more difficult for her parents to handle. Ronna came into care at age 17. The record indicates that the primary reason for placement was she "couldn't get along with parents." Overall, Ronna spent one year in state care, with two placements—one group home and one apartment. She completed a high school diploma and worked at several minimum-wage jobs. At age 19, she had her first child but remained unmarried. She earned less than $5,000 a year from ages 18 to 21. Ronna used several means-tested, safety-net programs, such as Aid to Families with Dependent Children (AFDC); food stamps; Women, Infants, and Children (WIC); and Medicaid.

Age 28

At the age 28 contact, it was learned that Ronna had made considerable progress toward self-sufficiency. She completed an AA degree with special training as a paralegal specialist. At this point, Ronna had a second child but remained unmarried. The birthfather helps out by taking care of the youngest child when Ronna is at work. The older child goes to day care. Ronna is currently employed on a full-time basis. Her hourly rate of pay is $15.63. She works as a civil rights representative in a state agency. Her job duties involve investigating complaints and allegations of discrimination and violations of civil rights. Her gross income for 1999 was approximately $35,000. Health and medical benefits are part of the employment package, and she has purchased a home with a 30-year loan.

Commentary

Ronna appears to be doing very well with respect to achieving economic self-sufficiency and family stability. A homeowner at age 28, an appointment as a state civil rights investigator, an annual income of $35,000, and a family arrangement that is suitable for her lifestyle are impressive achievements. Seven years earlier, at age 21, Ronna was heavily dependent on means-tested, safety-net support. At that time, her future self-sufficiency status was difficult to predict. She is now upwardly mobile and, at last contact, indicated that she plans to work toward a law degree.

Assessment: A 10-Year Follow-up Perspective

The aim of the Foster Care Independence Act is to prepare state wards for economic and social self-sufficiency. One criterion for gauging self-sufficiency is that people are economically independent of public assistance programs. The U.S. General Accounting Office (GAO), in conducting an evaluation of federal programs designed to facilitate self-sufficiency, concluded, "The earnings required for a family to become economically independent of housing and public assistance programs vary considerably across states and programs." (GAO, 1993, p. 2). The GAO report further pointed out that although a family may achieve independence from AFDC and food stamps, independence from rental or housing assistance is difficult for many families. Moreover, independence from Medicaid is hard to define because Medicaid can be used by people who are medically in need but have varying income levels.

With respect to self-sufficiency, empirical data from the University of Illinois Foster Youth project indicated the following:

Based on information obtained from 534 emancipated youth in Illinois, Ohio, and Indiana, virtually none in the sample met the self-sufficiency criterion of not using means-tested programs. One consequence of emancipation from placement is that on or about age 18, every ward must face the realities associated with becoming independent. Society expects wards to take an active part in creating their own futures. Readiness to take advantage of system opportunities is heightened. Turning 18 becomes a threshold point and suggests that the placement system should no longer have sole responsibility for a ward's future, nor should the system itself be totally responsible for producing positive results. Youth themselves must assume a major role in working toward self-sufficiency. Thus, it is important to have postemancipation opportunity structures in place for the transition years from ages 18 to 21.

The age 21 follow-up of the group surveyed at age 18 indicated a continuing pattern of reliance on means-tested programs. Of the 195 women in the sample, 44% were receiving public assistance grants, 41% received a housing subsidy, 93% were Medicaid recipients, and 69% used WIC. It is important to note that non-AFDC females were also significant users of means-tested resources. It is a mistake to equate nonwelfare status with zero use of public/community resources. Nearly 70% of the non-AFDC females relied on Medicaid as a health provider, one in three used food stamps, 19% used WIC, and 12% used public housing subsidies. Even at age 21, emancipated wards are vulnerable to continued dependence on public resources. For the majority, family, relative, or peer supports are tenuous. Most foster wards turn to societal safety net resources for assistance. Follow-up studies of foster wards that rely on measuring outcomes at age 21 can easily produce misleading results. Maturation, personal development, and life experience are factors that continue to influence outcomes. The 10-year follow-up, when wards were an average of 28 years old, provides a more balanced picture of the complexities of achieving self-sufficiency.

The age 28 follow-up consisted of a sample of 51 former foster wards, 26 female and 25 male. A random sample of 100 cases was drawn from the original (age 18) group of 534 cases. Within the six-week time period for the survey to be conducted, it was possible to locate and interview 51% of the sample group. Interviews were conducted by phone and tape-recorded with permission of the respondent. Interviews averaged 30 minutes. Participants received $20 for the interview. Overall, statistical results were as follows:

- **Income—Female Sample ($N = 26$).** In the aggregate for 1999, the annual income for females was $14,308. For females with no children, average income was $20,441. For females with one child, mean income was $13,914; for women with two or more children, the mean annual income was $13,541. For comparative purposes, an income level of $10,000 or less was used to assess poverty among female participants. Of the 26 participants, 7, or 27%, were in the poverty category. Looking back at the age 21 data for female participants, more than 90% were classified as at or below poverty level.

- **Health Insurance—Female Sample ($N = 26$).** With respect to health insurance, 18 of 26, or 70%, reported having health/medical insurance related either to workplace policy or to a spouse qualifying for insurance coverage as a job-related benefit. At the age 21 follow-up, only 10% reported health insurance coverage.

- **Education—Female Sample ($N = 26$).** The mean education level was 13.3 years. Of the 26 female participants, only one achieved less than a high school diploma or a GED. At the same time, only two participants completed a bachelor's degree. Again, compared with their educational progress at age 21, significant gains were demonstrated.

- **Income—Male Sample ($N = 25$).** For 1999, the mean annual income for men was approximately $24,000. Income reported ranged from a low of $6,000 to a high of $68,000. Only two men were below the operational poverty level of $10,000. Nearly one in three was at or above the $30,000 income level. Again, compared with income levels at age 21, these results are indicative of significant gains.

- **Health Insurance—Male Sample (*N* = 25).** Of the 25 male participants, 19, or 76%, reported health/medical coverage. That more than 7 in 10 participants were receiving health/medical coverage as an employment benefit represents a vast improvement over their status at age 21.

- **Education—Male Sample (*N* = 25).** Of the 25 male participants, only 3, or 12%, earned less than a high school diploma or a GED. With respect to four-year college outcomes, only one male (4%) completed a bachelor's degree. Overall, the mean education level completed was 12.24 years. Male achievement with respect to average years of education completed was one year below that of females. Yet despite an educational advantage, females on average earned 40% less per year than did their male counterparts.

Overall, on or about age 28, most former wards managed to attain some measure of economic self-sufficiency. However, economic self-sufficiency for females appears somewhat tenuous, particularly those with children. Most complete a high school diploma or a GED. Many initiate a postsecondary education plan, usually in a local community college, but are only able to complete one semester, or at best, one year of credit toward an associate's degree. For most, postsecondary education is an unrealized aspiration.

Even at age 28, the majority of respondents report plans to upgrade their employment, obtain additional education, or acquire a new skill. Much room exists for improvement. It is important to note that most participants in the age 28 follow-up were unable to identify or to credit specific elements in state independent-living programs that helped them to prepare for self-sufficiency. Accordingly, subsequent sections of this volume describe interventions that appear to be important elements in helping prepare foster wards for independent living.

Reference

U.S. General Accounting Office. (1993). *Self-sufficiency. Opportunities and disincentives on the road to economic independence* (GAO/HRD-93-23). Washington, DC: Author.

Chapter 6

Education, Employment, and Income

EDMUND V. MECH

> *The quest for excellence into the 21st Century begins*
> *in the schoolroom, but we must go next to the*
> *workplace....We must enable our workers to adapt*
> *to the rapidly changing nature of the workplace.*
>
> —*President Ronald Reagan,*
> *State of the Union Address, January 27, 1987*

The Education Imperative

Educational attainment is the centerpiece of any strategy that is aimed at preparing foster wards for economic self-sufficiency. Significant connections exist between the number of years spent in school and completion of requirements for a diploma, degree, certificate, or specialized credential and subsequent employment, career-track preparation, and income level.

In a democratic society, it is vital to ensure that our young citizens have access to a variety of educational and vocational opportunities. Too little has been done to open educational opportunities to foster wards or make certain that the placement system conveys a strong message as to the value it attaches to educational achievement. Moreover, the "expectations bar" for the educational attainment of foster wards has been too low. Based on a review of follow-up studies of foster wards who emancipated from placement, the U.S. General Accounting Office (GAO, 1999, p. 3) reports a number of discouraging outcomes. With respect to education, 37% to 46% of wards did not complete high school, and 30% to 46% were categorized as a cost to the community, which means that the wards use one or more public aid or means-tested programs. Too frequently, child welfare agencies tend to ignore the importance of educational attainment.

Legislative language in the Chafee Independent Living Bill refers to a high school diploma or completion of a general equivalency diploma (GED) as evidence of success. In a society that is witnessing rapid change in job-skill requirements and technological advancement, it is shortsighted to ask foster wards to settle for a GED or a high school diploma. In the University of Illinois Foster Adolescent Project (Mech, 2000) nearly 65% of foster wards in the multistate sample were enrolled in an all-purpose, general curriculum or in a special education program. Only 15% were enrolled in a college preparatory track and 19% in a vocational/technical curriculum.

These data suggest that most foster wards lack preparation for postsecondary education. State agencies are aware of the problem. The question becomes, What are the options, actions, and resources available that might help ameliorate educational deficits in foster care? If state agencies are to create "opportunity structures," education stands as a pivotal starting point. Table 6.1 summarizes enrollment distributions for high school curriculum options classified by type and race.

Education and Income

An important step in understanding the payoff value of educational achievement by foster wards is reviewing the statistical connections between education and income. The results are impressive, and in relative terms have been consistent year after year. Table 6.2 summarizes the relationship between education and income, classified by race.

As documented in Table 6.2, annual income increases with educational level. On average, college completers earn nearly twice as much as individuals with only a high school diploma. With respect to race, income shows a positive association with education completed, more so for white individuals than for Black or Hispanic people. Moreover, if education is viewed as an individual investing in his or her future, in terms of statistical outcomes, youth who complete a high school diploma are likely to earn 35% more than individuals without a high school diploma. A community college associate of arts (AA) degree is worth an additional 24% gain in income when compared with a high school diploma. A four-year college degree can return an additional 30% in income gain in comparison with an AA degree. Overall, education is a sound investment in one's future. In many instances, income returns on investments in education outperform stock market investments or other Wall Street ventures. Table 6.3 summarizes the gain in mean annual income for various combinations of educational completion.

TABLE 6.1

Enrollment in High School Curriculum Track Classified by Race/Gender (in percentages)

CURRICULUM TRACK	WHITE MALE	NONWHITE MALE	WHITE FEMALE	NONWHITE FEMALE	TOTAL
General	46	53	55	60	54
Vocational	22	24	20	12	19
College Preparatory	15	13	13	9	15
Special Education	17	11	12	9	12
Total	21	14	40	25	100
Total Number	83	55	156	99	393

TABLE 6.2

Annual Income Classified by Race and Educational Attainment (in dollars)

RACE	NO HIGH SCHOOL DIPLOMA	HIGH SCHOOL DIPLOMA	ASSOCIATE'S DEGREE	BACHELOR'S DEGREE	MASTER'S DEGREE
Black	13,569	20,991	28,772	37,422	48,777
Hispanic	16,106	20,704	29,329	36,212	50,576
White	16,957	25,847	32,955	47,401	55,799
Total	16,121	24,572	32,152	45,678	55,641

SOURCE: Adapted from Current Population Survey (1999).

TABLE 6.3

Comparison Between Levels of Educational Completion and Gain in Mean Annual Income

COMPARISON	GAIN IN MEAN ANNUAL INCOME	PERCENTAGE GAIN
High School vs. No High School Diploma	$8,451	35
Associate Degree vs. High School Diploma	$7,580	24
Bachelor's Degree vs. High School Diploma	$13,526	30
Bachelor's Degree vs. Associate's Degree	$9,963	18

Trends in the Employment Marketplace

The prevailing formula for success in U.S. employment markets is the following: Take substantive courses in high school, make good grades, do well on an admission test for college, and complete college with a bachelor's degree. Higher education is the path most often viewed as the solution for achieving upward mobility and economic stability. For the forgotten half—that is, youth headed directly into the job market without postsecondary education, the road to employment success is poorly marked. Employers are quick to point out that connections between a high school diploma or a GED and marketable skills is shaky. Whereas a college or university credential has value to employers, the value of a high school diploma in terms of marketable skills and work aptitude is unclear. The assumption that a high school diploma or GED is sufficient preparation for economic self-sufficiency is wishful thinking.

Signals from the new economy are clear—employment markets are making rational decisions—the best jobs, with the highest wages, are usually awarded to the best-trained and educated workers.

The National Alliance of Business has favored an employment policy that requires high school transcript checks for years. Although implementation has been spotty, transcript checking for grades, attendance, and related information is on the employment horizon. School administrators are hopeful that business and industry can overcome its inertia and use transcripts and school records to evaluate employment potential and work aptitude. Moreover, the American Federation of Teachers is in favor of transcript checking. The theory behind transcript checking is that if consequences are associated with good grades or poor grades and employability is at stake, students will be motivated to upgrade school performance. According to a multicity survey of employer views on the job market, there has been a general deterioration in the labor market for less-educated workers (Holzer, 1996). Male high school graduates "now earn 20% to 30% less per hour than such workers did in the early 1970's" (Holzer, 1996, p. 2).

What do employers want, and what do these trends mean for less educated workers? Increasingly, hiring practices are favoring people who possess higher levels of cognitive skills, including reading, writing, and computer skills. The growing importance of technology is a major factor, as is the phenomena of *deindustrialization*, which refers to job decline in areas such as manufacturing. In the new economy, less educated workers are at a decided disadvantage. Business and industry have consistently expressed concerns about the need for a skilled workforce. The implications for preparing foster wards for a workforce that is increasingly competitive are considerable. In addition to basic skills, such as literacy, youth need to possess computer and communication skills as well as suitable workplace habits such as reliability, perseverance, and accepting responsibility.

The United States has clearly moved from a manufacturing to a service economy. The U.S. Department of Labor estimates that 9 out of 10 new jobs will be in the service sector, not in manufacturing (U.S. Department of Labor/U.S. Department of Education, 1988). Analyses of work requirements in the new economy are contained in an influential report issued by the Hudson Institute. The Hudson Institute report, titled Workforce 2000 (Johnston & Packer, 1987), echoes familiar themes: (a) The wages of high school dropouts fell 42% between 1973 and 1986, (b) wages for youth with only a high school diploma fell by 28%, and (c) the current education system is failing. As a consequence, too many youth graduate with inadequate skills. Many have the mistaken idea that a high school diploma guarantees access to employment and economic stability. Unfortunately, youth now pass through an outmoded education system that worked best in past years at preparing graduates for a blue-collar manufacturing economy. Most new jobs require a high order of information processing skills. Concern in the Hudson Institute report is for youth who are unlikely to obtain a traditional four-year university degree. An influential report, titled *The Forgotten Half,* sponsored by the William T. Grant Foundation (1998), makes clear the importance of responding to the employment preparation needs of young people not headed for college.

School-to-Work Trends

A high percentage of foster wards fall into the nonacademic, non-college-bound category. The school-to-work movement represents real work activities conducted at actual work sites. This reform movement attempts to connect academic activities with occupational learning and workplace opportunities. Work-based learning is an attractive concept but is difficult to implement. The School-to-Work Opportunities Act (STWOA) was enacted by Congress in 1994. Its purpose is to enable states to establish comprehensive school-to-work transition systems.

The current wave of interest in reforming education began in the 1980s with the publication of *A Nation at Risk* (National Commission on Excellence in Education, 1983). The report gave low marks to America's schools, particularly when U.S. students were compared with students in Europe and certain parts of Asia. Criticism of schools emerged in three areas: (1) lack of discipline in schools, (2) low standards with "social promotion" as an unwritten policy, and (3) neglect of academic basics.

The education system in America continues to seek a consistent compass, one that points to genuine reform solutions. As things now stand, educators are very much aware of the magnitude of the challenge, but are uncertain and divided as to how to remedy school system deficiencies. Should schools educate for employment? For citizenship? For personal development? Tension exists among educators as to how to respond to the differing (and conflicting) demands that society has placed on schools. America's schools, both public and private, stand as the main youth development institution in society. Taxpayers expect schools to turn out young adults who are good citizens and productive workers. Although preparation for work, vocations, and careers is accepted as a major goal of American education, experts say that schools have made little progress in developing an effective school-to-work transition system (Mendel, 1995; U.S. General Accounting Office, 1991, 1993).

Many criticisms of America's schools are harsh. At the top of the list are irrelevant curricula, lack of incentives, and lack of career guidance. The specifics are these: Unless a student is planning to attend college, the optional tracks are general education and vocational education. Critics assert that curricula for vocational education typically do not reflect the needs of the labor market. Employers do not view vocational training in a typical high school as sufficient to prepare a skilled worker. Evaluations of the so-called general education track offer little hope for optimism. A report commissioned by Lilly Endowment, *The American School-to-Career Movement* (Mendel, 1995), concludes that the general education option offers little more than a mixture of "scholastic junk food," which includes diluted content that fails to prepare students for postsecondary education or for moving directly into the workplace.

Moreover, lack of career guidance is judged to be acute for students not headed for college. The non-college-bound student needs help but usually receives little in the way of occupational information or job market analysis. In the state of Indiana, only one in four counselors reported that their school's administrator believed that increasing the employability of work-bound students was an important goal for counselors (Orfield & Paul, 1994, as cited in Mendel, 1995). STWOA was intended to emphasize the importance of developing the employability skills of work-bound students for school administrators, teachers, and communities. Idealistic elements of the act include strong connections between school-based learning and the realities of workplace expectations (U.S. Congress, Office of Technology Assessment, 1995; U.S. Department of Labor, 1995). One symbol of industry recognition of work preparedness is certification of skill acquisition. Hamilton (1999) pointed out that to qualify as work-based learning, students must be engaged in tangible activities that require them to design and/or construct a product or to provide goods or services that result in acquisition of a skill. Passive activity such as listening to a guest speaker talk about career opportunities in a particular field does not count as work-based learning. One aspect of work-based learning is exemplified by the use of apprenticeships. Although the United States is not a mecca for youth apprenticeship opportunities, this model of experiential learning merits discussion.

Apprenticeships, Cooperative Education, and Career Academies

The school-to-work movement aspires to provide all students with information about careers in the workplace. Key elements in the work-based learning and school-based learning systems are: (a) youth apprenticeships, (b) cooperative education, and (c) career academies. These resources are available but are scattered throughout the United States. Regrettably, many areas are deficient in number, type, and quality of experiential resources necessary for young people to connect school learning with the realities of workplace requirements. Work-based learning typically requires students and/or teachers to go into actual community workplace situations to become familiar with key aspects of a business, service, or entrepreneurial venture and to make connections between workplace situations and the school curriculum. School-based learning attempts to bring business, industry, government agencies, labor unions, and nonprofit organizations into classrooms to assist in incorporating world-of-work situations into school curriculums (Rosenbaum, Stern, Hamilton, Hamilton, & Berryman, 1992).

Apprenticeships

Typically, an apprenticeship permits a high school student to obtain a paid training experience. Apprenticeships are task oriented and intensive and combine technical classroom training with on-the-job experience. Students can still work toward completing a high school diploma. Apprenticeships usually take one to three years to complete. Time spent as an apprentice varies with occupational specialty. At the end of training, the apprentice earns a certificate of proficiency. Apprenticeship certification is recognized on an industry-wide basis. It is estimated that apprenticeships are now available in more than 800 occupations. Apprenticeships were authorized by the Fitzgerald Act—The National Apprenticeship Act of 1937—and operate under the auspices of the Office of Apprenticeship Training, U.S. Department of Labor.

Registered apprenticeship programs operate in 23 states. Wisconsin is one of the states with a variety of youth apprenticeship programs, ranging from auto technician, financial services, graphic arts/printing, health services, hotel/motel management, computer services, freight movement, insurance, tourism, and animal sciences. Youth apprenticeships in Wisconsin are typically 24-month programs for juniors and seniors in high school who are interested in specific occupations in which apprenticeships are available. Student apprentices are paid for their work and receive training at the workplace from specialists in a particular occupation. Two outcomes occur when the program is successfully completed. Students are awarded a high school diploma and a Certificate of Occupational Proficiency. Other benefits accrue as well and include eligibility for advanced standing status in state technical colleges and fulfillment of admission requirements for many four-year colleges.

Eligibility factors include evidence that applicants have participated in career planning activities that enable students to make an informed career decision. Other requirements may be established, such as a minimum grade point average, school attendance standards, and demonstration of the ability to acquire the skills necessary in a particular apprenticeship occupation.

Apprenticeship opportunities exist in many other states. For example, New Hampshire uses a category that is referred to as a registered youth apprenticeship. Typically, the experience is paid and requires about 1,000 hours per year (approximately 20 hours per week) while a trainee is in high school. Following graduation, the same apprentice takes on full employment as a registered adult apprentice. The state of New Hampshire website on school-to-work programs provides an example of a registered youth apprenticeship. The following excerpt is a direct quote:

> While a junior at White Mountains Regional High School, a student began his apprenticeship in forestry. For the next two years, he worked an average of 20 hours per week while continuing to receive instruction in both forestry and his general education requirements. For one more year after graduation, he worked full-time and completed the remaining year of instruction in forestry to earn his apprenticeship certificate in forestry. (New Hampshire School to Work, n.d.)

One of the most frequently cited examples of a school-to-work based learning system is the German apprenticeship program. Hamilton (1999) described the German model as follows: "It is a massive institution, involving at least half of older teenagers in a combination of schooling and formal on-the-job training, typically for three years" (p. 304). According to Hamilton, the basic elements of the German apprenticeship system are the following:

- Information on the knowledge and skill requirements for approximately 360 occupations is documented in detail, as are the responsibilities of employer-sponsors of apprenticeship programs.

- Work-based learning requires four days per week over a multiyear period. Apprentices must pass a series of examinations before entering their field of choice.

- Once an individual has qualified by serving a successful apprenticeship and has passed requisite examinations, employers are required to give first preference to successful apprentices when hiring new employees.

The overall conclusion is that a comprehensive apprenticeship system offers continuity and opportunity to apply formal knowledge to workplace situations, and is sound preparation for excellence in a particular occupational area. The United States is flirting with a youth apprenticeship system. At the present time, apprenticeship resources are scarce and, despite the need to create apprenticeship opportunities for non-college-bound youth, many states have little to offer.

Cooperative Education

Whereas a typical apprenticeship placement is work intensive, cooperative education offers a proficiency credential in a recognized occupation that is far less demanding than apprenticeships in terms of time commitment, is more flexible in terms of applying occupational standards, and is oriented to responding to student interests. Cooperative education placements are jobs under the supervisory jurisdiction of a school. Typically, this form of experiential learning is linked to vocational learning in a specific occupation. In a cooperative education arrangement, teachers also coordinate and supervise paid placements. In a cooperative, school-arranged and -supervised field placement, teachers participate in formulating a training plan and are responsible for evaluating student performance. Students are paid for their work during placement and also receive school credit.

Two elements delineated by Stern (1994) are characteristic of a cooperative education arrangement: (1) There is a written training agreement between a school and employer—employers provide the job, and schools take responsibility for supervising students. (2) There is a written training plan. The plan is expected to specify learning objectives, indicating how objectives are connected to vocational courses. The field plan usually requires multiple signatures, including approval from the student trainee, the work supervisor, and the program coordinator. Cooperative education programs require resources sufficient to support a quality work experience for students. Teachers and coordinators need released time to supervise job sites and to prepare performance evaluations. Time is needed to develop new job placements. Employers are expected to make time for valued employees to assist in instructing student trainees.

Career Academies

The career academy concept constitutes another approach to preparing young adults for employment. Career academies are a partial response to a dilemma that faces most schools; namely, America lacks effective ways to assist young people to transition from the classroom to the workplace. The main idea of career academies is to organize the high school curriculum around a career theme. Local employers are vital; they assist in curriculum design and provide internships, summer employment, and on-the-job mentoring. Career themes are selected from occupations in which demand is increasing and employment opportunities exist. Students in this type of program combine technical and academic content. A career academy is typically described as a school within a school.

In terms of historical antecedents, modern versions of the academy movement began in 1979 in Philadelphia. A decade or so later, career academy programs started in California. California's state assembly enacted legislation that authorized career academies on a statewide basis (Stern, Raby, & Dayton, 1992).

Special aspects of the California academy model include the concept of a partnership between high schools and local employers, team teaching, small classes, a diploma at graduation, and development of vocational skills. The East Side Electronics Academy in San Jose, California, provides an example. Its purpose is to develop job and work skills and to help students stay on a career trajectory. The electronic curriculum is technological in nature and requires a hands-on practical approach that emphasizes career aspirations. The East Side Electronics Academy is part of the East Side Union High School in San Jose. Students are part of a team, in which the same staff stay with students throughout the three-year program. Teachers and industry experts are from the fields of mathematics, science, language arts, and electronics. Class size is small; there is much individualized, one-on-one, teacher/student contact. The career academy program is voluntary. For the most part, learning is guided by a series of project-based assignments. Employer-mentors are involved in all aspects of the program. Students are placed in monitored, paid jobs. With respect to the effectiveness of the career academy model, analysis of evaluative information by GAO concluded that "such academies are particularly helpful for students considered at high risk of school failure" (GAO, 2000, p. 5). Participants in academy programs demonstrate increased attendance, a reduction in school dropout rates, and an increase in credits earned toward graduation.

Forecasting Occupational Trends

Workforce 2000 forecasts occupational trends for the year 2000 and beyond (Johnston & Packer, 1987). Occupations predicted to lose ground in the future include agriculture worker, farmer, fisheries, machine operator, assembler, and fabricator. Occupations targeted as likely to show increases in job growth include service work, marketing and sales, and health-related occupations. Many of the projected increases in opportunities for workers are in computer services and computer support. Demand for computer scientists is expected to increase by more than 60%, whereas demand for laborers and helpers is projected to gain little more than 5%.

Educational expectations and skill requirements are steadily increasing. Of the new jobs being created, more than half will require postsecondary education, special training, or a higher education credential. Relying on a high school diploma or a GED is no longer sufficient. Some of the occupations such as farming are losing ground and are referred to as difficult job markets. There is considerable risk in preparing for work in job markets designated as difficult. Simply put, those markets are losing jobs. Each state has a research and statistics office that summarizes occupational trends. For example, in Minnesota, the Department of Economic Security has posted an employment outlook report for the period 1996 to 2006. This report classifies jobs by industrial category, such as services, manufacturing, finance, transportation, construction, government, mining, agriculture, forestry, and fishing. Table 6.4 summarizes employment projections in Minnesota for the period 1996 to 2006.

Jobs in service occupations head the list. Services are Minnesota's largest industrial category. Approximately 234,000 new jobs are predicted. This number is more than half of all projected new jobs in Minnesota for the period 1996 to 2006. Within this category, services most likely to provide jobs are business services, health services, educational services, and social services. Projections for job growth in manufacturing in Minnesota call for a 9% increase or 40,661 new jobs. This estimate runs counter to the national trend, which shows manufacturing losing ground. However, in Minnesota, job expansion is expected to increase in the manufacture of

TABLE 6.4

Employment Outlook in Minnesota, 1996 to 2006

CATEGORY	NUMBER OF JOBS	PERCENTAGE CHANGE
Services	233,866	+28
Trade	75,734	+13
Manufacturing	40,661	+ 9
Finance, Insurance, Real Estate	19,484	+14
Transportation/Public Utilities	15,241	+13
Construction	13,901	+16
Self-Employed (Nonagriculture)	11,114	+7
Government	9,272	+6
Mining	−215	−3
Agriculture, Forestry, Fishing	−2,764	−4

SOURCE: Adapted from Minnesota Department of Economic Security (1999).

medical instruments and supplies, commercial printing, and electronic components and accessories. Detailed state, substate, and regional information is available from the Department of Economic Security. Similar projections are available from other state economic security bureaus.

At the federal level, an excellent information source is the Bureau of Labor Statistics, U.S. Department of Labor. Information on employment projections nationwide for the period 1998 to 2008 are published in the *Monthly Labor Review* (Braddock, 1999). The main national trends cited are the following:

- Service-producing industries will dominate job growth for the period 1998 to 2008. Computer and data processing services are cited as the areas with the fastest wage and salary growth.

- Occupations requiring an AA degree are projected to grow 31%, faster than all other education categories.

- Health services are ranked among the top 10 industries in wage, salary, and employment growth.

- The fastest growing occupations from 1998 to 2008 are projected to be computer engineers, computer support specialists, paralegal and legal assistants, personal care and home health care aides, medical assistants, physician assistants, and social and human services assistants.

- The occupation with the largest projected job growth for 1998 to 2008 is computer support specialist; federal projections call for more than a 100% increase in demand for persons with computer support skills.

Career Planning: Occupational Profiles

A series of selected occupational profiles from the Minnesota database are summarized. Information is cited with respect to job duties, future job market, job requirements, and income.

Medical Assistants

Job Duties

Medical assistants may perform administrative, laboratory, and medical tasks to assist physicians in caring for their patients. Typical duties include scheduling and receiving patients, taking vital signs, assisting in examinations, sterilizing instruments, and keeping medical records. Medical assistants may collect samples for analysis, perform standard laboratory tests, give immunizations, and order and maintain supplies. They may also operate diagnostic equipment, do bookkeeping and billing, and handle insurance forms. The medical assistant's duties vary with employer and often overlap those performed by medical secretaries and other health care providers. Ophthalmic assistants and technicians work with eye doctors.

Future Job Market

Medical assistant is considered one of the fastest growing occupations in Minnesota and nationwide. Contributing to this growth is an aging population needing more medical care and the increased volume of paperwork associated with medical care. Medical assistants primarily work in outpatient settings, in which fast growth is expected. In addition, turnover is quite high, which creates job openings. Opportunities are best for those who have completed a formal program and have some related experience.

Wages

The estimated beginning salary range in Minnesota is $16,000 to $19,400 per year. Most experienced workers earn between $24,200 and $28,000.

Education and Training

High school courses in math, health, biology, word processing, and office skills are useful. Most employers prefer graduates of medical assistant programs, which are offered at technical colleges and private vocational schools. Some will train high school graduates on the job. Training programs vary in length from nine months to two years. Certification is not required in Minnesota but is available. One must graduate from an approved program and pass an exam to be certified. Taking courses in health, science, math, and word processing and computer skills while in high school can prove helpful. Certification in cardiopulmonary resuscitation (CPR) and advanced first aid is recommended.

Pharmacy Technicians

Job Duties
Pharmacy technicians prepare and dispense prescribed medicines under the direct supervision of a pharmacist. They enter prescription information into a computer and maintain records and inventories of drugs and other supplies. They order, stock, package, and price medications. They clean equipment, shelves, and work areas and may wash and sterilize bottles and beakers. Some pick up and deliver orders.

Future Job Market
In Minnesota, average employment growth is expected in the next few years. The growth in the number of older persons should spur demand.

Wages
Current data on Minnesota wages are not available for this occupation. Older data indicate that the estimated beginning salary range in the Twin Cities area is $8 to $9 per hour. Based on limited data, the estimated beginning salary range in greater Minnesota is $4.50 to $6 per hour. Estimated top salary range statewide is $10 to $12 per hour.

Education and Training
Useful high school courses include English, math, biology, chemistry, and computer operation. Apprenticeships, technology preparation, or cooperative learning opportunities may be available. Postsecondary training is available at technical colleges. Many skills are learned on the job.

Computer Support Specialists

Job Duties
Computer support specialists keep computer systems operating by providing technical assistance and training to system users. They load software into computers and set up printers. They test systems and diagnose problems in hardware and software. They make minor repairs, usually by replacing components or programs, and keep records of service and repairs. They instruct users on how to operate and maintain hardware and how to use software most effectively. They may help evaluate computer hardware and

software needs, purchases, and modifications. Some specialize in support-ing specific types of hardware or computer operating systems.

Future Job Market
Computer support specialist is one of the fastest growing occupations in Minnesota. The outlook depends on increased use of computers in busi-ness and government and on developments in computer hardware, soft-ware, and linkages to telecommunications equipment. Prospects are best for those who are familiar with products that integrate microcomputers, especially networks. Growth follows advances in telecommunications, medicine, education, and small business.

Wages
The estimated beginning salary range in Minnesota is $24,000 to $28,000 per year. The estimated top salary range is $41,000 to $52,000 per year. Nationwide, the median salary for computer training specialists is $39,000 annually. Most computer technical writers earn between $25,000 and $45,000 per year. Self-employed consultants may earn more depending on their expertise and clientele.

Education and Training
Useful high school subjects include advanced math, computer program-ming, electronics, and English. Postsecondary training is offered at voca-tional schools and at two- and four-year colleges. Employers increasingly prefer those who have a four-year degree. Preparation should include some programming as well as instruction on maintaining microcomputers and peripheral equipment, operating systems, and applications software. Ex-perience with database, spreadsheet, word processing, and graphics pro-grams is valuable.

Employers usually prefer applicants who are familiar with the particular types of hardware and software they use. Some hardware and software manufacturers offer short certification programs on their products. Because of rapid technological changes, experienced computer support specialists often attend training sessions to update their knowledge and skills.

Home Health Aides

Job Duties
Home health aides provide personal care and home management services to allow patients to live in their own homes. Duties vary with the specific needs of the patient. Home health aides usually work under the supervi-sion of a registered nurse. They may assist patients with baths and exer-

cise and do light housekeeping. They may check temperature, pulse, and respiration rates and report the condition of patients. Aides may monitor medications. They may teach patients how to adapt to changes caused by disability, frailty, or illness. Some aides are called homemakers. Homemakers do light housekeeping tasks, such as shop for groceries and household supplies, prepare meals, change bed linens, and do laundry. Some people combine home health aide and homemaker duties. An important task of both home health aides and homemakers is to give patients psychological support and companionship.

Future Job Market
In Minnesota, home health aide is one of the fastest growing occupations. Because turnover is high, it is also one of the occupations adding the most total job openings. Currently, there is a shortage of qualified workers in many places in Minnesota, including the Twin Cities area.

Wages
The estimated beginning salary range in Minnesota is $6 to $7 per hour. Top wages are $8 to $10 per hour. Wages vary depending on the location and level of responsibility.

Education and Training
Home health aides must complete a 75-hour training program to work in Minnesota. Training is available at community and technical colleges, hospitals, and health care agencies. Useful courses include math, home economics, health, biology, and CPR.

Medical Record Technicians
Job Duties
Medical record technicians, also called health information technicians, compile and maintain medical and statistical information about patients for hospitals and other health facilities. Technicians compile medical reports, prepare statistical reports, and review and analyze medical records for completeness and accuracy. Technicians code diseases, procedures, and other health information according to classification systems and maintain storage and retrieval systems. They work with doctors, nurses, and other health care professionals on planning research projects.

Future Job Market
Nationally and in Minnesota, this is one of the fastest growing occupations in the next few years. More medical tests will be ordered as baby boomers age and require more medical care. Good medical records are needed for

reporting and managing costs. Hospitals will remain the largest employer, but most growth will occur in HMOs, nursing homes, and large clinics.

Wages

Salaries vary by region and size and type of firm. The estimated beginning salary range in Minnesota is $14,000 to $17,500 per year. The estimated top salary range is $27,000 to $33,000. Wages are often a bit higher in the Twin Cities area.

Education and Training

Graduation from high school or the equivalent is required. Useful high school courses include English, math, biology, health, and computer skills. Most employers prefer applicants who have graduated from an accredited two-year program at a community college and have received an AA degree. Graduates of such programs can become Accredited Record Technicians by passing an exam offered by the American Health Information Management Association.

Assessment

It must be assumed that child welfare administrators, program managers, supervisors, direct service workers, and youth advocates, including members of the legal community, all understand the importance of education, training, and skill acquisition in preparing young people for self-sufficiency. The educational profiles, employment records, and income levels of emancipated wards are too often disappointing, and suggest, at least for these youth, that economic self-sufficiency is an elusive target. With respect to fulfilling the cardinal aim of preparing foster wards for economic self-sufficiency, America's independent-living programs are at the crossroads. Educational achievement does not appear to be a prime ingredient in state-generated opportunity structures. The new economy demands more than a GED or a general high school diploma. Numerous experts have voiced the opinion that a high school diploma is no longer the key to career employment. Feedback from the workforce, the employment marketplace, and successful samples of emancipated foster wards tells us that young people need to develop marketable skills and must be able to demonstrate occupational proficiency in jobs in which there is a demand for workers. An important question related to building effective opportunity structures is, What resources are available for the non-college-bound youth? Large numbers of young people head directly into the job market without postsecondary education or acquisition of a skill via specialized training. Parents, communities, teachers, guidance counselors, and young people themselves typically see college as the only solution. High schools are geared toward preparing its graduates for postsecondary study. As a consequence, non-college-bound youth are often left to fend for themselves.

The school-to-work legislation attempts to respond to the need for all youth to make connections between workplace requirements and classroom activity. School-to-work issues have immediate relevance for non-college-bound youth. It is necessary for child welfare workers and independent-living coordinators to familiarize themselves with skill acquisition resources at the local level. Are there apprenticeship programs available for young people? If so, in what specializations? To what extent are cooperative education programs functioning in area high schools? Are foster wards apprised of apprenticeship opportunities and/or other experiential school-to-work programs? To what extent is someone on staff informed about the nature and range of occupational resources in a particular service area? The essential advantages of apprenticeships are that certification of proficiency is earned and the award is recognized on an industry-wide basis. Overall, educational expectations and skill requirements are steadily increasing. Of all the new jobs being created between 2000 and 2010, the U.S. Department of Labor (Hecker, 2001) estimates that 42% will require postsecondary education, specialized/advanced training, or a higher education credential. Occupational trend and career-planning information is readily available from state, regional, and federal bureaus. Foster wards can learn to access occupational information sources and should be encouraged to incorporate pertinent information in formulating an independent-living plan.

References

Braddock, D. (1999). Occupational employment projections to 2008. *Monthly Labor Review Online, 112*(11). Retrieved from http://www.bls.gov/opub/mlr/1999/11/contents.htm

Current Population Survey. (1999). *Education attainment by total money earnings in 1999.* Washington, DC: Bureau of Labor Statistics and Bureau of the Census.

Hamilton, S. (1999). Preparing youth for the work force. In A. Reynolds, H. Walberg, & R. Weissberg (Eds.), *Promoting positive outcomes* (pp. 276–325). Washington, DC: CWLA Press.

Hecker, B. (2001). Occupational employment projections to 2010. *Monthly Labor Review Online, 124*(11). Retrieved from http://www.bls.gov/opub/mlr/2001/11/contents.htm

Holzer, H. J. (1996). *What employers want. Job prospects for less educated workers.* New York: Russell Sage Foundation.

Johnston, W. B., & Packer, A. (1987). *Workforce 2000. Work and workers for the 21st century.* Indianapolis, IN: Hudson Institute.

Mech, E. (2000). [University of Illinois Foster Youth Project]. Unpublished data.

Mendel, R. (1995). *The American school-to-career movement*. Washington, DC: American Youth Policy Forum.

Minnesota Department of Economic Security, Research and Statistics Office. (1999). *Minnesota job outlook to 2006*. St. Paul, MN: Author.

National Commission on Excellence in Education. (1983). *A nation at risk: The imperative for educational reform*. Retrieved from http://www.ed.gov/pubs/NatAtRisk/

New Hampshire School to Work. (n.d.). *School to work in NH*. Retrieved July 16, 2000, from http://www.ed.state.nh.us/SchoolToWork/wbl.htm

Reagan, R. (1987). *State of the union message: Message from the President of the United States transmitting a report on the state of the union*. Washington, DC: U.S. Government Printing Office.

Rosenbaum, J., Stern, D., Hamilton, S., Hamilton, M., & Berryman, S. (1992). *Youth apprenticeship in America: Guidelines for building an effective system*. Washington, DC: William T. Grant Foundation on Youth and America's Future.

Stern, D., Finkelstein, N., Stone, J. R., III, Latting, J., & Dornsife, C. (1994). *Research on school-to-work programs in the United States* (MDS-771). Berkeley: University of California, Berkeley, National Center for Research in Vocational Education. Retrieved from http://ncrve.berkeley.edu/AllInOne/MDS-771.html

Stern, D., Raby, M., & Dayton, C. (1992). *Career academies: Partnerships for reconstructing American high schools*. San Francisco, CA: Jossey-Bass.

U.S. Congress, Office of Technology Assessment. (1995). *Learning to work: Making the transition from school-to-work* (OTA-HER-637). Washington, DC: U.S. Government Printing Office.

U.S. Department of Labor. (1995). *What's working? A summary of research on the economic impacts of employment and training programs*. Washington, DC: U.S. Government Printing Office.

U.S. Department of Labor/U.S. Department of Education. (1988). *The bottom line. Basic skills in the workplace*. Washington, DC: U.S. Government Printing Office.

U.S. General Accounting Office. (1991). *Transition from school-to-work. Linking education and worksite training* (GAO/HRD-91-105). Washington, DC: Author.

U.S. General Accounting Office. (1993). *Transition from school-to-work. States are developing new strategies to prepare students for jobs* (GAO/HRD-93-139). Washington, DC: Author.

U.S. General Accounting Office. (1999). Foster care. Effectiveness of independent living services unknown (GAO/HEHS-00-13). Washington, DC: Author.

U.S. General Accounting Office. (2000). *At risk youth—School-community collaborations focus on improving student outcomes* (CTAO-01-66). Washington, DC: Author.

William T. Grant Commission on Youth and America's Future. (1998). *The forgotten half: Pathways to success for America's youth and young families*. Washington, DC: Author.

Chapter 7

Preparing Adolescent Wards for Independence in Foster Family Settings

EDMUND V. MECH AND
CARRIE CHE-MAN FUNG

> *Foster home was my best placement.*
> *I had lots of chances to practice what I learned*
> *in my independent-living classes.*
>
> —*Angela C., foster ward, age 21 follow-up*

Foster Homes: A Utilization Profile

At the age 21 follow-up of the University of Illinois Foster Adolescent Project, researchers asked youth to identify the types of placements they had experienced while in care and rate the placement that was the most helpful in preparing them for independence. Of the 390 youth in Illinois, Indiana, and Ohio who responded, more than 80% (*n* = 314) began their placement experience in a foster home setting. Of that 80%, nearly 45% rated foster homes as the most helpful placement in preparing them for independence. Foster homes are a vital threshold resource and an indispensable ally in preparing state wards for independence.

This chapter analyzes the role of foster families in preparing adolescents for independence. The analysis is directed toward improving the use of foster families in preparing adolescent wards to achieve self-sufficiency. The traditional process for acquiring independent-living skills is for youth to grow up in family settings in which parents, grandparents, and extended family members provide personal experience and ongoing exposure to what is required to succeed in life. When families are unable to fulfill this responsibility and children are put in out-of-home placement, the state must take on the role of substitute parent. Many youth are not likely to be reunified with their families prior to aging out of state care. For this group, the most expeditious service is independent living. During the 15-year period from 1982 to 1996, nearly 2 million adolescent wards received foster placement services (Tatara, 1997). This translates into an average of 133,000 teens in placement each year for the past 15 years.

Preparation for independent living is best viewed as a long-term, experiential process, not a tangible product that can be packaged into a formal curriculum, taught in a classroom structure, and dispensed to young wards in a matter of weeks or months. For more than a decade, the process of helping foster adolescents make a successful transition to self-sufficiency has been recognized as a new and valid challenge for child welfare services (Mech, 1988). Moreover, since publication of the Child Welfare League of America (CWLA) standards on independent-living services in 1989, the number of adolescents in placement has grown from 124,000 to approximately 200,000 per year (Tatara, 1997). With respect to foster families and independent-living services, CWLA Standard 5.6 stipulates that "foster parents should be recognized as having a unique opportunity to support adolescents throughout the process of gaining independence" (CWLA, 1989, p. 45). There is widespread agreement that foster parents are the single most important resource in the child welfare field. Practice theory suggests that foster families can serve as models for many skills that are needed for independent living. Council on Accreditation (COA) standard §23.5.01 stipulates that service plans for adolescents in foster care are to provide support that maximizes "independence in the least restrictive environment" (COA, 2001). Services to be provided include lifeskills training, vocational and technical training, education, employment preparation, housing, legal services, and a plan for aftercare services following discharge from placement.

As the independent-living movement is fueled by the demographic reality of increasing numbers of foster wards who are on the threshold of aging out of placement, it is imperative to develop a family-based model that responds to the need to prepare adolescent wards for independence. Nearly 4 in 10 wards in placement are in their teens. In addition, more than 75% of foster youth between the ages of 13 and 18 spend more than 65% of their time in care in a family-type home, and nearly 30% age out of care from a family-type placement. With so many adolescents in family foster care, it becomes clear that services for them deserve close attention. Yet, although the absolute number of adolescents in the placement system continues to rise, their share of available resources has dropped. In effect, the increasing number of younger children in substitute care has shifted attention, resources, and services away from adolescent wards.

Centrality of Foster Family Care

Much of the practice literature describes foster family placement in terms of its potential to prepare young wards for independence (Maluccio, Krieger, & Pine, 1990). Discussions on this topic are usually prescriptive and are typically framed in the context of future possibilities about what foster family care ought to accomplish. Little information exists as to what foster parents actually do to prepare adolescent wards for independent living, nor are there comparisons of services received in different types of family homes: relative, nonrelative foster boarding homes, and specialized or treatment foster homes. Belief in the centrality of foster family environments is anchored in several principles. Examples are:

- **Foster Parents Are Indispensable Resources.** Foster parents are considered to be integral elements in the service delivery team and should be viewed as partners who work in conjunction with social agencies in preparing young wards for independence.

- **Adolescent Wards Need Preparation for Independence.** Foster parents, social service specialists, and child care workers are consistent in reporting that young people who age out of placement are typically unprepared for independent living. The need for preparation extends to a variety of areas, including concrete skills and important intangible skills, such as effective interpersonal relationships, communication skills, and anger control. Foster families can provide youth with an environment conducive to learning independent-living skills.

- **Foster Parents Have Firsthand Knowledge of Wards.** The caregiving role of foster parents provides firsthand knowledge of the foster youth's adjustment to the placement, behavior, and level of maturity. The CWLA Task Force on Out-of-Home Care was entirely correct in concluding that it is the foster families "who provide the essential, consistent relationships with our children" (Barker & Aptekar, 1990). Foster families must handle difficult behaviors that are commonly associated with normal adolescent development as well as with the potential effects of the youth's separation from his or her birthfamily and subsequent experiences in foster care. Foster families can model independent-living skills and advocate for services most appropriate for the youth's developmental stage.

Transitioning to self-sufficiency is difficult to achieve at age 18, even for young adults who age out of their own (birth) homes. In comparison, the situation that foster wards face is infinitely more difficult and typically more hazardous in terms of being at risk for homelessness, incarceration, and/or extended reliance on public aid. Information based on short-term follow-up studies suggests that only 1 in 10 former wards in the age 18 to 21 cohort was able to live on his or her own without financial aid or in-kind assistance. For youth who are employed, the annual earning level is low, typically less than $10,000 (Mech, 1994). Low income, coupled with a need to survive, are potent reasons why so many newly emancipated foster wards must rely on food stamps, Medicaid, housing subsidies, and other safety net resources. Medicaid and food stamps are critical resources for youth who are in a transition period.

For nonfoster youth, aging out of the birthhome is characterized by gradualness and continued support. For foster youth, aging out can be an abrupt process, characterized by a lack of continuing support with few ties to community resources. Various reports state that 20% to 50% of foster youth return home after discharge (DeWoody, Ceja, & Sylvester, 1993). Data on more than 400 youth in the Foster Adolescent Project suggest that fewer than 1 in 4 youth returned to their birthhome after aging out. Moreover, those who returned to their homes did so for relatively short periods of time and ultimately moved away to "make it on their own" in the community.

Importance of Foster Families in Youths' Lives

Little information exists as to the perception of former foster wards regarding their placement experience. Follow-up research based on samples of emancipated foster youth in Illinois, Indiana, and Ohio confirm the salutary effects of foster family placement on the lives of emancipated foster wards. The University of Illinois Foster Adolescent Project collected information on former foster wards' postemancipation functioning. Based on nearly 1,000 interviews of the same cohort of youth at ages 18, 21, and 28, the results document the powerful influence foster families have on the lives of young people. In the age 21 follow-up, former wards were asked to rate their experiences in foster homes, group homes, and institutions. "Best placement" ratings were obtained from youth who had more than one type of placement setting. Typically, three choices were available: foster home, group home, or institution.

Almost 50% of all youth who experienced one or more foster placements as well as group and/or institutional care selected foster homes as the best placement; 45% chose group homes, and only 5% chose institutions. The main elements cited in favor of family foster homes included: (a) learning independent-living skills as a normal part of family life and having opportunities to practice specific skills were cited as a plus, as was participating in daily tasks associated with maintaining a household. (b) Family environments can provide a supportive structure for young wards. This includes encouragement to complete school, get a job, and save money. (c) Once emancipated from placement, family foster homes often provide an aftercare resource for young wards. Some youth stay with foster families after discharge until they have the resources to live on their own. One youth stated, "When I'm on my own I can always go back to them for help." The accounts provided us by former wards are characterized by conviction and poignant examples. Typical comments include:

> I liked my foster home the best because I was with adults who showed me what I had to do. Nobody else has given me a chance to get prepared for living on my own.

> My foster mother taught me about living, what it would cost, and how to get what you're entitled to.

> I liked my foster home the best. They taught me independent-living skills, being responsible, and a good work ethic.

> Foster home was best. Parents helped me with independent-living skills, gave me support. I have a good job now, and good skills to make it on my own.

> Foster home was best for me. They let me strike out on my own. Not as structured as a group home.

> I liked the "Smith" foster home best. They treated me like one of their own.

> Foster home was best. They taught me how to cook, clean, pay bills, and find jobs. I still live with my foster mother.

> Foster home was my best placement. I had a lot of chances to practice what I learned in my independent-living classes.

> Compared to the institution I was in, foster home was good because I learned to do things for myself.

Three case vignettes are cited here to illustrate the effect that a foster family can have on the lives of young people in placement. The vignettes are based on age 21 follow-up data collected by the University of Illinois Foster Youth Project.

Derek

I was in several foster homes from age 11 to about 14. Then stayed in one foster home for more than five years. I credit my foster father for preparing me best for independent living. I could never repay him for everything he has done for me. He taught me things my own father could not have done. I learned some good work skills. He taught me how to prepare for a job and to make good decisions.

Derek now has a good job, and his income is reported to be $31,000. He is an assistant manager of a tire outlet store. His foster father arranged for financial assistance for him to complete two years of postsecondary education at a technical school, where Derek studied auto mechanics. After emancipation, he lived with the foster family for a time. He has a savings account and a credit card, owns a car, has health insurance from his employer, and has goals for the future. One goal is to own an auto-tire store.

Brenda

I lived in two foster homes, one group home. I consider both my foster families as my family. At the top of my list is my first foster mother. Both foster mothers were very good to me— almost like relatives. I can go to either Foster Mother #1 or Foster Mother #2 if I had a big decision to make, if I needed money, or a place to go for the holidays. I keep in touch with both foster families, almost on a weekly basis. After discharge from care, I lived with Foster Home #2 for about three months. My foster sister helped me to find housing.

Margaret (Master Foster Parent)

The next vignette is based on an interview with master foster parent Margaret S. Margaret has been a foster parent for 25 years. She described her work with Karen, a former ward who spent four years in the "S" foster home.)

Karen was a marginal student when she came into our home. She was 15 years old at the time and getting "D" and "F" grades in school. When she left our home at age 19, she was getting "A" and "B" grades. When Karen graduated from high school we gave her a big party. We were so proud of her. She is now married and has two children. Her foster dad gave her away at the wedding. Her children think of us as their grandparents, and Karen has adopted us as her family. In the four years Karen was with us we taught her a lot of practical things like how to grocery shop wisely, how to fill out income tax forms, how to interpret apartment ads, how to fill out employment applications, also how to cook. Karen still calls us for recipes.

In the age 21 interviews, researchers asked foster youth to describe sources of social support. Questions relating to the social support of foster youths included the following: "Who are the people that are most important to you?" "How do you rate your relationship with selected individuals?" and "How often are you in contact with selected individuals?" Of the results that emerged, it is important to highlight the following: Youth rated their own parents as the least important people in their lives. Most important were peers and friends, relatives, foster families, and agency workers. Youth rated foster families and agency workers as more important to them than their immediate family members. The University of Illinois foster youth database indicates that nearly 50% of youth who spent time in a foster family setting cited foster families as "most important persons in their lives." Table 7.1 summarizes the distribution of responses to the question, "Who are the people that are most important to you?" Youth rated foster families and agency workers higher in importance than immediate family members (i.e., mother, father, sister, brother) (Fung, Mech, & Leonard, 1996).

In terms of rating the closeness of their relationship with various individuals, including birthfamily members, in almost 60% of the responses, youth depicted their relationship with birthparents as "not close." However, a relatively high proportion reported feeling close to relatives, including grandparents (57%) and siblings (68%). More than 60% of the youth rated a close relationship with former foster families. With respect to contact with various individuals, more than one-third of the foster youth sample reported weekly contact with foster parents. Half of the former

TABLE 7.1

Important People in Lives of Former Wards: "Who Are the People Who Are Most Important to You?" (N = 410)

IMPORTANT PERSON	NUMBER OF TIMES CITED	% OF TOTAL	RANK ORDER
Friend or Significant Other	554	36	1
Foster Family Member	215	14	2
Relative	196	13	3
Agency Worker	171	11	4
Mother	126	8	5
Sister	102	7	6
Father	66	4	7
Community Individual	62	4	8
Brother	58	3	9
Total	1,550	100	

SOURCE: Age 21 follow-up; Foster Youth-in-Transition Project, University of Illinois at Urbana-Champaign.

wards reported they planned to maintain contact with foster families and agency workers.

Prospects and Challenges for Foster Family Care: A 21st-Century Perspective

Foster care experts are devoting attention to the comparative merits of kinship versus nonrelative family foster care. Although the issue of preparation for independent living rarely receives mention in the context of kinship care, a study in Baltimore on a sample of foster wards is germane to this discussion (Benedict, Zuravin, & Stallings, 1996). The researchers made follow-up comparisons using two groups of former foster wards: Group 1 consisted of youth formerly placed in kinship care, and Group 2 consisted of youth formerly placed in nonrelative foster homes. The researchers compared participants on several outcome measures, including education, employment status, income, and housing arrangements. They concluded that "there were very few differences between groups in the adult outcomes studied" (Benedict et al., 1996, p. 545).

Although differences between kinship and nonrelative placements were not statistically significant, the direction of the outcomes is unsettling. Consider the pattern of results—nearly 40% of all participants failed to receive high school diplomas or to obtain a general equivalency diploma, nearly 50%

were not employed, and the majority (more than 50%) reported an annual income of less than $10,000. To what extent are the results for either group, kinship or nonrelative care, to be interpreted as a successful transition to independence? Are program managers, legislators, and decisionmakers likely to accept these outcomes as indicative of success?

At this juncture in the development of independent-living services, it may be important to provide foster caregivers with guidelines as to what constitutes a desirable set of outcomes. In the early beginnings of foster care in the United States, leadership in child care agencies was provided by middle-class females characterized as "women of good social standing" (Clement, 1985). The focus was on placing all homeless, institutionalized, and poor children in private foster homes. Their goal was to prepare young people for an "independent, useful life" (Clement, 1989). In the parlance of that era, "The best way to fit a child for an active, industrious, wage-earning life is to place it in an active, industrious, wage-earning family" (Clement, 1985). In short, the agenda of the early child-savers was clear, namely, to transform lower-class wards into responsible, middle-class citizens through conscious use of the foster care system. Their outcome standard was unambiguous; they wanted to avert system dependency and reliance on public aid. Social values appear to have shifted in the direction of setting lower expectations for young people classified as disadvantaged or poor, or otherwise viewed as marginal. This shift appears to include youth who experience out-of-home placement as wards of the state and carry the label "foster child."

If foster families are to better prepare adolescent wards for successful emancipation, the field needs to establish functional standards as to the elements that compose desirable outcomes. Although COA standards refer to the goal of "transition to full independence," and agency responsibility to prepare adolescent wards for a successful transition to independence, nowhere in the COA standards are these terms operationalized or are concrete examples provided. COA standards are excellent with respect to delineating "process" types of service activities, but are insufficient with respect to specifying outcome criteria. Behavioral-type criteria as to what constitutes readiness for independence and/or independent-living success are needed to provide guidelines for judges who make discharge decisions, foster caregivers who have the responsibility to prepare youth for independence, and program staff who must coordinate a diverse array of services. More than a decade has gone by since federal independent-living legislation was enacted. It is time to move toward consensus as to what elements constitute a successful transition to independence and how those elements should be measured. Moreover, the Independent-Living Initiative of 1987 under Title IV-E, Social Security Act §677, specifies that the objective is to "help the individual participating in such a program to live independently upon leaving foster care" (42 U.S.C. §677d). Although §677 describes program services that can be provided, this legislation stops short of establishing criteria for desirable outcomes.

A probable scenario for family foster care in the 21st century includes significant numbers of adolescent young people continuing to move into the placement system; many will remain in care for five or more years and experience multiple placements—often eight or more moves—school disruptions, and changes in caseworkers. It is difficult to conceive of a child welfare system without a strong foster family capability. In terms of future prospects, foster family care will become more complex, become more demanding on caregivers, and serve more adolescents, many of whom will require special attention, services, and resources. The probable result is additional pressure on an already overburdened system. Moreover, the current child welfare services structure is a maze, often beset by a host of coordination problems. Consider the fact that for each child or youth in out-of-home placement, an average of 10 to 12 adults can play a role or become involved in some aspect of the child's life. At a minimum, adult involvement can consist of the legal parent, multiple caseworkers, a court worker, a judge, a guardian ad litem, a mentor, school staff, and/or mental health workers, as well as case review administrators and a series of primary caregivers.

In recent years, emphasis has been on preventing institutional placements; encouraging the development of less costly, less restrictive community-based placements; and placing more youth with emotional/behavioral problems and medical needs in some type of family foster care. Characteristics that are typical of many older youth placed in out-of-home care include those having a history of hospitalization related to psychiatric/mental health problems, including suicide attempts; those who have a handicapping condition such as a learning disability; and those who have a conduct disorder, are destructive, or are aggressive. These trends indicate a need to recruit, train, and support foster families that can respond to young people with special problems.

Practice literature corroborates the need for new directions in recruiting, training, and supporting independent living–type family foster placements. The pool of foster families needed to help prepare adolescent wards for independence is insufficient. Colca and Colca (1996) asserted that "historically, foster family care placements have tended to isolate youths from their resources and inhibited them from accumulating the knowledge and skills needed for independent living" (p. 7). Recruitment strategies need to shift toward seeking foster families that possess special characteristics, including a strong value preference for educational achievement, world-of-work connections, and links to community resources that can assist youth in the transitional process. As noted in the recommendations of the CWLA Task Force on Out-of-Home Care, "The recruitment, selection, training, and retention of…foster parents must become a priority for the child welfare field." (Barker & Aptekar, 1990, p. 20).

Toward a Family-Based Placement Continuum

Resource specialists face the challenge of developing a continuum of family-based placements. These include relative/kinship homes, traditional foster family homes, as well as a range of specialized and treatment foster homes. What are the prospects for youth who are on the independent-living track? Although the need for aging-out preparation is real and innovative program structures are in place, progress in the area of independent-living services depends on a reorientation of system priorities. Independent-living services must be recognized as a vital permanency planning option. Among the issues to be confronted are:

- **Specialized Aspects of Adolescent Services:** Working with adolescents requires special attributes from caregivers as well as agency staff. Multiage caseloads and high workloads leave staff limited time to work with foster parents and are detrimental to the process of educating wards for independence.

- **Policy Revisions Needed:** There should be a limit on the number of adolescents living in a foster home. More emphasis is needed on providing respite resources and crisis support services, as well as upgrading training for staff and foster caregivers in preparing adolescents for independence.

- **Foster Caregivers:** If caregivers are to be effective in preparing adolescents for independence, special training is a critical element. Consideration should be given to the recruitment of foster families who hold strong beliefs about the value of education, are or have been connected to the workplace, and are committed to helping adolescent wards to develop links with the community, institutions, and organizations. Information collected by Westat, Inc., cited by Downs (1990), on the characteristics of foster parents who have cared for adolescents offers the following profile: (a) Nearly one in three foster mothers report less than a high school diploma, (b) more than 60% are or were full-time homemakers, (c) nearly 70% had more than one foster child in the home, and (d) although 84% were married, information on foster fathers was not reported. The extent to which these foster parents' profiles are correlated with helping adolescents transition to independence is a matter of conjecture. The relationship between foster parent characteristics and transitional outcomes is an area worthy of attention, particularly with respect to the educational commitment of foster caregivers.

- **Aftercare Services:** It is important to build a continuum of postdischarge services that can assist wards in transitioning to independence. Aftercare services are typically a low priority for most state-administered child welfare programs.

- **Follow-up Contact with Emancipated Youth:** An indispensable element in determining program quality is obtaining feedback on the experiences of youth who age out of placement. It is difficult to make accurate judgments about program effects without knowing how youth do after discharge. A report by Breed, Cook, and Irvine (1991) draws attention to the importance of periodic follow-up contact with former foster wards. Outcome information is needed on education, employment, housing, public assistance use, health status, social/relationship patterns, contacts with law enforcement, legal problems, and overall well-being.

Qualifications for foster caregivers must be geared toward teaching and modeling a series of achievement-oriented behaviors that are deemed necessary for preparing young wards to compete in a credentialed, information-based, technological society. The educational bar is likely to be raised. The new standard is likely to be completion of a high school diploma, plus two years of postsecondary education. With respect to world-of-work trends, many private sector employers are now requiring grade transcripts as a factor in deciding whom to hire. Also, many schools are starting to grade students on characteristics considered vital to job success including ability to cooperate and fit into a team approach, quality of work, positive attitude, attendance, punctuality, and responsibility. New developments in terms of increasing educational expectations and the certification of employability for high school graduates will likely be reflected in many areas of career employment. Unless program planners and foster caregivers heed these trends, foster wards will continue to fall behind in preparation for self-sufficiency.

Evaluation of New Foster Home Models

A series of new foster family placement models are expected to evolve. Many are already on the horizon and include a variety of options designated as transitional, independent-living foster homes. Transitional homes are based on the theory of providing older adolescents (ages 16-20) with real-life opportunities to learn and practice independent-living skills. The transitional model is based on the notion that young wards will make mistakes and should have opportunities to learn from those experiences. Variations in the transitional foster home model contain several options including mentor foster homes and boarder foster homes (Colca & Colca, 1996). Traditional views of foster parents as a "substitute family" may no longer fit the need posed by adolescent wards who are aging out. Shifting to a transitional mentor role might be beneficial, in that it would free foster parents from the need to compete with birthparents, and at the same time retain the characteristics of a least-restrictive environment. A focus on mentoring would permit foster families to assume objectivity in a teaching role and holds potential for continuation of a mentor relationship after youth leave care.

The mentor model uses young, single adults who are certified as transitional foster parents as mentors. Foster youth are expected to live with the mentor and "share the expenses and responsibilities of apartment life" (Colca & Colca, 1996). The boarder model uses a traditional foster parent arrangement in which foster caregivers set up a series of learning experiences for the adolescent, including responsibility "for his/her own finances, cooking, shopping, and decisions" (Colca & Colca, 1996). Foster parents are expected to be teachers and role models, and to provide a safety net when the need arises.

Prudent child welfare administrators will agree that preparing adolescents for independence represents a good investment. Investing in the development of human potential increases the likelihood that young wards will make a positive contribution to society. Simply put, it is common sense to make reasonable efforts to optimize youths' chances for independence and economic self-sufficiency. It is well to keep in mind that most young people in placement are there for reasons beyond their control, primarily because their families have in some measure failed to provide proper care. It is a virtual certainty that most foster caregivers are aware of this dilemma. Given proper system supports, foster caregivers can play a decisive role in influencing the futures of adolescent wards.

References

Barker, R. E., & Aptekar, R. R. (1990). *Out-of-home care: An agenda for the nineties. Report and recommendations of the CWLA Task Force on Out-of-Home Care*. Washington, DC: Child Welfare League of America.

Benedict, M. I., Zuravin, S., & Stallings, R. Y. (1996). Adult functioning of children who live in kin versus non-relative family foster homes. *Child Welfare, 75*, 529–549.

Breed, M. E., Cook, R., & Irvine, J. (1991). *Preparing youth in care for independence: A needs assessment study.* Unpublished report, State of Illinois Department of Children and Family Services.

Child Welfare League of America. (1989). *Standards for independent-living services*. Washington, DC: Author.

Clement, P. F. (1985). Families and foster care: Philadelphia in the late nineteenth century. In N. R. Hiner, & J. M. Hawes (Eds.), *Growing up in America: Children in historical perspective* (pp. 135–146). Urbana: University of Illinois Press.

Colca, L. A., & Colca, C. (1996). Transitional independent living foster homes: A step towards independence. *Children Today, 14*(1), 7–11.

Council on Accreditation of Service for Children and Family Services. (2001). *COA's standards and self study manual* (7th ed.). New York: Author.

DeWoody, F., Ceja, K., & Sylvester, M. (1993). *Independent-living services for youths in out-of-home care*. Washington, DC: Child Welfare League of America.

Downs, S. W. (1990). Recruiting and retaining foster families of adolescents. In A. N. Maluccio, R. Krieger, & B. A. Pine (Eds.), *Preparing adolescents for life after foster care: The central role of foster parents* (pp. 19–34). Washington, DC: Child Welfare League of America.

Fung, C. C., Mech, E. V., & Leonard, E. (1996, September). *Support networks of emancipated foster adolescents*. Paper presented at the National Conference on Child Welfare, Memphis, TN.

Maluccio, A. N., Krieger, R., & Pine, B. A. (Eds.). (1990). Preparing adolescents for life after foster care: The central role of foster parents. Washington, DC: Child Welfare League of America.

Mech, E. V. (Ed.). (1988). *Independent-living services for at-risk adolescents*. Washington, DC: Child Welfare League of America.

Mech, E. V. (1994). Foster youths in transition: Research perspective on preparation for independent-living. *Child Welfare, 73*, 603–623.

Tatara, R. (1997, March). U.S. child substitute care flow data and the race/ethnicity of children in care for FY1995, along with recent trends in the U.S. child substitute care population. *VCIS Research Notes, 113*. Washington, DC: American Public Welfare Association.

Chapter 8

Placement Restrictiveness and Educational Achievement Among Emancipated Foster Youth

EDMUND V. MECH AND
CARRIE CHE-MAN FUNG

> *It would be difficult to imagine a more at-risk population*
> *than adolescents in residential treatment centers (RTCs),*
> *the child welfare system's most restrictive level of care.*
>
> —Nan Dale, The Children's Village
> (Baker, Olson, & Mincer, 2000, p. ix)

Least Restrictive Placement Mandate

One of the central provisions of the landmark Adoption Assistance and Child Welfare Act of 1980 is the "least restrictive placement" mandate. Child welfare agencies are expected to include in client service records documentation that reasonable efforts were made to place children in the "least restrictive setting…available, and in close proximity to the parents' home" (Allen, Golubock, & Olson, 1983, p. 582). Congress intended that state child welfare agencies would develop a continuum of placements, ranging from least restrictive to most restrictive.

Placements Rated High in Restrictiveness

Placement settings that rate high in restrictiveness include child care institutions and residential treatment centers. These centers and group homes are characterized by high levels of restrictiveness in comparison with foster family homes or apartment settings. Kroner noted that "large institutional settings such as correctional facilities, psychiatric hospitals,…are probably the least equipped to prepare youth for independent-living" (Kroner, 1988, p. 549). High restrictiveness placements provide fewer opportunities for the acquisition of experiential, independent-living activities. Typically, emphasis is on the treatment of behaviorally difficult, disturbed youth.

Preparation for independence is not likely to be the cardinal aim of congregate-group placements. The fact remains that, despite high costs, such placements are needed and are widely used. In the University of Illinois age 21 follow-up study of emancipated foster wards, group and institutional placements were experienced by a significant percentage of youth. Overall, of the 390 wards for whom age 21 data was collected, 234, or 60%, reported placement in one or more group home settings. With respect to institutional/residential treatment facilities, 177, or 45%, reported spending time in one or more congregate facilities, often in a geographical location away from their home state. In terms of interpreting the ratings of wards as to types of placements judged to be most and least useful in preparation for independent living, the results are not surprising. In effect, much variability was noted—some group home experiences were rated highly, others received poor evaluations. Overall, of the 234 group home placements, 91, or 39%, were rated as most helpful compared with other placement options. Results for institutional placements were much less favorable. Of the 177 institutional placements, only 37 (21%) were rated as most helpful in preparation for independent living. Those results lend credence to the commonsense hypothesis that high levels of structure and restrictiveness make it more difficult to prepare young people for independence. Placements in congregate facilities are a necessary part of child welfare practice, and many institutional programs are seeking ways to incorporate independent-living services into their daily routine.

Recent developments suggest that residential treatment centers and child care institutions can respond to the challenge of preparing state wards for independent living. The Children's Village Program in Dobbs Ferry, New York, conducts an independent-living program called WAY (Work Appreciation for Youth). Initiated in 1984, the WAY scholarship program "targets the highest risk youth in the New York Child Welfare System—youths in Residential Treatment Centers—and provides mentoring by professionals for up to 5 years after youths leave treatment" (Dale, 2000, p. 189). Evaluation of the WAY program shows positive outcomes in education and employment. With respect to educational progress, approximately 80% of the youth studied "had graduated from high school, received their GEDs [general equivalency diplomas], or were still enrolled in school. Over one-quarter (29%) had gone on to college" (Baker et al., 2000, p. 79). Preparing youth for community living after discharge from institutional/ residential settings poses a serious challenge. Results associated with the Children's Village WAY Program provide a basis for optimism.

Researchers have devoted little attention to issues pertaining to the measurement of placement restrictiveness or the extent to which placement restrictiveness indices are related to aspects of educational progress, world-of-work participation, or elements of personal/social functioning for former foster wards. A U.S. General Accounting Office (1994) report on the status of residential care for high-risk youth concluded that "no consensus exists on which youths are best served by residential care rather than community-based care or how residential care should be combined with community-based care to best serve at-risk youths" (p. 4).

Practice theory, legislative intent, and community sentiment rest on the proposition that "least restrictive is best." As far as can be ascertained, the child welfare field lacks empirical information on relationships between placement restrictiveness levels and outcomes relative to education, employment, and world-of-work connections. In terms of practical application, restrictiveness scales provide a basis for documenting (on a case-by-case basis) the extent to which the placement record of foster wards shows a pattern of increasing restrictiveness or a trend toward placements rated low in restrictiveness. With respect to investigating relationships between restrictiveness levels and behavioral measures of outcomes, such as educational achievement, the child welfare field has been hampered by a lack of follow-up information on the well-being of foster wards. The study described here contains two essential elements: (a) measures of placement restrictiveness, and (b) postdischarge educational progress indicators for a sample of foster wards.

Our goal was to test several methods of measuring placement restrictiveness and analyze the relationship of each method to indicators of progress toward self-sufficiency at age 21. The essential question posed was, To what extent is placement restrictiveness a correlate of educational achievement?

Background Literature

Efforts to develop scales and/or measuring instruments to assess levels of placement restrictiveness in child welfare settings are relatively recent. The movement toward least restrictive environments has its genesis in deinstitutionalization philosophy and trends in service delivery for chronically mentally ill people, mentally retarded people, and people with learning disorders. *Deinstitutionalization* refers to efforts to avoid keeping disabled people in custodial settings and to eliminate physical isolation and exclusion practices as reflected in institutional care (Bachrach, 1985). Key terms in advocating for least restrictive environments are *normalization*, *mainstreaming*, and *inclusion*.

In the area of special education services for pupils with disabilities, pivotal court decisions led to the enactment of P.L.94-142, the Education of All Handicapped Children Act of 1975. This law provided federal endorsement of the principle that children classified as handicapped or disabled should be educated with children who are not handicapped.

Based on suggestions from practitioners and educators, the Scale to Assess Restrictiveness of Educational Settings (SARES) was published in 1994 (Epstein, Quinn, & Cumblad, 1994). The SARES is an 18-step scale that ranges from 0 (*least restrictive*) to 10 (*most restrictive*). Regular classroom settings are classified as least restrictive, with a mean rating of 0.5. Special education classes are rated 5.5 in restrictiveness, whereas home-based instruction is rated 8.0 in restrictiveness.

With respect to child welfare settings, Hawkins, Almeida, Fabry, and Reitz (1992) developed a scale to measure restrictiveness of living environments for "troubled children and youths." They defined *restrictiveness* in terms of limitations imposed by the placement facility on freedom of movement and contact with normalizing, community-based environments (i.e., shopping, recreation, social and peer relations, church, etc.), as well as the extent to which rules are used to control behavior. This instrument is the Restrictiveness of Living Environments Scale (ROLES). ROLES ranks 25 placement environments with regard to restrictiveness. Based on a scale from 1 to 10, in which 10 is most restrictive and 1 is least restrictive, *independent living by self* is rated as 0.5, *home of relative* as 2.5, *regular foster care* as 4.0, *group home* as 5.5, *residential treatment center* as 6.5, and *mental hospital* as 9.0.

In a similar vein, Thomlison and Krysik (1992) developed the Restrictiveness of Children's Living Environment scale, a modified scale based on ROLES. Thomlison and Krysik convened two separate expert panels, each of which independently rated 34 environmental settings using a 7-point scale. The rank of living environments reported by Thomlison and Krysik is similar to the ROLES instrument developed by Hawkins et al. (1992). Family-based settings are rated low in restrictiveness, with a self-maintained residence (independent living) judged to be the least restrictive on the scale. Treatment-focused settings, such as specialized foster care, are rated as middle range in restrictiveness, whereas placements characterized by psychiatric care in a ward, hospital, or institution are rated as most restrictive.

Database

The researchers derived the data used in this discussion from information on foster youth in Illinois. The permanency plan for each ward was independent living. The sample was part of a multistate, follow-up study on progress toward achieving independence among foster adolescents. The researchers collected data in two phases, Phase 1 at age 18 and Phase 2 at age 21.

In Phase 1, the Illinois child welfare system generated computer lists of wards between the ages of 17 and 19 who were preparing for emancipation and independent living. The researchers contacted youth by phone, letter, or caseworker to find out if they were interested in participating in the project. Each youth completed a university-approved consent form prior to data collection. Researchers obtained Phase 1 information from adolescent wards prior to emancipation at about age 18. Phase 1 data were primarily measures of cognitive competence in various independent-living skills areas. One of the purposes of Phase 1 was to establish the nucleus of a study group for the age 21 follow-up. The researchers also collected information for families, relatives, and friends. They offered an incentive payment of $35 for the follow-up and provided youth with a toll-free 800 number to keep project personnel informed of changes in residence.

The researchers collected Phase 2 data about three years later, when youth were about 21 years old; many were emancipated or were to be emancipated within six months at the time of the Phase 2 interview. Of the original 214 youth in the Illinois Phase 1 sample, researchers located and interviewed 171 youth. They collected information on a variety of indicators of well-being, including educational achievement, employment, and cost to community as measured by the use of means-tested, public aid programs.

In addition to data collected from Phase 2 interviews, researchers obtained placement information from state agency records for 211 of the 214 foster youths. Placement data were based on information extracted from placement/payment authorization forms used by caseworkers in the Illinois child welfare system. Caseworkers completed this form each time a change of placement took place for each ward. Placement data included: (a) all living arrangements in sequential order, (b) number of days spent in each placement, and (c) age of youth at time of first placement.

Measuring Placement Restrictiveness

Three methods of measuring placement restrictiveness were used. Researchers designated Method 1 as the *predominant placement type*. Method

2 was the cumulative restrictiveness level of all placements for each youth. Method 3 was derived from the proportion of time spent in each of three main placement types for each youth. An abbreviated version of the ROLES was used to calculate restrictiveness scores for each of the three methods cited. Table 8.1 summarizes a modified scale used to assign point values for placement restrictiveness. Computational applications of Methods 1, 2, and 3 are shown in Table 8.1.

- **Method 1—Predominant Placement Type.** Based on state agency records, it was possible to extract the number of days spent in various substitute care placements. The predominant placement example uses information for a young ward named Bill. Bill spent about three years in state care. Information was categorized by number of days in each placement type, along with the restrictiveness rating for each type of placement.

  Overall, Bill spent 1,097 days in placement. Because 53% of Bill's time in placement was spent in an independent-living apartment setting, this placement type was classified as the predominant placement and scored as a 1 (*low restrictiveness*). Bill started out in a relative's home (82 days), spent a total of 22 days in four foster homes, then 409 days in two group home placements, and 584 days in four apartment placements, for a total of 11 placements. Overall, the predominant placement score accounted for 65% of the total time spent in care.

- **Method 2—Cumulative Restrictiveness Level.** Continuing with Bill, a cumulative restrictiveness score was derived. In Method 2, each of the 11 placements was weighted according to the restrictiveness scale shown in Table 8.1. The sum of the restrictiveness level for the 11 placements equals 35 points; hence, the R score assigned was 35. Method 2 did not account for the time spent in each type of placement; instead, the R score emphasized the number of placements while in care.

- **Method 3—Proportion of Time in Three Main Placement Types.** The researchers used Method 3 to calculate the proportion of time spent in each of three main placement types. For Bill, the three main placements (based on number of days in each placement) were independent-living apartment (584 days), group home (409 days), and home of relative (82 days). The three main place-

TABLE 8.1

Restrictiveness Levels for Selected Placement Settings

PLACEMENT TYPE	RESTRICTIVENESS (R SCORE)
Independent Living/Apartment	1 (Lowest)
Home of Parent	2
Home of Relative	3
Foster Home—Regular	4
Foster Home—Specialized	5
Group Home	6
Shelter	7
Residential Institution	8
Medical Hospital	9
Psychiatric Facility	10
Detention Facility	11
Jail/Correctional Facility	12 (Highest)

ment types experienced by Bill accounted for 98% of this youth's time in substitute care. Accordingly, for Method 3, the restrictiveness score was calculated as follows: $0.53 \times 1 = 0.53$; $0.37 \times 6 = 2.22$; and $0.07 \times 3 = 0.21$, with a resultant R score of 2.96 ($0.53 + 2.22 + 0.21$). Using Method 3, the R score accounted for more than 90% of the total time spent in care.

Educational Achievement Indices

Educational achievement was measured by the highest grade level attained. Youth were classified into four possible groups: (a) less than high school, (b) GED, (c) high school diploma, and (d) postsecondary education (i.e., community college, four-year university, or vocational college). At the Phase 2 follow-up interview, 25.7% of foster youths had completed 11th grade or less, 7.6% had obtained a GED, 24% had received a high school diploma or equivalent, and 42.7% had completed some postsecondary education.

Using a 300-point educational achievement (EA) scale, each youth was assigned a score based on school achievement and future plans to continue his or her education. The possible range of scores was 0 to 300 points. Table 8.2 summarizes the point values assigned to each level of educational progress. Overall, the mean EA score was 135.24, with a standard deviation of 75.33. The scores ranged from 0 to 250 points ($N = 171$).

TABLE 8.2

The Educational Achievement (EA) Point Scale

OVERALL EDUCATIONAL PROGRESS	EA SCORE
11th grade or less	0
General Equivalency Diploma (GED)	50
Completed a High School Diploma	75
Completed GED and Has Plans for Postsecondary Education	100
Completed High School Diploma and Has Plans for Postsecondary Education	12
Completed GED and Is Enrolled in a College/University Program	150
High School Diploma and Acceptance to College/University program	175
High School Diploma and Completion of One Year in College/University Program	200
GED and Completion of Two Years in College/University Program	225
High School Diploma and Completion of Two Years in College/University Program	250
Completed a Bachelor's Degree	300

To test the association between placement restrictiveness and EA, youths were classified into three groups based on their restrictiveness scores (R score). The three restrictiveness groups were: Level 1 = least restrictive, Level 2 = moderately restrictive, and Level 3 = most restrictive.

Table 8.3 summarizes the educational progress of adolescent wards classified by level of placement restrictiveness. Chi-square tests of association indicate that placement restrictiveness is associated with level of education. The results were statistically significant for Methods 1 and 3. Regardless of the method of measuring placement restrictiveness, the percentage of youth who failed to complete high school increased as placement restrictiveness increased. A higher percentage of youth in Level 1 (low restrictiveness) were participating in postsecondary education as compared to other restrictiveness groups. With respect to Method 1 and Method 3, almost two-thirds of the youth in Level 1 attended some postsecondary education, compared with only one-third of the youth in the Level 3 (high restrictiveness) group. Based on Table 8.3, low placement restrictiveness was associated with higher scores in EA, whereas high placement restrictiveness was associated with lower scores in EA. The analysis of variance F ratios were statistically significant for Methods 1 and 3.

The importance of the finding that 73 (or 43%) of the group of 171 youth at the age 21 follow-up participated in postsecondary education should not be underestimated. Gaining acceptance in society is the belief

TABLE 8.3

Educational Progress Classified by Level of Placement Restrictiveness
($n = 158$) (in percentages)

RESTRICTIVENESS GROUP	HIGHEST EDUCATION LEVEL COMPLETED			
	LESS THAN HIGH SCHOOL	HIGH SCHOOL DIPLOMA	POSTSECONDARY	n
Method 1 (Predominant Placement Type) [a]				
Level 1 (low)	23.7	13.2	63.2	38
Level 2 (moderate)	25.0	33.0	42.0	88
Level 3 (high)	40.6	21.9	37.5	32
Method 2 (Cumulative Restrictiveness Level)				
Level 1 (low)	24.2	25.8	50.0	66
Level 2 (moderate)	26.5	24.5	49.0	49
Level 3 (high)	34.9	27.9	37.2	43
Method 3 (Proportion of Time in Three Main Placement Types) [a]				
Level 1 (low)	22.4	15.5	62.1	58
Level 2 (moderate)	29.3	32.8	37.9	58
Level 3 (high)	33.3	31.0	35.7	42

NOTE: Youth who completed only a general equivalency diploma were eliminated from this analysis because there were only 13 cases.

[a] Chi-square significance: Method 1—$X^2 = 9.85$, $p < 0.05$; Method 2—$X^2 = 2.25$, $p < 0.69$; Method 3—$X^2 = 10.00$, $p < 0.05$.

that completion of a high school diploma alone is no longer sufficient as a stepping stone to career opportunities in the workplace. Accordingly, of the postsecondary enrollees, nearly 64% ($n = 47$) selected a two-year community college program. For many youth, a community college provides a potential bridge to continuing in a regular college or university program. Of the remainder, only 9 reported taking courses in a vocational/ technical curriculum, and 17 were enrolled in a four-year college or university program. However, at the age 21 follow-up, educational attrition was noticeable. Of the 73 youth in the postsecondary group, nearly 27% were no longer enrolled in an educational program.

As shown in Table 8.4, less restrictive living arrangements during placement appear to be linked with more youth pursuing postsecondary education. Of the 73 postsecondary enrollees, nearly 85% came from placements rated low in restrictiveness (i.e., transitional apartments, home of relative, and foster family care). Only 15% of those in a postsecondary program emerged from placements rated high in restrictiveness. In short,

TABLE 8.4

Mean Educational Achievement (EA) Scores Classified by Placement Restrictiveness Level *(n = 168)*

RESTRICTIVENESS GROUP	METHOD OF CALCULATING RESTRICTVENESS		
	1	2	3
Level 1	163.5	143.5	156.5
Level 2	132.2	145.7	126.5
Level 3	113.3	115.2	121.1
F Ratio	4.3	2.6	3.8
p Value	0.015	0.081	0.025

[a] Chi-square significance: Method 1—$X^2 = 9.85$, $p < 0.05$; Method 2—$X^2 = 2.25$, $p < 0.69$; Method 3—$X^2 = 10.00$, $p < 0.05$.

educational progress among former foster youth appears to be inversely related to placement restrictiveness level.

Assessment

Practice wisdom suggests that a number of factors, including discontinuity in parenting, multiple living arrangements while in care, and disruptions caused by changing schools, can have a deleterious effect on the educational progress of foster youth. Numerous studies lend credence to the view that out-of-home placement poses a serious obstacle to the EA of foster wards. Based on a secondary analysis of the high-school-and-beyond data set from the High School and Beyond Survey of the U.S. Department of Education, Blome (1997) compared the educational experience of a group of older foster youth with nonfoster youths. Foster wards dropped out of high school at higher rates, were less likely to complete a GED, experienced more school disruptions, and were less likely to enroll in a postsecondary curriculum than nonfoster youth.

Other studies provide additional evidence that confirm the hazards of foster placement with respect to the education of foster wards. Westat, Inc., conducted a multistate, follow-up study of youth emancipated from placement. Among the results was the surprising finding that nearly 66% failed to complete a high school diploma (Cook, Fleishman, & Grimes, 1991). Also, investigators such as Festinger (1983); Fanshel, Finch, and Grundy (1990); and Barth (1990) reported a variety of educational deficits among foster wards, including difficulty completing a high school diploma, maintaining age-appropriate grade levels in school, and pursuing postsecondary education. A recent review of studies on outcomes among emancipated foster youth documents deficits in their educational preparation, low rates of labor market participation, overuse of public assistance, and insufficiency in housing provisions (McDonald, Allen, Westerfelt, & Piliavin, 1996).

Many suggestions have emerged for improving the odds for EA among older foster wards. Included on the list of corrective actions are:

- Extending the emancipation age for youth in placement to age 21. It should be noted that most state statutes already permit discretionary use of the age 21 guideline.

- Achieving closer connections between school—particularly junior high and high school programs—and child welfare service providers. Cooperative programs that bring together schools, caregivers, and agencies in terms of guiding and monitoring the educational progress of foster wards exist but are rare.

- Strengthening postemancipation services following discharge from the placement system. Services that are classified as tangible are sorely needed. These include postsecondary scholarship programs for wards (i.e., tuition, books, etc.), employment supports, and housing assistance.

When P.L. 96-272, the Child Welfare Adoption and Assistance Act, was enacted in 1980, issues related to preparing foster wards for self-sufficiency and/or independent living received little attention. Subsequent legislation under P.L. 99-272, the independent-living initiative of the Social Security Act, placed responsibility on states to prepare foster wards for adult living. It is misleading to assume that most wards are reunified with their birthfamilies or return to their own homes following emancipation from placement. Much can be done to upgrade independent-living services while wards are still in state care. It should be noted that independent-living legislation (P.L. 99-272) emphasizes the importance of providing adequate preparation prior to emancipation.

Despite the need for a continuum of transitional, postemancipation services, aftercare programs alone cannot be expected to compensate for service deficiencies prior to discharge. Although society expects young people to take on many adult responsibilities as soon as possible after reaching the age of majority, developmental evidence suggests that in terms of attaining economic self-sufficiency, the transition to adulthood is uneven and continues well into the mid- and late 20s. Historically, the placement system has devoted its efforts to child protection, safety, and reduced risk of endangerment. The influx of older adolescents into the placement system, and the need to develop services to facilitate their progress toward self-sufficiency, constitutes a new agenda item for child welfare practice.

One area of importance is the topic of placement restrictiveness and its potential effect on EA. The topic of placement restrictiveness has received scant research attention. Yet, basic child welfare practice revolves around the edict that least restrictive placement is best. The data for adolescent wards suggests a pattern of progressive insertion into the restrictiveness system—home of relative, then foster home, followed by group home, and then residential, institutional, and hospital settings. Whatever the restrictiveness level, a continuum of living arrangements is necessary. Statistical associations between restrictiveness levels and educational progress suggest that less restrictive apartment and/or family-type living arrangements are correlated with better educational progress. Although this result was not unexpected, the implications for child welfare practice are several.

First, when tested against highest grade completed, Method 1 (predominant placement) and Method 3 (proportion of time in placement) produced a statistically significant relationship with the criterion measure of EA. Overall, low placement restrictiveness scores were associated with higher EA. The most useful method of calculating restrictiveness was the predominant placement formula, at least for the sample of Illinois youth discussed here. It is important to note that cross-validation studies are needed using other samples of foster youth who are preparing to emancipate from placement.

Second, the results cited are based primarily on the assumption of "homogeneity of restrictiveness" within placement type. Although the variability within similar types of placement settings is unknown, it is probably considerable. The study results quite likely reflect average effects. This raises the following questions: Does Foster Home A provide the same independent living environment as Foster Home B? Does Group Home C offer youth the same preparation for self-sufficiency as Group Home D?, and so on.

In this data set, most foster adolescents experienced a combination of placement settings that varied in restrictiveness from low to high. Many were exposed to placements rated as high in restrictiveness. Overall, placements rated as low in restrictiveness, such as foster family homes and transitional apartments, are probably the most effective settings in which to prepare foster wards for independence. In this sample, a high percentage of older wards who experienced placement in foster family homes and in apartments, as well as in other more restrictive settings, tended to choose family homes and transitional apartments as the best placements. Empirical results confirm their perceptions.

Third, much has been written about social services as an investment in children, youth, and families (Edelman, 1991; Ozawa, 1993). The child welfare field has a financial stake in selecting placements that provide effective independent-living preparation. The fiscal costs of long-term care are high, particularly so in residential/institutional settings. There is agreement that residential placements are expensive and typically reflect high levels of restrictiveness. Based on 1993 information, the U.S. General Accounting Office estimated that it cost from $20,000 to $132,000 a year to serve one youth in a residential setting, with a median cost of about $44,000. Hence, dollar costs vary directly with placement restrictiveness levels; that is, less restrictive placements cost less than more restrictive placements.

Regardless of restrictiveness level, the extent to which youth-serving agencies offer productive preparation for adult living is uncertain. Wide variability exists among placement settings. Although much has been written about what foster parents and group/institutional caregivers can do or ought to do to prepare youth for independence, evidence is sparse as to what actually is done. The extent to which independent-living programs are implemented according to plan is an area that requires monitoring.

Accordingly, for the thousands of adolescents now in placement, the issue is not one of downgrading the usefulness of highly restrictive group/institutional facilities, but one of upgrading independent-living services in all types of placements. Improvement is needed in settings classified as low in restrictiveness as well as in placements rated as high in restrictiveness. An important next step in self-sufficiency research for adolescents in placement may be one of analyzing, documenting, and measuring the effectiveness of different environments in preparing foster youth for independence.

New welfare reform legislation under the Personal Responsibility and Work Opportunity Reconciliation Act of 1996 (P.L.104-193) is based on the premise that individuals and families no longer are entitled to receive welfare assistance on a long-term or permanent basis. Emphasis now is on temporary assistance and stringent work requirements. State child welfare independent-living programs, administrative case review panels, judges, court administrators, and community-based advocacy groups need to establish mechanisms to monitor the educational preparation of foster wards.

Responsibility for educational advocacy and the process of monitoring connections between schools, foster wards, and caregivers resides with the state agency. Accreditation standards established by the Council on Accreditation of Services for Families and Children (1992; COA) spell out guidelines for services to youth who are preparing to emancipate from the placement system. COA standards stress the importance of including life skills training, vocational training, and work experience in preparing wards for economic self-sufficiency. Typically, administrative policy guidelines for state child welfare departments underscore the importance of education for foster wards. Youth are expected to be enrolled in school until they graduate. When youth move to a different placement, caseworkers are responsible for working with school personnel to see that young wards are enrolled.

Often, foster parents and other caregivers are expected to serve as educational advocates for youth in their care. The role of educational advocate by foster caregivers includes (a) assisting with homework, (b) attending parent/teacher conferences, and (c) encouraging participation in school/community activities. Schools, surrogate homes, and agencies are expected to communicate with respect to any problems wards might be experiencing in school. The progressive insertion of wards into placements rated as high in restrictiveness poses a special hazard for satisfactory EA. The relationship between placement restrictiveness and educational progress deserves close attention from child welfare personnel, surrogate caregivers, and administrative case review panels.

References

Allen, M. L., Golubock, C., & Olson, L. (1983). A guide to the Adoption Assistance and Child Welfare Act of 1980. In M. Hardin (Ed.), *Foster children in the courts* (pp. 575–601). Boston: Butterworth Legal.

Bachrach, L. L. (1985). Deinstutionalization: The meaning of the least restrictive environment. In R. K. Bruininks & K. C. Lakin (Eds.), *Living and learning in the least restrictive environment* (pp. 23–26). Baltimore: Paul H. Brooks.

Baker, A., Olson, D., & Mincer, C. (2000). *The WAY to work. An independent-living aftercare program for high-risk youth*. Washington DC: CWLA Press.

Barth, R. (1990). On their own: The experiences of youth after foster care. *Child and Adolescent Social Work, 7*, 419–440.

Blome, W. W. (1997). What happens to foster kids: Educational experience of a random sample of foster care youth and a matched group of non-foster care youth. *Child and Adolescent Social Work, 14*, 41–53.

Cook, R., Fleishman, E., & Grimes, V. (1991). *A national evaluation of Title IV-E foster care independent living programs for youth: Phase 2, Final Report, Part I* (U.S. Department of Health and Human Services). Rockville, MD: Westat.

Council on Accreditation of Services for Families and Children. (1992). *Accreditation policies and procedures manual*. New York: Author.

Dale, N. (2000.) What works in employment programs for youth in out-of-home care. In M. Kruger, G. Alexander, & P. Curtis (Eds.), *What works in child welfare* (pp. 187–193). Washington, DC: CWLA Press.

Edelman, M. W. (1991). Social services. In D. W. Hornbeck, & L. Salamon (Eds.), *Human capital and America's future: An economic strategy for the '90s* (pp. 269–293). Baltimore: Johns Hopkins University Press.

Epstein, M., Quinn, K., & Cumblad, C. (1994). A scale to assess the restrictiveness of educational settings. *Journal of Child and Family Studies, 3*, 107–119.

Fanshel, D., Finch, S., & Grundy, J. (1990). *Foster children in a life course perspective*. New York: Columbia University Press.

Festinger, T. (1983). *No one ever asked us: A postscript to foster care*. New York: Columbia University Press.

Hawkins, R., Almeida, C., Fabry, B., & Reitz, A. (1992). A scale to measure restrictiveness of living environments for troubled children and youths. *Hospital and Community Psychiatry, 43*, 54–58.

McDonald, T., Allen R., Westerfelt, A., & Piliavin, I. (1996). *Assessing the long-term effects of foster care: A research synthesis*. Washington, DC: CWLA Press.

Ozawa, M. N. (1993). America's future and her investment in children. *Child Welfare, 72*, 517–529.

Thomlison, B., & Krysik, J. (1992). The development of an instrument to measure the restrictiveness of children's living environments. *Research on Social Work Practice, 2*, 207–219.

U.S. General Accounting Office. (1994). *Residential care: Some high risk youth benefit but more study is needed* (GAO, HEHS-94-56). Washington, DC: Author.

Chapter 9

Preparing Foster Wards with Disabilities for Self-Sufficiency

Edmund V. Mech and
Carrie Che-Man Fung

> *Comparisons with non-disabled populations reveal that youths*
> *with disabilities are characterized, on the average, with lower grades,*
> *with greater absenteeism, and with a higher dropout rate.*
>
> —Harnisch and Gieri (1995, p. 21)

> *The disability movement, unlike other civil rights causes,*
> *remains rarely recognized and little celebrated.*
>
> —Shapiro (1994, p. 339)

Perspective on Youth with Disabilities

The Individuals with Disabilities Education Act of 1990 requires an individualized education plan for each child who has a disability. With this legislation, Congress rejected an assembly-line approach to education and instead mandated that education be individualized for each disabled child. The act's intention was to assist youth with disabilities to participate in the regular, state-prescribed curriculum. When children and youth were judged not capable of benefiting from the regular curriculum, the next step was to "maximize his/her education potential" (Hurder, 1997, p. 5).

Findings from the National Longitudinal Transition Study of special education students (Blackorby & Wagner, 1996) indicate that youth with disabilities remain behind their peers in the general population. Based on information in the first five years after high school, the researchers reported the following results: Youth with disabilities had a significantly lower employment rate and were less likely to enroll in postsecondary education than youth in general. Blackorby and Wagner (1996) cited the following comparative statistic: "Three to five years after leaving secondary school, 78% of graduates in the general population had attended postsecondary schools in contrast to 37% of youths with disabilities" (p. 408). They also stated that "with respect to the goal of independent living, the

level of residential independence among youths with disabilities was significantly below that of youths in the general population—37% versus
60%" (p. 409). Blackorby and Wagner concluded that substantial gaps in
education and income exist between youth with disabilities and their peers
in the general population. Low levels of educational attainment do not
bode well for the economic futures of disabled youth. Accordingly, this
chapter emphasizes the preparation of foster wards with disabilities for
independence.

Study Focus

Helping young people with disabilities make a successful transition from
placement to community living poses major challenges to state agencies.
In Illinois, the Department of Children and Family Services (DCFS) has
jurisdiction over children and youth who are neglected, abused, aban-
doned, or otherwise seriously maltreated. Of the approximately 50,000
children in placement in Illinois, nearly 20% are classified as disabled. Little
is known about the extent to which foster adolescents with disabilities
are prepared for economic self-sufficiency and community living. Three
questions were posed for analysis:

- What is the level of placement restrictiveness for disabled foster
  youth as compared with placement restrictiveness levels for
  nondisabled wards?

- How are placement restrictiveness levels distributed with respect
  to race, gender, and disability status?

- Is educational progress a correlate of placement restrictiveness?

Database

The main source of information was the DCFS Program/Client Information System. The DCFS database contains information on children and
youth in state care. This study used information available in the state database for fiscal year 1996. The researchers concentrated on the 16- to
18-year-old age group because the federal independent-living legislation,
Title IV-E of the Social Security Act, Section 477, authorizes state child
welfare programs to provide independent-living services to all wards starting at age 16.

The Children/Youth Information Base collects disability information
on foster youth. The DCFS disability codes for state wards adhere to the
definitional guidelines outlined in the Americans with Disabilities Act of

1990. A disability is described as a "physical or mental impairment that substantially limits one or more of an individual's major life functions" (Americans with Disabilities Act, Sec. 3.2.a).

Information collected included: (a) placements in sequential order, (b) the number of days spent in each placement, (c) age at first placement, and (d) the reason for each placement change. Placement data were generated from the Placement/Payment Authorization Form. This form was completed by caseworkers each time a change of placement occurred. Education data were also reported by caseworkers and included the grade level completed and type of school program the child was in.

Results

Permanency Goal

The concept of permanency of living arrangement is central in all child welfare legislation. The most valued permanency plans emphasize reunification with the child's own family, a relative/kinship arrangement, or permanency through adoption (Taylor, Lakin, & Hill, 1989). Table 9.1 summarizes the distribution of permanency goals for youth in placement by age and race.

There are significant differences between race and permanency goals across age groups. For all age groups, a significantly higher percentage of nonwhite youth have a goal of long-term relative care than white youths. A significantly higher percentage of white youth in both the 13 to 15 and 16 to 18 age groups have a goal of returning home compared with nonwhite youth. Race differences diminish with the 19- to 21-year-old youth. With respect to disability and permanency goal, Table 9.2 summarizes the findings, classified by age group and disability status.

For 16- to 18-year-olds, less than 15% of youth have the goal of returning home. From ages 19 to 21, this goal virtually disappears. The permanency option of kinship care is significantly lower for disabled youth than nondisabled youth. For nondisabled 13- to 15-year-old foster youth, more than 30% have a goal of long-term relative care, compared with only 14% of disabled youth. By age 16, only 3% of disabled youth have a permanency goal of relative care, compared with 14% of the nondisabled population. The permanency goal of relative care drops to 2% for the 19- to 21-year-old disabled youth and 3% for nondisabled youths. It should be noted that adoption is not a significant permanency goal for disabled or nondisabled youth across age groups. For disabled 13- to 15-year-old youth in placement, long-term foster family home care (48%) is the goal of choice, compared with 29% for nondisabled youth in this age group.

TABLE 9.1

Permanency Goals Classified by Race and Age (N = 15,680) (in percentages)

PERMANENCY GOAL	AGE CATEGORY					
	13–15		16–18		19–21	
	WHITE	NONWHITE	WHITE	NONWHITE	WHITE	NONWHITE
Return Home	37	19	20	10	4	4
Adoption	9	15	2	4	<1	<1
Home of Relative	11	34	5	15	1	4
Foster Home	40	30	15	13	3	3
Congregate Care	2	1	2	2	3	2
Independent Living	1	<1	56	57	88	89

TABLE 9.2

Permanency Goals Classified by Disability Status and Age (N = 15,680)

PERMANENCY GOAL	AGE CATEGORY					
	13–15		16–18		19–21	
	DISABLED	NONDISABLED	DISABLED	NONDISABLED	DISABLED	NONDISABLED
Return Home	27	22	14	13	4	4
Adoption	7	15	2	4	<1	<1
Home of Relative	14	33	3	14	2	3
Foster Home	48	29	20	11	5	2
Congregate Care	1	<1	5	1	9	1
Independent Living	4	1	56	57	80	90

The option that becomes increasingly important as youth get older is independent living. For 13- to 15-year-old teens, the independent living goal is 4% or less. From ages 16 to 18, this goal increases to more than 55% for disability and nondisability groups. It overshadows all other permanency goals. By age 19, independent living dominates all permanency categories and, regardless of disability status, is the goal for more than 80% of foster youth.

By age 16, permanency goals of returning home and relative/kinship care for disabled youth are virtually nonexistent. Adoption received only minor emphasis as a permanency goal. Once disabled youth reach the transitional age of 16, independent living takes over as the primary goal for more than 80% of the sample. This result confirms the idea that eventually, all foster youth need to adapt to community life and prepare for eventual independence from system resources.

Placement Restrictiveness and Disability Status

All living arrangements are restrictive to some degree. Some are more restrictive than others, such as congregate/residential care versus living in a regular foster home. Placements rated high in restrictiveness are believed to delay progress toward independence. Tables 9.3 and 9.4 compare disabled and nondisabled youth with respect to placement restrictiveness. Table 9.3 summarizes information for foster wards ages 16 to 18. The results are consistent for race/gender comparisons and overall trends. Placement restrictiveness scores for youth with a disability were on average more than two times higher than placement restrictiveness scores for nondisabled youth.

All race/gender comparisons for disabled and nondisabled youth were statistically significant. State wards have difficulty overcoming barriers to achieving independence. Foster youth with disabilities face additional barriers of living in more restrictive placements with the prospect of receiving limited emphasis on developing skills needed for daily living and self-sufficiency.

Restrictiveness, Disability, and Education

Educational attainment is pivotal in preparing for economic self-sufficiency. Table 9.5 contrasts grade level status for disabled and nondisabled youth.

Higher grade-level attainment was associated with placement in settings of low restrictiveness. The researchers noted a systematic effect for predominant placement as a factor associated with grade-level attainment. Youth whose predominant placement was an apartment or foster boarding home attained the highest grade level. Youth in congregate placements achieved lower education levels than apartment-dwelling youth. Youths in relative placements did least well in terms of grade level status. The results are consistent regardless of disability status or age category.

An unsettling finding surfaced from the analysis of educational attainment. Table 9.6 shows the percentage of Illinois wards below grade level for their age. Regardless of disability status, age, or race, a high percentage of foster youth were below the normal grade level for their age. The grade level/age discrepancy effect was most prominent for nonwhite youth, of whom 80% to 90% were classified as below grade level. Youth in apartment placements achieved somewhat higher grade levels than youth in alternate placements. Although foster homes and apartment placements appear to provide youth with an advantage in educational attainment, a majority of foster wards ages 17 to 21 were below Grade 12, regardless of disability statistics.

Table 9.7 summarizes this result in dramatic fashion. For both disabled and nondisabled foster youth ages 17 to 21 in congregate care, more than 80% were recorded as below Grade 12 attainment. These statistical pat-

TABLE 9.3

Mean Placement Restrictiveness Scores by Disability Status and Race/Gender: Ages 16–18

RACE/GENDER	DISABLED	NONDISABLED	MEAN DIFFERENCE	T VALUE
White Male	51.8	40.5	+11.3	4.9
Nonwhite Male	36.6	23.9	+12.7	6.1
White Female	39.8	29.3	+10.5	3.9
Nonwhite Female	31.7	18.5	+13.2	4.8
Overall	40.0	28.1	+12.0	9.6
n	586	2,231		

TABLE 9.4

Mean Placement Restrictiveness Scores by Disability Status and Race/Gender: Ages 19–21

RACE/GENDER	DISABLED	NONDISABLED	MEAN DIFFERENCE	T VALUE
White Male	49.9	30.9	+19.0	7.3
Nonwhite Male	39.1	22.7	+16.4	6.7
White Female	41.7	22.2	+19.5	6.6
Nonwhite Female	33.3	16.6	+16.7	5.4
Overall	41.0	23.1	+17.9	12.8
n	461	1,984		

TABLE 9.5

School Grade Level Classified by Placement Restrictiveness Level, Disability Status, and Age

PREDOMINANT PLACEMENT TYPE	MEAN SCORE	AGE CATEGORY			
		16–18		19–21	
		DISABLED	NONDISABLED	DISABLED	NONDISABLED
Apartment	1.0	10.0	10.6	10.5	10.8
Relative Home	9.0	8.4	8.3	9.5	9.7
Family Foster Home	19.4	9.1	9.1	10.6	10.3
Congregate Care	65.6	9.3	8.9	10.2	9.8
F Value		4.1	22.8	4.3	15.4
Significance		$p < .007$	$p < .0001$	$p < .005$	$p < .0001$

TABLE 9.6

Percentage of Illinois Foster Wards Below Grade-Level by Age, Disability, and Race ($N = 15,331$) (in percentages)

AGE GROUP	DISABLED	NONDISABLED	WHITE	NONWHITE
13–15	65	78	62	80
16–18	84	86	77	90
19–21	73	74	61	80
Total Below Grade Level	2,182	9,933	3,283	8,832

TABLE 9.7

Distribution of Foster Youth Below Grade 12 by Predominant Placement and Disability Status: Ages 17-21 ($n = 4,742$)

PREDOMINANT PLACEMENT	DISABLED		NONDISABLED	
	n	%	n	%
Apartment	17	65	221	54
Relative Home	114	89	1,781	84
Foster Home	296	73	1,018	72
Congregate Care	495	81	770	82
Total	952		3,790	

terns need to be reviewed and rechecked. Accuracy of caseworker entries requires validation.

Although many explanations can be offered to explain the high percentages of foster adolescents achieving below grade level for their age, placement instability is a factor not easily dismissed.

Placement Instability

One of the differences between children in out-of-home care and children living in their own homes is placement change. Few wards remain in one placement. Wards often experience multiple changes in their placement careers. It is important to note that analysis of placement movement data for 5,273 foster wards ages 16 to 21 recorded a total of 36,303 placement changes. Table 9.8 summarizes placement changes classified by disability status, race, and restrictiveness for wards ages 16 to 18.

Analysis of administrative data indicated that 19,205 placement changes were recorded for the sample of 2,824 foster youth ages 16 to 18. This is an average of seven placements per youth. Disabled youth experienced a significantly higher number of placement changes than nondisabled youth.

TABLE 9.8

Placement Changes Classified by Restrictiveness Level, Disability Status, and Race: Foster Youth Ages 16–18

STATUS/RACE	n	LESS RESTRICTIVE (%)	NO CHANGE (%)	MORE RESTRICTIVE (%)	TOTAL	MEAN
White Disabled	327	38	24	38	3,484	10.7
Nonwhite Disabled	260	35	30	35	2,473	9.5
White Nondisabled	563	41	22	37	4,529	8.0
Nonwhite Nondisabled	1,674	36	30	34	8,719	5.2
Overall	2,824	38	27	35	19,205	7.0

Disabled youth recorded an average of 10.1 placement changes. Nondisabled youth averaged 5.9 changes. The result was an approximate 40% differential between disabled and nondisabled youths. The number of years spent in care, however, did not differ between disabled and nondisabled youth; both spent approximately five years in care. With respect to restrictiveness levels associated with each placement change, the odds were that youth would move into a more restrictive placement 35% of the time. Table 9.9 summarizes similar information for wards ages 19 to 21.

Nineteen- to twenty-one-year-old youth averaged 7.0 placement changes overall. For disabled youth, the placement change mean was 10.1; for nondisabled youth, the average was 6.3. Although disabled and nondisabled youths both spent about six years in care, the result was 39% fewer placement changes for nondisabled youth than disabled youth.

Assessment

Despite an extensive literature on children and youth with disabilities, little attention has been devoted to foster youth classified as disabled. Surveys of children in placement lack consistency in terminology. Some use the broad category of "special needs" which can mean need for a minority child to be placed in an adoptive home. The drawback to the special needs classification is that the needs cited are not necessarily equivalent to a handicap or a disabling condition. Others use functional descriptors, such as "physical," "emotional," or "mental handicap," or diagnostic categories such as mental retardation or visual impairment. Also used are broad indicators such as "psychological handicap" or "learning" problem.

Recent surveys of handicapped children in foster care tend to use the following categories: (a) mentally retarded, (b) emotionally disturbed/mentally ill, (c) learning disabled, (d) physically handicapped, and (e) hear-

TABLE 9.9

Placement Changes Classified by Restrictiveness Level, Disability Status, and Race: Foster Youth Ages 19-21

Status/Race	n	Less Restrictive (%)	No Change (%)	More Restrictive (%)	Total	Mean
White Disabled	257	44	22	34	2,744	11.0
Nonwhite Disabled	205	37	30	33	1,928	9.4
White Nondisabled	562	41	26	33	4,431	7.8
Nonwhite Nondisabled	1,425	38	31	31	7,995	5.6
Overall	2,449	40	28	32	17,098	7.0

ing, vision, speech disabled. Emotional disturbance/mental illness accounts for 38% of the five disability categories listed. Approximately 20% of all children in foster care are classified as handicapped. State-by-state estimates for foster children with handicaps range from a high of 40% (Arkansas, California, and Kansas) to a low of 2.9% (District of Columbia) (Hill et al., 1990).

Evaluations by service providers as to how well the placement system works for children with handicaps produced the following: 42% rated the system "average," 16% said "poor," and 10% responded "very well." It is significant that 32% did not answer (Richardson, West, Day, & Stuart, 1989). Increasingly, the literature on youth with disabilities emphasizes the importance of developing transition teams with links to local community resources. The community resource model suggests that reliance on a family and friend network is insufficient. Seeking assistance and support from knowledgeable community resource people is recommended (Reiff & deFur, 1992). Transitional programs for youth with developmental disabilities are growing at a rapid rate. Yet the overall effectiveness of transitional services is unclear. Rojewski (1992) pled for service providers to "conduct follow-up...as part of service delivery" (p. 148). In addition to the component of "follow-up/follow-along services," Rojewski's transitional model includes academic remediation, vocational preparation, support systems, and job search assistance.

In terms of application to the Illinois sample, the three main disability categories were learning (45%), emotional (34%), and mental (21%). The extent to which these numbers represent valid estimates depends on the accuracy of the state administrative database. Nearly 20% of Illinois foster wards in the 16- to 21-year-old age group had a disability condition. Of this number, doctors diagnosed one in three as emotionally disabled, nearly one in two had a learning disability, and doctors classified one in five as mentally disabled. Youth with an emotional, learning, or mental disability are not prime candidates for a successful transition to independence. Illinois faces a difficult task in helping disabled wards prepare for self-sufficiency. Consider Louis, a typical example.

> *Louis is a state ward with a diagnosis of having a learning disability and behavior disorder, and being mentally handicapped. He came into care at age 15. Relatives no longer wanted to care for Louis. In most of his school years, Louis was in special education classes. At the request of foster parents, he was given a psychiatric evaluation. The clinical report described Louis as hyperactive, undersocialized, and overly aggressive. A doctor prescribed medication for hyperactivity. While in care, Louis was involved in a retail theft. As a consequence, a social worker moved him to a specialized group home. By age 18, Louis's client service plan indicated a permanency goal of independence. A year or so prior to discharge, a worker placed Louis in a vocational rehabilitation program for youth with disabilities conducted by the Department of Rehabilitation Services. Little is known about Louis after discharge from state care.*

The need exists for information about disabled wards once they emancipate from state care. It in important to study the extent to which families (birth- and/or foster) are involved in transition planning, and the part each plays in the period following discharge from state care (Morningstar, Turnbull, & Turnbull, 1995). Based on administrative data, the prognosis for successful transitions to independence is cloudy. For youth with severe developmental disabilities, complete independence may not be a realistic goal (Hayes, Bain, & Batshaw, 1997). Faced with a disability along with multiple barriers such as working below grade level and experiencing an average of seven placement changes (and for each re-placement, one in three youth is likely to experience a more restrictive setting than the previous arrangement), the cumulative record does not provide an optimistic picture regarding potential for economic self-sufficiency. Improvement in programs that serve disabled foster youth depends on knowing more about the transitional services provided and collecting follow-up information on the postemancipation progress of former wards. Youth disability experts recommend that independent living services emphasize educational or vocational preparation, including assistance in obtaining employment via unsubsidized jobs or sheltered workshop programs, along with teaching survival skills (Wood, 1987). Analysis of client profiles and transitional plans, as well as follow-up contact after emancipation, is vital to program improvement.

References

Americans with Disabilities Act, P.L. 101-336 (1990). Retrieved from http:/www.usdoj.gov/crt/ada/pubs/ada.txt

Blackorby, J., & Wagner, M. (1996). Longitudinal post-school outcomes of youth with disabilities: Findings from the National Longitudinal Transition Study. *Exceptional Children, 61*, 399–413.

Harnisch, D. L., & Gieri, M. J. (1995). *Factors associated with dropping out for youths with disabilities.* Paper prepared for the 1995 Council for Exceptional Children (CEC) Annual Convention, Indianapolis, IN.

Hayes, A., Bain, L. J., & Batshaw, M. L. (1997). Adulthood: What the future holds. In M. L. Batshaw (Ed.), *Children with disabilities* (4th ed., pp. 757–772). Baltimore: Paul H. Brookes.

Hill, B. K., Hayden, M. F., Lankin, K. C., Menke, J., & Novak Amado, A. R. (1990). State-by-state data on children with handicaps in foster care. *Child Welfare, 69*, 447–462.

Hurder, A. J. (1997). The Individuals with Disabilities Education Act and the right to learn. Legal analysis of IDEA. *Human Rights, 24*(1). Retrieved from http://www.abanet.org/irr/hr/hurder/html

Morningstar, M. E., Turnbull, A. P., & Turnbull, H. R., III. (1995). What do students with disabilities tell us about the importance of family involvement in the transition from school to adult life? *Exceptional Children, 62*, 249–260.

Reiff, H. B., & deFur, S. (1992). Transition for youths with learning disabilities: A focus on developing independence. *Learning Disabilities Quarterly, 15*, 237–249.

Richardson, M., West, M. A., Day, P., & Stuart, S. (1989). Children with developmental disabilities in the child welfare system: A national survey. *Child Welfare, 68*, 605–613.

Rojewski, J. W. (1992). Key components of model transition services for student with learning disabilities. *Learning Disability Quarterly, 15*, 135–150.

Shapiro, J. P. (1994). *No pity. People with disabilities forging a new civil rights movement.* New York: Times Books.

Taylor, S. J., Lakin, K. C., & Hill, B. K. (1989). Permanency planning for children and youth: Out-of-home placement decisions. *Exceptional Children, 55*, 541–549.

Wood, L. (1987). *On their own: The needs of youth in transition. Final report.* Elizabeth, NJ: Association for Advancement of the Mentally Handicapped.

Chapter 10

Effectiveness of
Transitional Apartments

EDMUND V. MECH[1]

*All of the classes and training in the world
do not have the impact of a month living alone
in an apartment.*

—*Kroner (1999, p. 18)*

Perspectives on Housing Options

Preparation for adult living refers to a constellation of attitudes, skills, and behaviors that improve the life chances of foster adolescents. Lifeskills knowledge and the ability to carry out a variety of daily tasks constitute the major elements needed for self-sufficiency. The lifeskills strategy includes orientation to the world of work, emphasizes economic self-reliance, and is consistent with the societal value of avoiding prolonged dependence on public aid. Other areas of development are also vital in preparing foster adolescents for successful careers and family life. These include building self-esteem, maintaining positive relationships with others (Maluccio, Krieger, & Pine, 1990), and helping adolescents form attachments with adults and significant others (Downes, 1988).

The study discussed in this chapter assumed that lifeskills acquisition would be highest in apartment settings and foster boarding home placements and lowest in group home/institutional settings. In foster boarding homes, youth are exposed to lifeskills situations on a daily basis. Foster parents can serve as role models for managing practical living situations. Kroner (1988) noted that institutions are "probably the least equipped to prepare a youth for independent-living" (p. 53). Institutions emphasize adjustment to group norms and tend to follow highly structured routines. Institutional living tends to limit

---

[1] Based on an article by Mech et al. (1994).

opportunities for trial-and-error learning. In congregate placements, young people are less likely to gain practical experience in tangible lifeskills, such as decisionmaking, time management, employment, shopping, or assuming financial responsibility for paying bills. Youth who spend extended periods of time in institutional placements usually encounter fewer opportunities to acquire the lifeskills needed in society.

Because apartment placements are realistic and practical, they provide experiences that help prepare young people for independence. Apartment programs for foster wards represent a developmental focus and a new direction for the child welfare field that, heretofore, has emphasized placement primarily to protect children from harm.

Apartment placements offer important opportunities to acquire and apply lifeskills knowledge. Youth placed in cluster-site and scattered-site arrangements assume major responsibility for purchasing food, planning and preparing meals, and getting themselves to school, work, and appointments. Getting a job is a necessity, because the youth have to help pay for living expenses.

In a cluster-site apartment arrangement, several apartment units are located in one building. Youth may live alone or share a unit with another person. One of the cluster units is usually allocated to a staff person who resides in the building and acts as a supervisor. Scattered-site placements are apartments that are located in various neighborhoods of a community. Youth receive less supervision than they do in cluster-site placements. Scattered-site supervision varies, in that service workers may have contact with youth that ranges from several times a week to one contact per month. Some service workers make unannounced random visits, whereas others make planned visits and establish a visiting schedule. Although the scattered-site model provides less supervision than other models, this plan creates a realistic situation for youth who are learning to live on their own. Youth in both scattered- and cluster-site placements are expected to save a portion of their monthly income. They must also prepare for the eventuality that when state aid is phased out, they are expected to become self-supporting. Kroner (1999) provided an updated definition of a scattered-site apartment as follows: "A privately-owned apartment rented by an agency or youth in which a youth lives independently or with a roommate, with financial support, training, and some monitoring" (1999, p. 3). Empirical information regarding the effectiveness of apartment placements in assisting youth in the acquisition of lifeskills is virtually nonexistent. This chapter discusses evidence for the effectiveness of apartment placements draws implications for program and policy. Information was collected from five data sources:

1. Ratings of the effectiveness of placement options, as seen by foster wards

2. Life-Skills Inventory—A 50-item, multiple-choice instrument

3. Case-Record Review—Extraction of case-record information with emphasis on school grades

4. Readiness for independent living—scores at age 18

5. Outcome indicators—Age 21 follow-up (education, employment, finances, etc.)

Database

Researchers collected information from more than 500 older adolescents in out-of-home placements. Each youth had the goal of independent living. Agencies in Illinois, Indiana, and Ohio participated in the follow-up series. Youth were interviewed on or about age 18 and again at age 21. Living arrangement classification was determined by the youth's placement at the time of the first interview. Conducted under the auspices of the University of Illinois, the participants completed a consent form approved by the Institutional Review Board. Participants received $15 for the age 18 interview and $35 for the age 21 interview. Of nearly 600 youth contacted, 90% agreed to participate.

Perceived Effectiveness of Placement Options

This section discusses placement options in terms of their effectiveness in preparing wards for independent living. The options are foster homes, group homes, residential/institutional facilities, and scattered-site and congregate apartments. The evidence indicates that foster family homes and scattered-site apartments are the most effective placements in preparing wards for independence. Group homes also receive support as placements that provide preparation for independent living. Institutional facilities rate lowest. Table 10.1 summarizes ratings of placement options classified as "most helpful" in preparing for independent living. The data source for Table 10.1 was 336 emancipated foster wards who were approximately 21 years old at follow-up.

It is clear that youth who experience various placement options preferred transitional apartments and foster family homes. Approximately two-thirds

TABLE 10.1

Placement Options Rated as "Most Helpful" in Preparing Foster Wards for
Independent-Living: Age 21 Follow-up (N = 336)

GENDER	APARTMENT	FOSTER HOME	GROUP HOME	INSTITUTION	TOTAL
Male					
n	42	30	28	10	110
Percentage	38	27	25	9	
Female					
n	76	77	49	24	226
Percentage	34	34	22	10	
Total					
n	118	107	77	34	336
Percentage	35	32	23	10	

of the "most helpful" ratings were for apartments and foster homes. Only
10% of the youth rated institutional programs as most helpful.

Lifeskills Inventory

A lifeskills inventory was administered as part of a battery of instruments
designed to assess readiness for independent living. The researchers tested
the youth individually. The study used a 50-item, multiple-choice inventory to assess lifeskills knowledge. Each item was weighted 4 points, for a
maximum score of 200 points. The inventory included the following areas: rental arrangements, checking accounts, practical finances, shopping,
meal preparation, job seeking, job holding, nutrition, alcohol and drug use,
contraception, health, consumer rights, and household management. Independent-living coordinators working in state/county foster youth programs pretested the inventory.

   An example of a lifeskills item is, "Which one of the following is usually
included in a lease?"

- A requirement that you are not allowed to have overnight guests.

- The right of a landlord to evict you within 72 hours.

- The length of time that you are required to rent the apartment.

- A requirement that you must turn lights off after midnight.

- The requirement that you are responsible for providing your own
  security-alarm system.

The placement options contained a total of five specific living arrangements. The comparison between the cluster-site model and the scattered-site model was of special interest. Table 10.2 summarizes the distribution of lifeskills scores for each of five living arrangements classified by race and gender.

Comparisons of lifeskills knowledge for the two apartment models yielded a mean score of 158.7 points for the scattered-site apartment model; the cluster-site apartment mean was 150.1 points. The direction of the difference in favor of the scattered-site apartment model was consistent for all race and gender subgroup comparisons.

This result confirms that foster wards in apartment placements and foster home settings acquire a broader range of information related to daily living than they do in residential/institutional settings. Exposure to practical lifeskills is more likely to occur in foster homes and apartment placements.

Case Record Review

The researchers conducted a case record review based on caseworker notes in state files. Information on school grades, health status, and social-emotional adjustment was collected. Table 10.3 summarizes the findings.

School Grades. With respect to school progress, a higher percentage of transitional apartment youth and foster home residents received school grades categorized as "above average" (B or better). Group home/institution youth were more likely to receive "C" grades in school. The comparison of C grades was 55% for group home/institution youth, 47% for youth living in foster family homes, and 40% for youth living in transitional apartments. Youth in group home/institutions were more likely to receive "below average" grades (D or lower) than youth in foster family homes.

Health Status. A similar pattern was evident with respect to health status. For each living arrangement category, health status was reported as "good" for most of the foster youth. Good health ratings were reported for 79% of youth living in foster family homes and 80% of youth living in group homes and institutions. In comparison, 74% of those living in apartments received health ratings of "good."

Social-Emotional Adjustment. The highest percentage of foster wards with adjustment problems were in group home/institutional placements. Within this category, 76% of participants had adjustment problems compared with 49% in the foster boarding home category. The results showed adjustment problems for 62% of youth in apartment placements. Overall, the researchers found percentages of foster wards having adjust-

TABLE 10.2

Mean Lifeskills Scores for Foster Adolescents Classified by Living Arrangement, Race, and Sex (*N* = 534)

Race/Gender	Foster Home	Group Home	Institution	Cluster-Site Apartment	Scattered-Site Apartment
White Males	145.09	129.39	135.13	151.75	160.33
Nonwhite Males	133.07	130.00	133.48	138.00	148.50
White Females	154.63	145.14	142.38	154.95	165.36
Nonwhite Females	145.46	133.50	138.23	150.09	158.70
Overall	149	134	138	150	158

TABLE 10.3

School Progress, Health Status, and Social-Emotional Adjustment Comparisons for Foster Adolescents Classified by Type of Living Arrangement (in percentages)

CASE RECORD VARIABLE	FOSTER HOME	GROUP HOME/INSTITUTION	APARTMENT
School Progress (n = 246)			
Above average	31	19	34
Average	47	55	40
Below average	22	26	26
Health Status (n = 249)			
Good	79	80	74
Fair	21	20	25
Poor	0	0	1
Social-Emotional Adjustment (n = 256)			
Adjustment problem present	49	76	62
No adjustment problem present	51	24	38

ment problems ranged from 49% in the foster boarding home category to a high of 76% in the group home/institution category. Based on case review estimates that 49% to 76% of the study group manifests social-emotional adjustment problems, it is difficult to conclude that those in apartment placements are selectively different from youth in other placement settings.

Readiness for Independent Living: Age 18 Measures

The age 18 interview collected information on six indicators: (1) life-skills knowledge, (2) health information, (3) community resources, (4) following directions, (5) future plans, and (6) readiness for independence.

Using the measures cited plus the cumulative score for the six baseline indicators, youth who exited care from scattered-site apartment placements scored highest, followed by foster home placements and cluster apartment placements. Youth who exited care from group home and institutional placements scored lowest—on average, 80 to 90 points below scattered-site apartment placements. The Life-Skills Inventory, the health information survey, and the following directions test clearly delineated differential effects across placement settings. Table 10.4 summarizes the results.

Outcome Indicators: Age 21 Follow-up

Overall, youth who emancipated from placement at age 18 and lived in scattered-site apartment settings when they left care scored well on the age 21 outcome measures. They did best in educational achievement, employment, orientation toward self-sufficiency, and income. On average, youth who exited care from residential/institutional settings did least well. An average of 155 points per youth separated scattered-site placements from institutional/residential placements. Table 10.5 summarizes the results.

Assessment

The results confirm that readiness measures and subsequent outcomes for adolescents in scattered-site apartments and foster-boarding placements are higher than among youth in group home and/or residential/institutional placements. Institutional and congregate placement environments tend to emphasize set schedules and conformity to rules and regulations. Exposure to practical lifeskills is more likely to occur in foster family homes than in congregate placements. With respect to apartment placements and lifeskills knowledge, the association appears to be promising.

No external reference group was available against which to compare apartment results. Based solely on within-sample observations across placement settings, the association between apartment placements and indicators of lifeskills knowledge was positive. The average length of stay in apartment placements was about four months, ranging from one to nine months. Youth who experienced apartment placements (in addition to foster home, group home, or institutional placements) tended, on average, to do statistically better on measures of lifeskills knowledge than youth who experienced only foster boarding home or group/institutional placements. This may be because apartment arrangements place responsibility for planning and implementing important day-to-day activities directly on foster youth. Moreover, some combination of school and work

TABLE 10.4

Readiness Scores for Independent-Living Measures at Emancipation Classified by Housing Arrangement (N = 534)

Area	Foster Home	Group Home	Institution	Scattered-Site Apartment	Cluster-Site Apartment	Significance Level (p Value)
Life Skills	148	134	138	150	158	.024*
Health Information	98	91	87	93	105	.015*
Community Resources	60	58	59	62	62	.781
Following Directions	97	85	78	96	111	.007*
Future Plans	131	126	121	128	130	.016*
Readiness for Independent Living	72	71	69	77	81	.344
Self-Rating Cumulative Baseline	694	650	640	689	732	.001*

*Indicates significant findings.

TABLE 10.5

Status of Foster Wards at Age 21 on Selected Outcome Measures Classified by Placement Type at Emancipation

Outcome Area	Foster Home	Group Home	Institution	Scattered-Site Apartment	Cluster-Site Apartment	Significance Level (p Value)
Education	122	106	106	102	149	.001*
Employment	107	113	85	99	118	.030*
Self-Sufficiency	96	98	91	96	112	.012*
Community Links	33	30	32	22	34	.346
Public Aid Costs	99	105	124	107	87	.280
Income/Housing	52	56	41	53	58	.044*
Cumulative Measures	611	598	530	564	685	.001*

*Indicates significant findings.

is usually mandatory. In apartment settings, youth are typically responsible for purchasing and preparing food, maintaining the apartment, deciding when to go to sleep and when to get up, saving a portion of their earnings to build up an emancipation fund, and assuming responsibility for paying rent, utilities, and other bills.

The researchers obtained a consistent statistical progression in support of apartment placements for each race/gender subgroup. Within the white male group, the apartment lifeskills mean was 31 points, or 24% higher than the group home mean. Within the nonwhite male group, the apartment mean was 18 points, or 14% higher than the group home mean. Within the white female group, the apartment mean was 20 points, or 14% higher than the group home mean. For nonwhite females, the apartment mean was 25 points, or 19% higher than the group home mean. Overall, among adolescents in apartments, those placed in scattered-site units did best on the Life-Skills Inventory.

The percentage of youth who scored below 50%, or less than 100 points, on the Life-Skills Inventory is further indication of the association between apartment settings and lifeskills knowledge. The study found the following relationship with living arrangements: scattered-site apartments = 1/126, or less than 1% below 50%; cluster-site apartments = 3/67, or 4.5% below 50%; foster family homes = 16/156, or 10.3% below 50%; institutions = 15/104, or 14.4% below 50%; and group homes = 14/81, or 17.3% below 50% correct on lifeskills items. Only 2% of the youth in transitional apartments scored below 50% on the Life-Skills Inventory compared with 10.3% of the foster family placements and 15.7% of the youth in group home/institutional placements.

These data suggest that when foster homes, group homes, and institutions are supplemented by apartment experiences, lifeskills knowledge may be enhanced. Many older adolescents are discharged about age 18 without the benefit of an apartment experience, perhaps missing an opportunity to practice independent-living skills and learn from their own mistakes. Most young people view living in their own apartment without continuous adult monitoring as a symbol of independence. Extending apartment opportunities to a wider range of foster youth may be beneficial to them.

Results favoring apartment placement may be linked to selection bias and/or creaming practices when placing foster wards in apartment settings. It is not clear to what extent placement selectivity alone can explain the statistical differences among foster boarding home, group home/institutional, and apartment placements. Children who caseworkers remove from their homes because of abuse, neglect, sexual exploitation, or parental inadequacy can justifiably be characterized as at-risk or high-risk. Although selectivity exists in allocating youth to specific placements, the decision process represents a composite of youth needs, practitioner judgment, and resources available. This study assumed that most young people in out-of-home care are drawn from high-risk, difficult, or otherwise unfavorable backgrounds. The backgrounds of most youth in placement cannot be construed as recipes for success. Accordingly, this study attempted to identify the nature and direction of possible placement selectivity bias in the study group. The researchers extracted case-record pro-files for nearly 50% of the study group. They reviewed placement-related characteristics to determine if systematic differences existed between youth in apartments and youth in foster boarding and group home/institutional placements. Case reviews provided information on reason for placement, school progress, health status, and social-emotional adjustment.

Survey results are often difficult to interpret. Statistical associations reported are correlational in nature, not causative. In the absence of allo-cating participants to placement options by random procedures, causal arguments are futile. Despite positive findings with respect to apartment placements as an effective resource for preparing adolescent wards for independent living, the results are preliminary. Based on the overall data profile, including the behavioral outcomes obtained in the age 21 follow-up, foster home placement followed by a scattered-site apartment experi-ence is a good way to prepare state wards for independence.

The comparative results suggest a need to devote special attention to upgrading independent-living skills of foster wards in congregate/institutional settings, to target minority males for lifeskills enhancement in all placement settings, and, whenever possible, to offer apartment placements to older adolescent wards for whom the goal is independent living.

References

Downes, C. (1988). Foster families for adolescents: The healing potential of time-limited placements. *British Journal of Social Work, 18*, 473–487.

Kroner, M. (1988). Living arrangement options for young people preparing for indepen-dent-living. *Child Welfare, 67*, 51–55.

Kroner, M. (1999). *Housing options for independent-living programs*. Washington, DC: Child Welfare League of America.

Maluccio, A., Krieger, R., & Pine, B. (1990). Adolescents and their preparation for life after foster family care: An overview. In A. Maluccio, R. Krieger, & B. Pine (Eds.), *Preparing adolescents for life after foster care* (pp. 5–17). Washington, DC: Child Wel-fare League of America.

Mech, E., Ludy-Dobson, C., & Hulseman, F. (1994). Life-skills knowledge: A survey of foster adolescents in three placement settings. *Children and Youth Services Review, 16*, 181–200.

Chapter 11

Effectiveness of Mentors for Adolescents in Placement

EDMUND V. MECH AND
ELIZABETH L. LEONARD

> *Mentoring relationship[s] with young people can be*
> *effective if they extend over time and if mentors*
> *themselves have clear goals, adequate training, and*
> *adequate support from the sponsoring organization.*
>
> —*National Research Council (1993, p. 214)*

Mentoring: An Emerging Social Movement

Child Welfare League of America standards encourage the involvement of citizens and community-based resources in assisting foster wards to move toward self-sufficiency. Youth-serving organizations have responded by developing community-based mentor services. Numerous child welfare agencies, facilities, and organizations currently operate mentor programs. The mentoring movement in child welfare is relatively new, but the concept is catching on rapidly (Mech & Leonard, 1988). Mentor programs are highly visible in public and private schools, in various professions, and in business organizations. They are also emerging with special populations.

Efforts to mentor at-risk and disadvantaged youth on a large-scale pose a public policy dilemma. Pertinent literature shows that successful mentoring relationships typically involve well-motivated individuals. Little is known about the effects of mentoring disadvantaged or difficult-to-reach youth. Freedman (1993), in the volume *The Kindness of Strangers*, pointed out that Americans hold a heroic, idealistic image of mentoring. To many, mentoring represents a quick fix for youth in transition. To others, mentoring is cost-effective because mentors are typically citizens who volunteer to work with young people. Enthusiasm for mentoring is anchored in a belief system that exudes optimism, applauds individualism, and is anxious to cheer on society's underdogs to succeed against all odds.

One of the misleading selling points in recruiting mentors for disadvantaged youth is the message that mentoring is easy. Does just a few hours a month plus a motivated youth equal success? A variety of mentor programs for disadvantaged youth suggests otherwise.

Obstacles in Mentoring Disadvantaged Youth

Many factors influence a mentor-mentee relationship. When mentors are assigned or matched with a youth, the mentor is usually a stranger to the youth. Mentors are usually from socioeconomic backgrounds that are different from the mentees' backgrounds. Mentors often differ from mentees with respect to race and sometimes gender. Volunteers usually enter a mentoring agreement with high expectations of what can be accomplished. Too often, they assume that mentees have a goal-driven agenda that matches that of the mentor. Mentor-mentees matches are often plagued by broken appointments and irregular contact. Some matches are never activated. Therefore, the high expectations model often embraced by mentors may be ill-suited to the backgrounds of youth who have different life circumstances than mentors.

Foster Youth Mentor Project

The investigators derived the findings reported here from a multistate survey of mentor programs for youth in foster care. They collected information from 29 programs in 15 states. The researchers conducted the survey at the University of Illinois (Grant No. 90CW1026), U.S. Department of Health and Human Services, Children's Bureau (Mech, 1999).

The investigators conducted in-person interviews with 280 mentor and 272 mentees (N = 552). They paid mentees $20 for participating and offered mentors a $10 participation stipend. Mentors and mentees completed a consent form before the interviews. The project goal was to collect information for 250 mentor/mentee pairs, with an overall target of 500 interviews. The project completed 552 interviews; of that number, only 354 interviews consisted of mentor/mentee pairs. Table 11.1 summarizes the distribution of mentor/mentee pairs for 177 matches classified by race and gender. Nearly 70% were female pairs, 27% were male mentor/mentee matches, and 3% were cross-gender and cross-racial pairs. Of the female group, 75% of pairs were the same race, and 25% were cross-race. Within the male group, the majority of matches (55%) consisted of nonwhite mentor/mentee pairs. Overall, nearly 25% of the matches were cross-racial.

With respect to measuring the effectiveness of matches, the investigators used qualitative information, which they generated by asking

TABLE 11.1

Mentor/Mentee Pairs Classified by Race and Gender (N = 177 pairs/344 interviews)

RACE/GENDER OF MENTEE/MENTOR	NUMBER OF PAIRS
WF/WF	44
WF/NWF	27
NWF/WF	4
NWF/NWF	47
WM/WM	9
WM/NWM	9
NWM/WM	4
NWM/NWM	27
WM/WF	1
WF/WF	3
NWM/NWF	1
NWF/WM	1

NOTE: W = white; NW = nonwhite; F = female; M = male.

mentors and mentees to separately rate satisfaction with the match. The mentor/mentee satisfaction inventory contained such questions as, "How satisfied are you with your relationship with your mentee (or mentor)?" The researchers scored ratings on a scale of 1 to 10, with 10 equaling extremely satisfied and 1 equaling extremely dissatisfied. Other items rated were, "How much do you think you have accomplished with your mentee (or mentor)?"; "How responsive is the mentee (or mentor)?"; "To what degree does your mentee trust you and think that you want to help?"; and "To what extent do you trust your mentor?" Investigators asked mentors and mentees to rate subjective qualities that included trust in each other, closeness of relationship, and satisfaction with the match.

Effectiveness of Mentor/Mentee Matches

Mentors and mentees each rated their match on a series of eight factors, as follows: (1) goals, (2) skill development, (3) responsiveness, (4) trust, (5) improvement in school performance, (6) readiness for independent living, (7) satisfaction with the match, and (8) effect on mentee development. Each factor had a point value. The maximum point value possible for a match was set at 2,000 points, with 1,000 points for mentor ratings and 1,000 points for mentee ratings. Table 11.2 summarizes the scoring format used with respect to the point values for the eight factors.

The analysis emphasized the cumulative point scores of mentor and mentee ratings. Researchers gauged success by the distribution of mentor/mentee reciprocal ratings. They conducted an analysis of success levels for mentor/mentee matches using a 2,000-point format. The cumulative mean score was 1,424 points, which was 71% of the maximum 2,000-point standard. Overall, cumulative scores ranged from a low of 537 points (27% of the maximum) to a high of 2,000 points (100% of the standard). Based on the data cited, researchers devised a four-level classification system. Table 11.3 summarizes the four levels and point values associated with each level.

In terms of global assessment of success, Table 11.3 data illustrate the following. Researchers rated nearly 60% of the matches as highly successful or above average in success. About one in three were functioning at a marginal level. Less than 10% were classified as unsuccessful.

Results were consistent with respect to the influence of gender on match success. Of the female matches, 58% were either highly successful or above average in success. Of male matches, 61% were high or above average in success. Only 8% of female pairs were unsuccessful; 13% of male pairs were unsuccessful. In the male pairs, of the six unsuccessful matches, four were from a cross-racial match (i.e., white mentor/nonwhite mentee or nonwhite mentor/white mentee). Of the 23 pairs of white female mentors and nonwhite female mentees, 4, or 18%, were unsuccessful.

The evidence suggests that cross-racial matches are associated with a higher likelihood of failure. In particular, mentors were prone to experience low satisfaction with a cross-racial match or to view their efforts as having limited effect. One of the areas that proved difficult for mentors/mentees was rating readiness for independent living. A huge gap existed between mentor perceptions of mentee readiness and the inflated view that mentees held of their readiness for independent living. The results indicate that mentors were more realistic than mentees in their evaluations in terms of calling attention to the low readiness levels of mentees for independent living.

Quality of Relationship

The eight outcome indicators were divided into two subareas: (1) quality of relationship for mentor/mentee pairs and (2) preparation for independent living, which emphasized skill development, educational preparation, work experience, and tangible factors associated with achieving economic self-sufficiency. Mentor and mentees made separate ratings for each of eight factors. Four elements were considered in the quality of rela-

TABLE 11.2

Scoring Format to Assess Effectiveness of Mentor/Mentee Matches

FACTOR	MAXIMUM POINTS
Goals	50
Skill Development	50
Responsiveness	100
Trust	100
Improvement in School Performance	100
Readiness for Independent Living	100
Satisfaction with Relationship	250
Effect on Mentee Development	250
Match Total	2,000 points

NOTE: Mentor total = 1,000 points; mentee total = 1,000 points.

TABLE 11.3

Distribution of Effectiveness Levels for Mentor/Mentee Matches

LEVEL	EFFECTIVENESS LEVEL	POINT RANGE	% SUCCESS LEVELS
1	Highly Successful Match	1,600-2,000	22
2	Above Average Success in Match	1,400-1,599	37
3	Match Functions Marginally	1,100-1,399	32
4	Unsuccessful Match, Key Elements Have Disrupted	<1,100	9

tionship analysis: goals, responsiveness, trust, and satisfaction. Somewhat surprising was the result that mentees assigned higher quality of relationship ratings than did the mentors. The discrepancy in mentor/mentee ratings is evident in cross-racial matches. Quality of relationship ratings for cross-racial matches were consistently lower than the same-race matches. In cross-race matches, the point difference between mentors and mentees was wider than in same-race matches. Overall, mentors were less satisfied with match outcomes than mentees. A consistent finding within the nonwhite matches was that for each comparison in which nonwhite mentors rated each factor lower than mentees, their respective rating levels were higher than the cross-race pairs. Table 11.4 summarizes these findings. It appears that in same-race pairs, mentors are less constrained to establish higher expectations for mentees and can do so without the potential barrier of race coming between mentor and mentee.

TABLE 11.4

Comparative Mentor/Mentee Point Ratings for Quality of Relationship Classified by Race/Gender

MENTOR/MENTEE	RELATIONSHIP AREAS			
	GOALS	RESPONSIVENESS	TRUST	SATISFACTION
WF/WF	43/38	81/92	81/91	182/233
WF/NWF	42/40	87/91	90/89	162/221
NWF/WF	42/44	88/88	72/88	170/220
NWF/NWF	42/38	86/97	83/95	181/226
WM/WM	43/37	93/86	93/89	222/227
WM/NWM	43/41	68/89	75/91	164/214
NWM/WM	44/32	60/80	60/80	144/181
NWM/NWM	45/41	77/95	76/86	176/209
Maximum Points	50	100	100	250

NOTE: W = white; NW = nonwhite; F = female; M = male.

Overall, mentors were more satisfied with the goals that had been established than mentees. With respect to responsiveness, mentors rated their mentees much lower than the mentees rated mentors. A similar rating pattern was obtained in the areas of trust and satisfaction.

Independent-Living Preparation

The question was, To what extent did mentoring prepare mentees for independence with regard to skill acquisition, improvement in school performance, readiness for independent living, or effect on mentee development? The most consistent difference in mentor/mentee ratings was in readiness for independence. Based on a 100-point format, the mean for female mentors was 29 points; the mean for male mentors was 34 points. In contrast, the average readiness score for mentees was 68 points. An approximate 40-point differential existed between mentor/mentee ratings. Overall, mentor ratings were drastically lower than mentee ratings. In comparison with mentor evaluations, mentees tended to overestimate readiness levels for independence. This result suggests a need to establish realistic standards for readiness that will serve as guidelines for mentors as well as mentees. Table 11.5 summarizes mentor/mentee comparisons for readiness for independence.

Table 11.5 highlights the discrepant mentor/mentee ratings with respect to readiness for independent living and effect of mentors on mentees. Mentors rate mentees readiness for independence as low and rate their own ef-

TABLE 11.5

Comparative Mentor/Mentee Point Ratings for Independent-Living Preparation
Classified by Race/Gender

MENTOR/MENTEE	INDEPENDENT-LIVING PREPARATION			
	SKILL DEVELOPMENT	SCHOOL PERFORMANCE	READINESS FOR INDEPENDENT LIVING	EFFECT ON MENTEE
WF/WF	29/36	46/52	28/68	142/189
WF/NWF	31/32	39/57	27/67	146/150
NWF/WF	32/36	56/64	28/62	130/150
NWF/NWF	32/34	50/67	33/65	148/170
WM/WM	31/32	51/62	42/76	150/183
WM/NWM	26/27	53/53	42/73	116/172
NWM/WM	28/33	60/70	20/52	150/150
NWM/NWM	33/36	67/64	32/73	178/174
Maximum Points	50	100	100	250

NOTE: W = white; NW = nonwhite; F = female; M = male.

fect on mentees as low. An average of nearly 100 points separates mentors
and mentees on effect on mentees and independent-living preparation. The
message that foster youth mentees appear to be sending is that mentors are
helpful and are having a positive effect on youth. Mentors apparently are
unaware of the value that many mentees place on the relationship.

Mentor/Mentee Profiles

In Profiles 1 and 2, both mentors are lawyers. Mentees are female foster
youth at age 17. One mentee is Hispanic, the other mentee is African
American. Profile 3 describes a white mentor who is a legal secretary
matched with a nonwhite mentee. In Profile 4, the mentor is an administrative clerk. Both mentor and mentee are African American. Profile 5
describes a male mentor, an Air Force pilot on surveillance duty, and a 17-
year-old mentee.

Risk factors associated with matches cited are noted. In the aggregate,
these include: (a) poor school performance by mentee; (b) mentee distorts
(lies) events; (c) mentee is a runaway from placement and breaks contact
with mentor; (d) mentee seldom initiates contact with mentor, which places
responsibility on mentors to sustain contact; and (e) mentee is unable to
trust adults and/or to develop a relationship with adults. The researchers
estimated the difficulty level of each match on a scale of 1 to 10; 10 equals
high difficulty and high risk, and 1 equals low difficulty and low risk. The
researchers rated Profile 1 as 2, a low risk. They rated Profile 2 as 9, a high-

risk match. They classified Profiles 3 and 4 as 4, in the low- to moderate-risk category. In Profile 5, the mentor is confident that this relationship is helping his mentee. The difficulty level of match was low, a 2 or 3.

Profile 1—Anna and Esmeralda

Anna is a 31-year-old Hispanic patent attorney, who has been matched with her mentee, Esmeralda, for more than a year. Esmeralda, age 17, is Mexican and Puerto Rican. She is a junior in high school in a college-preparatory curriculum. According to Anna, the volunteer coordinator matched them because they were "same sex, same race." Anna says, "I work as a trademark lawyer. It's not a social job, and I'm a very social person." She decided to become a mentor when she received a flyer on being a mentor to youth on parole. She views her role as a friend, saying, "She knows I'm there," and "We are alike." "I want to be there to help her in her transition from high school to a junior college. Esmee likes having a mentor and introduces me as her sister. We are really close." Esmee was placed in care at age 14 because of physical abuse by her mother. She has had several placements prior to living with her aunt.

Anna and Esmeralda spend about eight hours a month together (average of two weekends a month). Both would like to spend more, but their schedules do not permit it. They have gone to the beach, hiked, visited a university campus, gone to a rock concert, and gone to several dinners and movies. Esmeralda also spent a night at Anna's home. They are both looking forward to going to Great America. With respect to lifeskills, emphasis has been on educational planning, job search, and budgeting. Anna feels Esmeralda has made progress in the education area. However, her rating of Esmeralda's readiness to live on her own is very low. Anna reports, "Esmee is very sociable, has good values, is easygoing, light-hearted, and positive, but has had some problems in preparing herself for college." At first, Esmeralda did not think she could do it because her grades were not high enough. With Anna's help, Esmeralda worked hard to improve her grades and now has high goals for her future—"to be a doctor, psychiatrist, or an obstetrician." This has been their major area of work together. Esmeralda has never had any job experience, but Anna feels she will be "a natural." Although Esmeralda has good potential, she is definitely not ready to live on her own without financial help. Anna feels that Esmeralda's many friends will not be able to help her financially. Anna rates Esmeralda's and her accomplishments a 10, citing a strong relationship and the fact she has been a role model for Esmeralda. Anna says, "We are the type of friends that don't have to spend a lot of time together." Anna believes she has made a difference in the life of her mentee and wants to continue the relationship because "I love this kid. She's more than a mentee. I want to help set her up in an apartment and help her head for college." Esmeralda felt she made progress in areas of responsible sexuality and in education. Both mentor and mentee want to continue the relationship after Esmeralda is emancipated. They will continue as long as possible and are already setting goals for the future. "Mentoring Esmee has been a great experience and helping her to succeed has been especially rewarding." As for Esmeralda, she likes everything about her mentor. "She encourages me. I feel better, and am definitely more comfortable in school now." She rates her mentor a 10 in helping to prepare her to live on her own. "She gives me pointers, we talk about things that make me think and that changes my attitude."

Profile 2—Valerie and Nedra

Valerie, age 30, is a white practicing attorney in corporate law. She has worked at her present position for three years and reports her income at $70,000 per year. Valerie's volunteer work has included offering legal services to women in prison, helping in soup kitchens, and working with high-risk youth groups. While in law school, she became interested in work with women in prison. She volunteers because she wants to be of service to her community. Valerie wants to work in areas of prevention, where she may be able to make a difference. She mentors Nedra, a nonwhite female who lives in a group home. Valerie views her role as that of an "older friend." After Nedra turned 18, her group home had a hard time holding onto her. Valerie reports, "We never got as far as helping her through the transition period to independent living." In the beginning, Nedra was interested in all kinds of things; "She was enthusiastic and outgoing, and affectionate, and we were alike in these respects." The first year, Nedra enjoyed the activities they did together—eating at the International House of Pancakes and talking, visiting, and walking around the neighborhood near Golden Gate Park. "She liked to walk around, and we both liked hiking, went to movies. She visited me in my home and we made cookies." For the first year, Nedra thought it was great, and they did have significant contact. However, she started having problems later on.

She started running away all the time, even before she turned 18. She just took off from the group home and would disappear for 3 or 4 days at a time. Just before she ran away the last time, the group home had put her on restriction because she wouldn't go to school. No one has heard from her or knows where she is.

Valerie could tell that the relationship was deteriorating. After having gotten off to a good start, problems seemed to arise. Nedra started to withdraw from the mentor, the group home staff, and her friends. She seemed to lose interest. She began to turn to older men who were hanging around the house. Group home staff think she had some sort of sexual problem. Nedra's relationships with people who cared about her the most, who would have helped her, were deteriorating. She began to let people take advantage of her, and her performance in school dropped from barely average to poor. She apparently had a learning disability. Then, she dropped out of school. She did the same thing with her summer job. She started out okay and then petered out. She never saved any of the money she earned.

> She had been lying to me all along about a lot of things. For example, she told me she was a track star. As it turns out she was not good in track. At first she seemed to like the group home, then she told me she was tired of living there and they were not nice to her and didn't like her. Her behavior changed dramatically—both at school, in the group home, and in our relationship. Something was very definitely going on. I felt she was in need of professional help. I felt ill-equipped to help her.

Valerie rated Nedra's progress toward independent living as a 2, which is very low, and satisfaction with the match as a 5. Valerie felt that Nedra was not ready to live on her own and that she was not even "street smart." Valerie believes Nedra has been living on the street for the past six months.

Despite her disappointment in the relationship, Valerie would be willing to continue as mentor mainly because she wants to let her mentee know that someone cares.

> I liked her, I really loved her, and we had a good time together. I thought we were building a friendship so that when she went out on her own, I could actually continue to be of help with the more practical skills I knew she needed. I mean, for a while that was what we were building toward. I would let her back into my life if she showed up, but I'd be more wary of whom she's hanging out with. I want to wait out this year before I take another mentee, just in case Nedra does show up.

Risk Factors

- Poor school performance and serious learning disability (dyslexia). At age 17, she refused to go to school.

- After a good start, mentee's behavior changed dramatically. Lost interest in relationship.

- Mentee was hanging out with the wrong people, letting them take advantage of her and make decisions for her.

- Mentee seldom initiated any contacts with mentor. Mentee began running away from the group home and disappeared for days at a time.

- Mentor feels the relationship has deteriorated, and the mentee needs psychiatric help, and mentor is not equipped to handle this.

- Mentor discovered mentee had lied to her and that mentor no longer could trust her.

Profile 3—Irena and Marcia

Irena is a legal secretary. She is 26 years old with two years of college majoring in criminal justice and is married. She estimates her income between $36,000 and $39,000. She has had no previous volunteer experience. Her husband and her friends think it's great that she is a mentor. She describes a mentor as "a friend and a guide." Marcia wanted a mentor and seems to like it. They were matched several months ago. Mentor usually initiates the contact.

They spend time on job searches and eating out. Getting a job and keeping it is the most important skill they work on, although decisionmaking/ problem solving, social relations skills, and education preparation are also cited as important. Irena reports Marcia is making progress in preparation for employment, some progress in social relations, and progress in responsible sexuality. Irena rates Marcia as highly prepared in knowledge of community resources, including job searches, although she does not have a job yet. Irena rates Marcia low in education planning, decisionmaking, social relations, and readiness to live on her own without financial assistance. Marcia has no network of friends, but her family might help after emancipation. She lives with a grandmother who is a foster parent.

Irena rates satisfaction with the match a 7, but feels it is too early to be certain. She wishes Marcia would open up more. Marcia is beginning to trust Irena, although she rarely initiates contact. In spite of modest progress, Irena feels she has made a difference, especially in areas of job search. Irena wants to continue the relationship because she wants to see Marcia get a job. Irena says, "She likes me, and I want her to make something of herself. She feels she may not be able to get close to anybody, and lack of trust is still a problem." For Irena, "It is self-satisfying, a great experience, but the challenge is to get her to open up and talk more. I make a difference by just being there."

Risk Factors

- Short duration of match (less than six months).

- Mentee's dependency on others and inability to make decisions on her own.

- Mentee never initiates contacts.

- Mentee's inability to get close to anyone or trust others.

Profile 4—Teresa and Chekesha

Teresa has been a mentor to "Kesha" for about three months. She decided to become a mentor because "I had someone in my life during my teen years." They were matched by the program coordinator who felt they "would hit it off." They see each other two hours a month and spend three hours in phone contact. Teresa works as an administrative clerk. She has one year of college, majoring in legal administration. Her annual income is approximately $20,000. Teresa's prior volunteer work has been with a hospital and three years of work in her church. Some of her friends have been mentors. She thinks of a mentor as "someone in your life to vent to, to help you, and someone a teenager can relate to."

When together, they talk about decisions Kesha must make, such as going home or not going home, her relationship with her mother, and her behavior in the group home. How they will spend their time and what they talk about is decided by mutual agreement. Everyone is very supportive of their relationship.

Teresa cites decisionmaking/problem solving, educational preparation, and money management as important skills to work on. Kesha has made some progress in budgeting and educational planning, but virtually no progress in finding a place to live once she is discharged from care. Teresa described Kesha as "committed to getting an education." Although Kesha wants to go to college, Teresa mentioned nothing about school.

Kesha has made poor choices in the past, and the pair work on this. She is learning to save money. Kesha has to decide whether to try living on her own or go home. Everything depends on her relationship with her mother. She does not have a strong network of friends or relatives to whom she can turn for help. Satisfaction with match is rated as 4 because, "I haven't had enough time to spend with her." Teresa needs more time to see some changes. Kesha's progress is rated as 3 for the same reason—"not enough time and it is still a new relationship." Although match is new, Teresa feels she has made a difference, but is not sure how long it will last.

Risk Factors

- Short duration of match (only a few months).

- Because mentee is having difficulty with her mother, she might not be able to relate to an older female mentor. This does not appear to be the case, however.

Profile 5—Randy and Bryan

Randy is a white male, age 26, and is an airborne warning and control pilot. His job is surveillance of Department of Defense targets. He is a college graduate with a major in management/human resources. He has been a volunteer in a program in Florida, has worked with Boy Scouts, and was a summer youth camp counselor. He has been a mentor to Bryan for about a year. His former mentee, who was living in a shelter, ran away from placement.

Randy says, "I have always wanted to work with kids who are in the foster care system, and being a mentor was my chance." He describes Bryan as a bright youth who wants to do a lot for himself. Bryan needs encouragement from someone on a one-on-one basis. "I was picked as a mentor for Bryan with the hope that I would be able to help him prepare for emancipation." Bryan, although 17, is only in the 9th grade. He has been in foster care since age 5. He has no family or relatives. At first, Bryan was on restriction, and they did not get much done together. Since then, they have gone to movies, eaten out, gone to an air show, and gone to the mall. Randy describes what he does as a mentor as similar to being a Big Brother. The difference is that youth are in the foster care system, have no real family, and have to deal with emotional pressures.

Two skill areas they have worked on most are job acquisition and job holding. In addition, they have worked on communication and education preparation. Bryan has made some progress in education planning and in decisionmaking. He has made progress in the job area. Randy rates Bryan's skills in problem solving and social relations as high. Randy rated Bryan's knowledge of community resources, education planning, and school achievement as low. Bryan's prognosis for living on his own following emancipation is cloudy. Bryan has a job as a dishwasher and has been a reliable worker. He is saving money "to a point," because he wants to get out of his group home placement. Bryan lacks a support network and lacks family, relatives, and friends.

Randy rates satisfaction with his mentee a 10, saying,

> He has told me and others that he trusts me and that he is glad I am around for him. One time he even gave me a hug, which surprised the hell out of me—this from a 17-year-old.

The mentor rates school progress an 8, saying, "He needs to work on getting an education." Randy is convinced that he is more effective in helping Bryan than the system and wants to continue the relationship.

> I want him to know that I will be there for him as long as I can. He needs a lot of help in getting his education and being on his own. I'm trying to help him get into a vocational technical program.

On Bryan's part, he views Randy as a big brother "who you can tell things to and share a bond together." Bryan decided to have a mentor to see if he could "stay out of trouble," and "it is working so far." "We talk about what is going on in my life and what is happening." Bryan likes the fact that his mentor is a pilot and would like to do flight simulation with him. Bryan said, "You don't have to talk to your mentor about court, or tell him what's going on in your head if you don't want to, and he helps you prepare for life."

> He won't tell people what you tell him. We have a bond where we can talk about personal things and can sleep at night knowing it is between us. I consider him my friend, and I wouldn't ever walk out on him. (Bryan)

Bryan rates the match an 8, saying his mentor has made a difference in his life. "Before him, I was always getting into trouble...fighting...now I rarely do."

Randy, the mentor, views the support he has received from the agency as "extremely inadequate. There is no supervision." Randy sums up his mentor experience as follows:

> This is not a piece of cake. Being a mentor is a challenge since youth are not always responsive to you. They might come around or they might not. They run away a lot. They enjoy being with you even though they may not show it or tell you.

You do make a difference to them at that time and for many years later on in their life. You can help them achieve goals that they might not be able to do in the placement system.

Risk Factors

- Mentor's prior experience with runaway youth could have disillusioned him.

- Having been in foster care for 11 years, it might be hard for youth to bond with a mentor. This appears not to be a barrier, however.

- Mentor's job as an AWAC surveillance pilot takes him away for extended periods of time. Mentor has to change meeting dates with mentee because of flight schedule conflicts.

Assessment

Mentors for older adolescents in placement appears to be a feasible intervention. Despite the difficulties inherent in forming and sustaining meaningful relationships with foster wards, 29 programs in 15 states demonstrated that satisfactory matching is possible. The researchers found that mentors were more likely to express dissatisfaction with a match than mentees. Age differences between mentors and mentees do not pose a barrier to a successful match. We found that mentors age 35 and older were more successful than mentors younger than age 35. In terms of results, a higher percentage of matches in the younger than age 35 group were rated as low in success (45%) as compared with those in the older mentor group.

Ratings in cross-racial matches were lower than for same-race matches. Differences were most striking in the male category, in which white male mentor and white male mentee matches were, on average, 168 points higher than white males paired with nonwhite males. A similar result was noted with nonwhite mentors and white mentees. A comparable pattern was noted in cross-racial pairs with female mentor/mentee matches. The point difference in cross-racial female matches, however, was not as large as for male cross-racial pairs. Table 11.6 summarizes the comparative ratings for same race and cross-race mentor/mentee pairs classified by gender.

The average rating for same-race matches was nearly 1,500 points for male pairs and 1,440 points for female pairs. For cross-racial matches, the average for male pairs was less than 1,300 points; for cross-racial female pairs, the average was 1,379 points. Overall, cross-racial matches for male pairs were rated about 200 points lower per match than same-race pairs.

TABLE 11.6

Cross-Race and Same-Race Mentor/Mentee Mean Ratings Classified by Gender

MENTOR/MENTEE	MENTOR	MENTEE	CUMULATIVE MEAN
WF/WF	632	798	1,430
WF/NWF	624	747	1,371
NWF/WF	625	752	1,377
NWF/NWF	656	793	1,448
WM/WM	727	802	1,529
WM/NWM	559	761	1,350
NWM/WM	566	679	1,245
NWM/NWM	685	780	1,465

NOTE: W = white; NW = nonwhite; F = female; M = male.

The average ratings were about 60 points lower for female cross-race pairs. The results suggest that cross-race mentoring can be difficult. Thomas (2001) noted that racial minorities who have white mentors tend to advance further when their white mentors understand and acknowledge race as a potential barrier to communication. In addition to negative stereotypes that may interfere, Thomas called attention to an element he referred to as "protective hesitation." In protective hesitation, both mentor and mentee tend to avoid raising issues that might be viewed as sensitive. It should be noted that in the 15-state survey, 25% of the mentor-mentee matches were cross-racial. Because cross-racial mentoring is an important element in providing mentor resources for youth in placement, special training and preparation may be required.

References

Freedman, M. (1993). *The kindness of strangers*. San Francisco: Jossey-Bass.

Mech, E. V. (1999). *Mentors as resources in preparing foster adolescents for independent-living* (Final report, Grant No. 90CW1026). Washington, DC: U.S. Department of Health and Human Services, Children's Bureau.

Mech, E. V., & Leonard, E. L. (1988). Volunteers as resources in preparing foster adolescents for self-sufficiency. *Child Welfare, 67*, 595–608.

National Research Council. (1993). *Losing generations: Adolescents in high-risk settings/ Panel on High Risk Youth, Commission on Behavioral and Social Sciences and Education*. Washington, DC: Author.

Thomas, D. A. (2001). The truth about mentoring minorities—Race matters. *Harvard Business Review, 79*, 98–107.

Chapter 12

Wraparound Services, Subsidies, and Mentors as Social Capital

EDMUND V. MECH

> *In the past two decades*
> *social capital...has emerged as one of the*
> *most salient concepts in social sciences.*
>
> —*Nan Lin (2001, p. 3)*

What is meant by *social capital*? How is it different from *human* capital or *cultural* capital? The term *capital* refers to an investment with expected returns. Human capital represents an investment by individuals in themselves. People invest in themselves to acquire knowledge, technical skills, and competencies that are likely to increase their individual earning potential.

The concept of capital as an investment with expected returns fits well with what many refer to as *social capital*. One type of social capital is when communities and organizations invest in resources and social networks to improve productivity and quality of life for its citizens. This interpretation is probably idealistic. Most people are familiar with such terms as *physical capital*, which refers to the acquisition of machines, hardware, buildings, and so forth. *Venture capital* and *financial capital* are familiar terms in the business world. Why should social capital be an unfamiliar notion? With respect to youth well-being, the goal of a social capitalist might be to enhance the developmental potential of children and youth in a particular community. Foster young people are the population of concern; many of them can be described as underdogs in American society. Social analysts often refer to youth growing up at the margins as the "underclass." If social capital represents a community investment with expected returns, can such expected returns be measured in monetary benefits? Our response is in the affirmative. It is well-documented that educational achievement carries a financial payoff. Likewise, reductions in school dropouts, which affect delinquent and antisocial behavior, adolescent pregnancy, and family violence, can be converted to financial returns on investments in community resources.

Building a bridge, a highway, a school, a sports complex, a marina, or an airport, and naming whatever is built after an influential person or a well-known business entity represents a capital investment. Society is not shy about investing taxpayer dollars in these tangible assets. The usual rationale is that whatever is built is an investment and is "good for the community." By the same token, the development of resources, social networks, and assets that contribute to the positive development of children and youth should be viewed as good for the community.

Theorists in sociology are debating the boundaries of the term *social capital* (Lin, 2001). When introduced by Coleman (1988), it was defined as any societal resource that provided beneficial returns for individuals and communities. If communities desire to create "opportunity structures" for young people, including youth who are former, current, or potential foster wards, action is needed that creates resources that enhance these youths' preparation for self-sufficiency. A unifying principle for the social capital movement is the view that "people who do better in society are somehow better connected...social capital structures...can create for certain individuals or groups a competitive advantage in pursuing their ends. Better connected people enjoy higher returns" (Burt, 2001, p. 32). The elements that compose a comprehensive social capital approach include:

- Specific assets and resources are available in a community,

- Information about assets and resources is available to target youth,

- Guidance informs youth how they can access community resources, and

- The youth use the available resources.

In addition, a transitional resource specialist or advocate would be an asset in helping youth establish, solidify, and sustain connections with community resources.

It is difficult to argue against the proposition that youth in transition with good networks and a variety of connections are more likely to achieve economic self-sufficiency. Caseworkers, foster parents, and allied agency staff can help foster wards build social capital connections. As a long-term strategy, however, reliance on agency staff and independent-living coordinators is insufficient. As youth transition into their communities, contacts with former agency staff may taper off, workers leave jobs, and connections with foster caregivers may be disrupted. It is essential that foster wards connect with individuals who are not employees of the placement system. At some point, "natural system" connections must fill the gap. It is important to link foster wards with citizens who represent a cross-section of the community in which youth will live and work. It is in the best interests of all foster wards to gain experience in building a natural-system network for themselves. Independent-living plans should describe efforts to develop a transitional network. Although there are no hard and fast rules as to what resources should be available, it is possible to identify several resources that can be decisive in helping youth move toward economic self-sufficiency such as wraparound services, subsidies for housing, education, medical/health care, and citizen-mentors.

Wraparound Services as Social Capital

Theory
In the field of child welfare, *wraparound* is interpreted as a pattern of individual care in which a variety of services are targeted to the needs of a particular youth. Wraparound services are typically used to: (a) prevent out-of-home placements or (b) to avoid inserting youth into a more restrictive placement. Placement in a more restrictive setting usually means an institutional facility, often away from the youth's local community.

Skiba and Nichols (2000) described the evolution of the system of care approach as a response to the increase in children placed in residential/institutional facilities. Impetus for wraparound services resulted from a federal initiative in the 1980s by the National Institute of Mental Health under the Children and Adolescent Service System Program (CASSP). CASSP focused on developing a network of community- and family-based services so that youth with emotional and behavioral problems could be served in their local communities. Skiba and Nichols summarized wraparound services as an alternative to "expending local and state resources on expensive residential placements" (p. 23). The wraparound alternative refers to developing a network of services that enable children in need of treatment to remain in their home community and to live in environments that are less restrictive than residential/institutional placement. Early evaluative studies "uniformly report modest gains for children and families receiving wraparound services" (Maluccio, Ainsworth, & Thoburn, 2000, p. 103).

Wraparound programs require a dramatic shift in philosophy—one that moves from a categorical, uncoordinated, "one-service-at-a-time" approach to a community-based, team approach for service delivery.

Criteria for a Wraparound Plan

Conditions considered essential in providing a wraparound service are:

1. Service must be community-based, with emphasis on interagency cooperation.

2. A team approach is essential. Wraparound teams of five to seven members should include nonprofessionals and professionals. Most team members should be nonprofessionals (i.e., natural-system people), preferably including parents and family members.

3. The service must focus on an individualized service plan.

4. The team must designate a team coordinator who takes responsibility for activating the plan.

5. The team implements the plan and periodically reviews its progress.

Application of Wraparound Criteria: Analysis of Three Plans

This section focuses on analysis of three service plans that have been designated as wraparound plans. Which ones appear to meet the criteria for wraparound? Which ones do not?

Wraparound Plan 1—John

The White family is a wraparound family that was referred to the child and adolescent screening committee by a school social worker. The school was concerned about John, a 9-year-old boy who was experiencing serious problems in school. Following an interview with the family, the screening committee found the Whites suitable for wraparound services based on several criteria:

- John was at risk of school failure.

- John has emotional problems diagnosed as attention deficit/hyperactivity disorder (ADHD).

- There are five children in the family younger than 10 years old.

The mother is young (23 years old), and the Whites are a blended family. Bob (25 years old) is the father of Mike (10 years old) and John (9 years old) from his first marriage. Sally (23 years old) brought her 6-year-old daughter, Catherine, to this union from her first marriage. Sally is the primary caregiver while Bob works. They are loving, caring parents with many strengths and a strong commitment to helping their children and improving their current family situation. The family rents a small, two-bedroom house and struggles to make ends meet on Bob's salary. The Whites have limited emotional support from extended family. Their relationship with Bob's parents is strained, and Sally's father resides halfway across the country. A few close friends and members of the church they attend compose their natural support system.

The team members are Bob and Sally White, the wraparound coordinator for the local area network, the social worker from John's school, John's teacher, and a therapist who had previously worked with the family during a crisis with John. The team identified the following needs: (a) special help for John in school, (b) help for Sally in the home with household duties, (c) someone to spend extra time with John and Mike after school, (d) training and education for the parents on how to deal with John's behaviors, and (e) assistance in purchasing necessary supplies (diapers, detergent, cleaning items, etc.).

The child and family team developed a plan to address the family needs. They requested a meeting with school personnel to get extra help for John in school in several areas. The team located a person in the community who was hired to help Sally with household duties (laundry, dishes, etc.). Fortunately, this individual was also qualified to teach Sally how to work with John's ADHD and negative behaviors. A male with child welfare experience was hired to serve as a mentor for John and Mike to work on anger management, social skill development, and relationship development. The team requested financial assistance to buy cleaning supplies, diapers, and items like shelves and baskets to better organize the house and make efficient use of limited space. Finally, the church that the Whites attend sponsored the family and helped with meals, babysitting, and clothing donations.

Analysis of Plan 1

Most purists would not rate the plan as a genuine wraparound service. On a scale of 1 to 10, with 10 representing a high wraparound score, Plan 1 would be near a 5. Plan 1 represents a quasiwraparound effort, but is an effort that the agency can be proud of. Positive results have occurred. A wraparound purist might argue for improvement in the following areas: (a) John must be on the team, (b) friends of the family should be on the team, and (c) a church member should be on the team. The plea for nonprofessionals is that a natural-system team is needed when the professionals leave. (d) After six months, community area network members should take over the team. Professionals should be secondary. (e) It appears that many team members are being paid to be there. The team lacks volunteers from the community. Professionals appear to lead the team, which may hamper the involvement of a natural support system for a long-term effort.

Wraparound Plan 2—Latoya

Latoya is a 17-year-old African American female who currently is in placement at a residential facility. Her presenting reasons for entering a behavior disorders program included: running away from home, drug and alcohol use, poor relationship with her mother, truancy from school, gang involvement, fighting with peers, poor anger management, and lack of self-esteem. Latoya has worked on all of the areas listed and has the tools to help when she returns home to live with her mother. This case describes a wraparound plan to help Latoya and her mother build a support system and obtain necessary services to aid Latoya in returning home. This family has multiple needs and has agreed to participate in the wraparound team process.

Latoya's church pastor was assigned to serve as facilitator of the team. The pastor schedules a meeting that includes Latoya, her mother, her grandmother, her uncle, a neighbor, Latoya's mentor, a couple of church members, and Latoya's school counselor. The team includes people who the family invited as a natural support system—community members, professionals, and a facilitator. The first meeting included introductions and an explanation of the team. The team was to help this family build from their strengths, set goals with the family, help them achieve their goals, provide a support system, and provide the necessary help this family needed. Strengths that were identified include: determination, desire to succeed, willingness to put forth the effort to achieve goals, and a trusting relationship between Latoya and her mother. Goals this family have set for themselves include:

- Latoya will graduate from high school.

- Latoya will maintain a positive circle of friends.

- Latoya will use appropriate anger management tools.

- Latoya's mother will use appropriate parenting skills.

- The family will build on their positive relationship.

- The family will avoid drug and alcohol use.

The team meets two to three times a month to discuss the family's needs, goals, and solutions. Resources are located or developed within the community to provide the necessary aid to this family. The following are services and resources that have been activated since the family's initial meeting. Latoya's school counselor meets with her weekly to check on how things are going in school. Tutoring is provided by the school when Latoya needs extra help with her homework assignments. A YMCA pass is provided to family for extracurricular activities. Latoya has joined a sports team and the church's youth choir to help establish a positive support system. Latoya has weekly meetings with her mentor to discuss how she can handle daily stresses. Church members, her grandmother, and her uncle check in with family weekly. The family attends support groups for drug and alcohol use. The wraparound team continues to meet monthly. The goal is to review family progress and to support the gains that have been made. The support system consists mainly of nonprofessionals, drawn from family and natural-systems individuals.

Analysis of Plan 2
Plan 2 is likely a convincing application of wraparound theory. Several reasons substantiate a high wraparound rating. First, power is given to natural systems that are derived from the local community. Second, authority and leadership resides in large part with the family; agencies are in the background. Third, this wraparound team is family and community based, is flexible, has wide participation, and meets as needed. This team appears to work. Because the team has a natural-system nucleus, it may sustain itself on a long-term basis, whereas teams dominated by agency staff are usually time-limited and fall short of providing continuity of service.

Wraparound Plan 3—April
April is a 15-year-old African American female. She has been in a residential placement for more than three years. The approximate cost to the state is $210,000. Prior to residential placement, April was in a relative home, then in a nonrelative foster home. While in a relative home, an uncle sexually abused April and her younger sister. Relative foster care was identified as April's permanency goal. There were four attempts to link April with various relatives identified by the state as appropriate resources. Each attempt reached the point of testing weekly extended home visits but ended when relatives gave excuses why April could not visit on a particular weekend. Finally, relatives would not return agency calls. Shortly after the last identified relative resource was eliminated, a

24-year-old sister with four children of her own emerged as a resource. April's sister, Toni, had previously been noted for neglect of three of her four children. The children were returned from foster placement a few months before Toni contacted April. In an administrative decision, the agency's placement review team notified April's caseworker to activate "step-down" wraparound services for her (i.e., transition from residential placement to a less restrictive, less costly setting). When presented with the idea of a step-down wraparound plan, April refused. Despite April's refusal, the state child welfare agency ordered the worker to put together a wraparound plan. The wraparound team consisted of the state agency administrator, the caseworker from the residential facility in which April was placed, and April herself. The following series of events transpired.

April was asked to submit information about her sister, Toni, as a possible resource, and to provide a list of people she wanted on the team.

The state agency caseworker who had been involved with April in her previous foster home placement was invited to assist in preparing a plan.

The state agency completed a background check on Toni and approved weekend visitations. No other placement resources were identified. A number of relatives were recontacted, but each declined having April in their home, stating that the sexual abuse charges had divided the family, causing arguments and bad feelings.

Weekend visits with April and Toni were reportedly going well. The team met with Toni to determine if April could be placed in her home. Toni accepted this plan but indicated that April would need to find a job that would pay enough so that she would be self-sufficient. The tentative plan for April to move in with her older sister was stymied because Toni was not eligible to be licensed as a relative foster home because of the substantiated neglect reports.

At this point, the child and adolescent local area network became involved and provided a coordinator for the wraparound plan. One proposal was that April be placed with her sister with a permanency goal of independent living. By that time, there were reports from April that weekend visits at her sister's home were not going as well as had been reported. April complained that she was used as a babysitter while Toni and a boyfriend went out. Also, Toni and her boyfriend were involved in several fights while April was at home.

Little progress was made on a step-down wraparound plan. April reported that she wanted to stay at the residential facility through the school year so she could graduate. She resisted moving from residential placement because it might delay graduation from high school.

The wraparound team arrived at a compromise. They requested licensing approval to place April in a supervised independent-living program when she graduated from high school. Reportedly, the step-down wraparound committee was not entirely satisfied with the independent-living plan, although April was looking forward to moving into a supervised independent-living placement.

Analysis of Plan 3

Plan 3 has severe limitations. There was little or no community participation. A wraparound purist would point out that if April's plan was genuinely community based, many local, nontraditional resources would be offered. A reasonable step would be to initiate contact with church groups and attempt to involve church leaders and members in the team. In situations like April's, when there is little or no family potential or friends as resources, it is important to look to the community. Ideally, community education for resource development is an ongoing process and should precede decisions to re-place youth in less restrictive settings. It takes time to develop relationships and trust within communities. Wraparound Plan 3 receives low marks because community involvement is virtually nonexistent.

Subsidies as Social Capital

Political theorists draw a distinction between a subsidy and welfare. One definition of *subsidy* is "a transfer payment from the public treasury to a private enterprise or person" (Stone, 1980, p. 253). The term *welfare* also refers to transfer payments. What differentiates the two terms?

A key element is that a subsidy is a form of contract between donor and donee, with the expectation that benefits will accrue to both parties. Governments offer subsidies to organizations and individuals to accomplish certain objectives. With respect to welfare, and in particular to entitlement programs, recipients are usually not obligated to engage in activities viewed as beneficial to society.

Issues of obligation and mutual responsibility in entitlement programs have received little public policy attention. A notable exception is the political scientist Lawrence Mead, who concluded, "Federal programs that support the disadvantaged...have been permissive in character, not authoritative...they have given benefits to their recipients, but have set few requirements for how they ought to function in return" (Mead, 1986, p. 1).

Whereas a welfare recipient is under no obligation to do anything in exchange for receiving transfer payments, subsidies require recipients to meet performance standards specified in a contract. Subsidy advocates assert that expenditures are of general benefit to society. Welfare advocates usually do not address the issue. As a consequence, subsidy as a policy instrument is viewed with far more political favor than is welfare. Although the myriad of means-tested welfare programs ask little of those who receive benefits, can there be doubt that benefits accrue to society? The much maligned Aid to Families with Dependent Children (AFDC) program has helped needy families stay together and quite likely has prevented thousands of children from placement in foster care for "reasons of poverty." Unfortunately, little has been written about the benefits that accrue to society via means-tested programs. Consider the following example.

Based on data from the foster youth project at the University of Illinois, researchers interviewed a sample of 194 females who formerly were state wards approximately two years after their emancipation from state care. The researchers collected information on AFDC status, Medicaid, public housing subsidies, food stamps, and WIC, the Women, Infants, and Children program. Nearly 45% of participants were AFDC recipients at the age 20 to 21 follow-up. What was apparent, regardless of AFDC status, was that emancipated female foster wards were significant users of mean-tested resources. To equate non-AFDC status with zero use of public resources is a mistake. Consider the following use of means-tested programs by non-AFDC females: 69% relied on Medicaid, 33% used food stamps, 19% used WIC, and 12% benefited from housing subsidies. These data suggest a continuum of need. Nearly 80% of foster wards reported having to rely on one or more programs or services in the social safety net. Without assistance from existing social safety net programs, the short-term effects on emancipated foster wards would have been quite damaging. Social safety net programs are a vital resource for foster youth in transition. Means-tested programs are a form of subsidy and provide valuable assistance to foster wards who are becoming self-sufficient.

Two prominent examples of subsidy programs in the field of independent living are independent-living subsidies and tuition waivers for education and training. One of the early models is the transitional independent-living subsidy. An example of structure, language, and elements that may appear in an independent-living subsidy plan is as follows:

Purpose

The independent-living subsidy permits a young person 17 years of age and older who is in the custody of the Department of Human Services to live without daily substitute parental supervision. The purpose of the program is to provide an avenue through which the youth can learn to live independently and responsibly.

Eligibility

- Youth is at least 17 years of age but not yet 21 years of age.

- Youth has been in the custody of the department or other state agency for at least six months prior.

- Youth has written approval from parent or legal custodian, if younger than 18.

- Youth has a plan for self-sufficiency that is achievable within 18 months.

- Youth has demonstrated an ability to handle independence, as evidenced by responsible behavior during placement, such as sustaining part-time employment, maintaining a savings account, and demonstrating regular attendance at school or a training program.

- Youth is capable of contributing a minimum of $100 per month to his or her financial support.

- Youth has obtained the basic life skills necessary for beginning independent living, as evidenced either by satisfactory completion of independent-living training provided by the foster parents, service provider, worker, school, or community volunteer, or by demonstration through the practical application of these skills.

- Youth is willing to work with a responsible adult from the community who will be the youth's volunteer independent-living advisor until the goal of independence in achieved.

Standards for Living Arrangement

Independent-living residences shall meet the following minimum standards:

- Be located so as to provide reasonably convenient access to schools, places of employment, or services as required by the individual.

- Comply with applicable state and local zoning, fire, sanitary, and safety regulations.

- Provide a setting that is conducive to progressing toward independence as determined by the state agency.

Worker must determine that the residence meets minimum standards before a lease is signed or a commitment made to use the residence.

Transitional Independent-Living Plan

Once the worker has identified a youth for whom independent living may be appropriate or a youth requests an independent-living arrangement, a plan is developed and submitted to the area administrator and the administrative review committee for approval, along with documentation that all other eligibility requirements have been met. The plan is a written agreement developed by the worker, the youth, and the volunteer independent-living advisor.

The written agreement shall include, but is not limited to the following:

- The responsibilities of the youth, the worker, and the advisor.

- The anticipated length of time independent-living support will be needed until the youth is fully independent (not to exceed 24 months).

- An education/training and work plan that will provide full-time activity for the youth.

- A plan for assisting youth in increasing his or her knowledge and skills in such areas as budgeting and household management.

- A plan for supervision of the youth, including worker contacts, other agencies to be included, and contacts with the advisor.

- A plan for financing independent living specifying the amount the youth will contribute and the amount to be provided by the department.

- A statement explaining how the department's portion will decrease as the youth's income increases.

- Target dates for when the youth's income will increase and when he or she will become self-sufficient.

- A budget outlining the youth's proposed monthly expenditures.

- A statement confirming the youth's responsibility to inform the agency within 72 hours of any major changes in his or her situation (i.e., loses job, leaves educational/training program, moves, is arrested, etc.)

Subsidy Agreement

Expenses related to setting up a household may be partially subsidized by the department. Initial expenses may include such things as rent deposits, utility deposits, bedding, and kitchen equipment. Requests for assistance with start-up costs should list specifically what is needed. The requests are submitted to the coordinating social services supervisor for approval. The coordinating social services supervisor can authorize payment up to $450.

The youth may elect to save up to 35% of his or her earned income without affecting the independent-living subsidy. The maximum combined income a youth in the transitional independent-living subsidy program is allowed is $500. The $500 includes the youth's earned income, minus the savings, any unearned income, and the department's subsidy payment.

For example, Jack earns $160 per month as a checker at a local supermarket. He elects to save 30%, or $48. His total contribution for rent per month is $112. The $112 is subtracted from the allowable monthly income of $500, leaving $388, which is the amount of the subsidy.

Youth electing to save a percentage of their earned income must establish a savings account. This account will be jointly held with the area administrator or coordinating social services supervisor and requires both signatures for withdrawal of funds. Money accrued in the savings account can be spent only if the worker and youth have established a plan for such expenditures. Expenditures might include the purchase of special work equipment, household equipment, additional furnishings, and so forth.

The agreement prepared by the worker, youth, and advisor will indicate the time period in which the youth will require the subsidy payment and the target dates at which his or her income will increase. It is expected that the youth's income will gradually increase and that the subsidy payments will gradually decrease during the time allotted in the written agreement.

Tuition Waivers

The tuition waiver for education/training is an area in which subsidy expansion is rapidly progressing. Educational achievement appears to be the main strategy used by states to help foster wards move toward economic self-sufficiency. The costs of postsecondary education or specialized train-ing are escalating. College tuition costs have virtually doubled in the past decade (Codrey, 1999). Various kinds of financial assistance are available, including grants, scholarships, work-study stipends, and tuition waivers. Tuition waivers for foster youth are receiving significant attention. A num-ber of states have enacted legislation that permits foster wards to enroll in state-supported institutions, including vocational programs with a tuition fee waiver. Table 12.1 summarizes eligibility guidelines for three tuition-waiver states: Texas, Florida, and Maine.

Across the three states, tuition waivers apply only at state-supported vocational schools, colleges, and universities. Variability exists on other criteria such as number of youth who can receive a tuition waiver and whether or not waivers are time-limited. A *time-limited waiver* refers to the number of semesters the state will support students via a tuition waiver. For community college and vocational schools, the limit is four semesters or approximately two years. Eight semesters (or approximately four years) is the maximum for a four-year university program. Tuition-waiver policy usually stipulates that recipients must maintain a satisfactory grade point average. The typical requirement is a minimum grade average of C. Other tuition-waiver benefits may include financial aid to help pay for room and board. When translated into monetary costs, tuition-waiver sub-sidies amount to thousands of dollars invested in the educational futures of foster wards.

Citizen-Mentors as Social Capital

Since enactment of the landmark independent-living legislation in 1987, there has been a dramatic increase in support for mentors for adolescents in placement. Mentors for foster youth represent a diverse spectrum of citizen-volunteers. Positive results are likely to occur when natural-systems citizens are recruited as mentors. Nearly 50 years ago, speaking before the Volunteers Personnel Committee of the YWCA in New York City, Eduard C. Lindeman, a noted social philosopher, posed the ques-tion, "What would happen if, in the United States, all citizens who…serve as volunteers were suddenly to 'go on strike'" (Mech & Leonard, 1988)? Lindeman's response to his own question was that professionals would continue to operate their programs, institutions, and agencies in a vacuum. They would find themselves insulated from society. Support for public and private programs would erode, and "democracy will have committed suicide" (Schindler-Rainman & Lippitt, 1971).

TABLE 12.1

Tuition Waiver States

ELIGIBILITY	TEXAS	FLORIDA	MAINE
Youth must still be in foster care or independent-living arrangement.	No	Yes	No
Youth must have been in custody at the time of high school graduation or general equivalency examination.	Yes or was in care at the time of his or her 18th birthday	No	Yes
Adopted youth are eligible.	Yes if the youth was in care on his or her 14th birthday	Yes if adopted after 1/1/98	No

GUIDELINES			
Tuition waiver only valid at state-supported vocational schools, colleges, and universities.	Yes	Yes	Yes
Tuition waiver is time limited.	Yes	Yes	No
Tuition waiver may only be used after other resources are exhausted.	No	Yes	Yes, but a change is pending
Tuition waiver is available to a limited number of youth.	No	No	Yes—presently limited to 25 youth per year

SOURCE: Codrey (1999).

Citizen-volunteers fill important roles in society. The message for state child welfare agencies and allied tax-supported programs is clear. Public social services should involve volunteers in their work. Typically, citizen-volunteers are underused and, in many instances, are ignored. There is an element of elitism in the notion that professionals and experts have decisive answers to social problems. Citizen-volunteers should be recruited as members of teams to help transition foster wards to self-sufficiency. Considerable evidence points to the finding that a significant adult in the lives of young people can be a protective factor and an asset in helping wards transition to adulthood.

It is difficult to envision one-to-one mentoring without using community citizens. The trend toward the personalization of social services cannot be met by available agency personnel. Citizen-volunteers are needed because the economy and budget restrictions will not permit large increases in the ratio of agency workers to clients. Volunteerism in America has solid roots. At this particular moment in political history, endorsements for use of citizen-volunteers in human services emanate from all segments of society. Volunteers may be a critical factor in linking foster wards to vital community resources.

Mentors are drawn from several sources, including former foster youth, college students, and peers. Evidence tends to focus on adults as mentors. Other than the University of Illinois project, *Mentors as Resources in Preparing Foster Adolescents for Independent-Living*, little empirical information exists on the topic of mentoring services for youth in foster care (Mech, 1999).

Based on information collected from 29 programs in 15 states, including in-person interviews with 280 mentors and 272 mentees ($N = 552$) the following conclusions were drawn:

- Mentors for older adolescents appear to be a feasible intervention. One finding that was impressive was the extent to which mentor/mentee pairs rated matches as effective. Nearly 60% of the matches were rated as "highly successful" or "above average" in success.

- Age differences between mentor and mentee were not a barrier to a successful match.

- Cross-race match ratings were significantly lower and more problematic than same-race matches.

- Key elements required for effective mentor services appear to be missing. A majority of program coordinators reported administrative support as weak. Because most programs use citizen-volunteers, administrators tend to think that such programs can be operated on a shoestring budget. One major shortcoming in mentor programs is the high percentage of part-time program coordinators. For many, 50% time is a luxury. For most, time allocated for coordination was described as insufficient.

- The mentoring system emphasized contact and relationship building prior to emancipation. Little emphasis was placed on continuing mentor/mentee contact after discharge. Many mentor-mentee pairs remained in postemancipation contact, but did so as a natural outgrowth of the relationship, not as a result of system expectation. Continuity of mentoring after youth leave state care continues as a need.

- It is imperative that agencies scale down expectations that foster wards can make large lifestyle changes in short periods of time. Mentors need to be provided with continuous support and training throughout the match, as opposed to a brief orientation at the beginning.

- Emphasis is needed on selecting mentees who understand and accept the premise that if mentoring is to work for them, each youth has to make a commitment to active participation.

Assessment

A vital element in creating opportunity structures for youth is the need to connect foster wards to sources of social capital. To do so, public and private agencies must first document the types of social capital resources available in the community. Public and private agencies need to assume advocacy roles and specify the resources needed to achieve an effective social capital network. Examples of social capital resources that can be decisive in helping foster wards progress toward economic self-sufficiency are:

- wraparound services, with emphasis on community-based, natural-systems participation;

- independent-living subsidies;

- educational assistance via tuition waivers and related supports; and

- citizen-mentors, with emphasis on mentor continuity for a minimum of one year after a foster ward emancipates from state care.

In effect, placement agencies and service providers will be saying to a community, "Help us help foster youth who are aging out of the system to become productive citizens." Key agencies and youth-serving organizations need to assume leadership roles in directing community attention to the importance of citizen participation in contributing to the future of its youth.

References

Burt, R. (2001). Structural holes versus network closure as social capital. In N. Lin, K. Cook, & R. Burt (Eds.), *Social capital. Theory and research* (pp. 31–56). New York: Aldine De Gruyter.

Codrey, M. (1999). Tuition waivers: One way states are helping youths prepare for the future. *Daily Living, 13*, 1–3.

Coleman, J. (1988). Social capital in the creation of human capital. *American Journal of Sociology, 94*, 95–121.

Lin, N. (2001). Building a network theory of social capital. In N. Lin, K. Cook, & R. Burt (Eds.), *Social capital. Theory and research* (pp. 3–29). New York: Aldine De Gruyter.

Maluccio, A., Ainsworth, F., & Thoburn, J. (2000). *Child welfare outcome research in the United States, the United Kingdom, and Australia* (pp. 101–106.) Washington, DC: CWLA Press.

Mead, L. M. (1986). *Beyond entitlement. The social obligations of citizenship*. New York: Free Press.

Mech, E., & Leonard, E. (1988). Volunteers as resources in preparing foster adolescents for self-sufficiency. In E. Mech (Ed.), *Independent living for at-risk adolescents* (pp. 99–100). Washington, DC: Child Welfare League of America.

Mech, E. V. (1999). *Mentors as resources in preparing foster adolescents for independent-living* (Final report, Grant No. 90CW1026). Washington, DC: U.S. Department of Health and Human Services, Children's Bureau.

Schindler-Rainman, E., & Lippitt, R. (1971). *The volunteer community: Creative use of human resources*. Washington, DC: Center for a Voluntary Society.

Skiba, R., & Nichols, S. (2000). What works in wraparound programming. In M. Kluger, G. Alexander, & P. Curtis (Eds.), *What works in child welfare* (pp. 23–32). Washington, DC: CWLA Press.

Stone, A. (1980). Subsidy as a policy instrument. In J. Brigham & D. Brown (Eds.), *Policy implementation* (pp. 249–269). Beverly Hills, CA: Sage.

Chapter 13

Transitional Services for Emancipated Foster Youth

JANET LEGLER LUFT

The Texas Profile

Since 1986, Texas has been providing independent-living services to older teens in foster care. The program is known as Preparation for Adult Living (PAL), and the Texas Department of Protective and Regulatory Services administers it. Texas is divided into 11 regions. Each region has at least one PAL program coordinator who ensures that youth are provided services in collaboration with local community organizations. In 1999, 3,110 youth ages 16 to 21 years old received PAL services. The core of the program is the provision of lifeskills training, made up of the following elements: personal and interpersonal skills, housing, transportation, planning for the future, job skills, health, and money management.

Texas provides a transitional living allowance to PAL participants to help them make successful transitions to independence. As of December 2000, the total stipend per youth was $800, which is divided into allotments and distributed over three to four months, depending on the needs of the youth. With passage of the Chafee Foster Care Independence Act, increasing the stipend to $1,000 per youth is under consideration. The allowance is an integral aspect of foster youth money management training. The stipend has two aims: (a) to provide an incentive for youth to participate in and complete lifeskills training, and (b) to help youth make the transition from foster care to independent living. Youth must attend training in five of the core areas to qualify for PAL transitional funds. PAL staff visit youth at their apartments and complete an aftercare report that includes a budget. The state agency provides qualified participants with a one-time $200 stipend for household supplies including sheets, towels, and cooking utensils. This amount is projected to increase to $300 per youth. Youth must provide receipts for the items purchased. PAL staff, caseworkers, PAL contractors, or foster care providers often accompany youth to stores to assist them with comparative shopping.

With respect to postsecondary education policy, a youth is exempt from tuition and fees at state-supported colleges and universities if in foster care under the supervision of the Texas Department of Protective and Regulatory Services on or after:

- the day of the student's 14th birthday, if the student was also eligible for adoption (parental rights have been terminated) on or after that day; and

- the day the students enrolls in college as an undergraduate student, not later than the third anniversary of discharge from foster care; the date the student graduated from high school or received a general equivalency diploma, whichever is earlier; or the student's 21st birthday.

Tuition Waiver Legislation

The original Texas tuition waiver legislation was enacted in 1993, followed by a series of amendments in 1997. In fiscal year (FY) 1993 to 1994, only 76 foster wards used a tuition waiver. In FY 1998 to 1999, 339 foster wards used a tuition waiver, a 400% increase in participation. Of this number, 196 attended community college, 22 enrolled in technical institutes, and 121, or 36%, matriculated at a four-year college or university. Information for numbers of youth completing degrees or certificates in the various programs is unavailable.

The tuition waiver legislation has created opportunities for former foster care youth who previously had little or no hope of obtaining postsecondary education. Tim, age 20, uses a tuition waiver. He stated that at age 17, he had a strong interest in going to college but did not want to stay in foster care. He was tired of the rules and the hassle. He said that PAL and the tuition waiver kept him from leaving foster care early. Looking back, he now realizes that he would not have been able to make it on his own at 17. He said,

PAL helps, but it hits you hard once you are on your own. You are standing in the middle of the rat race and you don't know what to do. Anybody can survive, but I wanted to live. Friends gave me tips, and my foster family helped, but you have to do it yourself.

Tim found the transitional living allowance and household supplies stipend invaluable in getting him started on the road to independence. He now has his own apartment, is working at a state school for youth with disabilities, and plans to return to college in a few months.

Several Texas universities, including Texas A&M at Commerce, offer enhanced support for foster care youth. Texas A&M at Commerce convenes an annual college orientation conference each February for foster youth who are high school juniors and seniors. The university offers residential housing scholarships of $500 per semester and provides faculty and staff mentors for all PAL students. Residential housing costs range from $1,200 to $1,500 per semester. Meals cost approximately $1,000 per semester. Staff at the university assist youth in obtaining federal financial aid to cover the costs of room and board. Organizers at the university also host a barbecue, at which PAL students informally meet potential mentors. Many of the PAL students obtain part-time jobs with the help of mentors. PAL students receive support and encouragement that helps them make the transition from foster care to college.

Connie, who earned a degree in social work, and Derek, who is studying for a degree in counseling, feel that the extra support has made a real difference in their lives. They want to help others and to give something back to their communities. Connie is now a caseworker with child protective services, and Derek helps to coordinate the annual college conference. The PAL program will continue to seek partnerships with more colleges and universities so that youth can more easily transition to higher education.

Texas Youth Leadership Committee

The more opportunities youth have to be involved in positions of leadership and responsibility, the more they rise to the occasion. One such opportunity is the Texas Youth Leadership Committee (YLC), which is an advisory group. This committee includes one current or former foster care youth, age 16 to 21, from each region of Texas. A youth may serve for up to two years on the committee. The group meets quarterly to work on improving services to children and youth in the foster care system. Providing a voice for Texan youth, the members of this committee are energetic, insightful, and a gratifying addition to the program. Youth on the YLC are role models, advocates, and leaders within their communities. Regional PAL staff keep casework staff and care providers informed about committee issues. Each year, four youth from the committee present YLC recommendations to the board of directors. Since, 1994, the committee has (a) developed of a video called "From the Youth Perspective" that is used in training care providers, staff, and mentors; (b) made a policy change to allow youth to stay in paid foster care an additional three and a half months (typically in the summer), if they are scheduled to begin college or enter the military or vocational training; and (c) expanded mentor programs and social support systems.

Darlene, age 24, was an outspoken leader on the YLC for two years. She received a degree in finance from Texas A&M University at College Station in 1999. While attending the university, she worked as a PAL regional youth specialist and in the university president's office. She had a positive attitude and encouraged other youth to hold their heads high and not use their past as a crutch. She used the transitional living allowance, household supplies stipend, and college tuition waiver. She worked as a management trainee for Wal-Mart in Atlanta. She is now a caseworker with child protective services. Darlene stated,

> I would like youth in foster care to get more recognition for the good they do. You always hear about the bad, and that adversely affects them. The [YLC] is influential. If the YLC representatives stay up to date and are a proactive voice, they can find ways to make people aware of the concerns and contributions of youth in foster care to our society.

Expanding Transitional Resources

The Casey Family Program and the Center for Public Policy Priorities are conducting a research study called the Foster Care Transitions Project, regarding youth who transitioned from foster care to independence in the Austin and San Antonio areas of Texas. The purpose of the study is to identify the challenges young people face when leaving the foster care system. Based on follow-up contacts, the major barriers include:

- Lack of a "home base" to use for emergencies, holidays, and other emotional support;

- Lack of experience in job skills/training;

- Mental and physical health problems, and difficulty accessing health care; and

- Lack of safe, affordable housing.

In the summer of 2000, the Casey Family Program opened a transitional living center in San Antonio that offers one-stop help and support for former foster youth. The essential elements in the San Antonio program are:

- A staff person from the local community college to help with enrollment and financial aid;

- A job counselor;

- Assistance finding safe, affordable housing; and

- Assistance accessing community resources.

Another valuable resource is "For Youth/By Youth." The Casey Family Program developed this foster care alumni project. This program is located in the San Antonio and Austin areas. It advocates for and supports former foster care youth. This grassroots organization has had growing pains, but the possibilities are exciting for developing a statewide support network of former foster care youth.

Although Texas has been a leader in preparatory services for youth transitioning from foster care, resources remain limited to aid youth once they emancipate from the system. Because a majority of youth are not attending institutions of higher education after emancipation, there is concern for their futures. The literature indicates that not only are more services needed for this population, but better collaboration and support is needed for these young adults. In an attempt to address this need in 1999, Texas began a pilot program in the Beaumont area designated Project YES (Youth Emancipating from the System). An advisory committee was formed that consisted of child protective services staff, PAL staff, local and state agencies, private industry, foster parents, universities, and faith-based institutions. The YES committee enhances current services, provides support and mentoring services, and makes services for youth more coordinated and user-friendly. In addition to the regional committee, a statewide Project YES advisory committee establishes partnerships with other state agencies and foster care providers to identify reforms that improve services. Members of this committee include: the Texas Workforce Commission, the Texas Department of Mental Health and

Mental Retardation, the Texas Education Agency, adult protective services, the Texas Rehabilitation Commission, and the Texas Department of Housing and Community Affairs. One of the goals of Project YES is to develop formal protocols among agencies to streamline the delivery of needed services to young adults.

The Beaumont region's collaborative effort is providing youth emancipating from the system with the following services: intensive transitional living case management for up to one year after discharge from foster care, a resource bank, sponsor families or mentors, and supervised transitional housing. A *resource bank* is a database that contains contact information on available local community resources for housing, employment, education, vocations, child care, health, and other needs. A sponsor family can be a church member, former teacher, former coach, or employer. They are members of the community who have a concern for helping foster youth become productive members of society.

The PAL special project in the Austin, Texas, region is a collaboration of private agencies dedicated to providing a system of support for youth aging out of foster care. The Casey Family Program, Lifeworks, Marywood Children and Family Services, Presbyterian Children's Home, and Caring Family Network work together to assist youth with ongoing case management and independent-living services. Assistance includes helping youth obtain a suitable living arrangement and a job, access health care, manage money, and plan for the future.

In addition, five other regions in Texas have implemented special projects aimed at providing similar services to youth leaving care. Local community organizations assist by providing matching funds for various independent-living projects. The PAL program plans to identify what works and replicate effective components of these projects throughout the state.

Future Plans

Support from external stakeholders is invaluable in helping foster care youth transition into independent living. Plans for the future include expanding aftercare services in all areas of Texas. The state held a public meeting in April 2000 to obtain input from its external partners for implementation of the Chafee Foster Care Independence Act. Many people, including former foster care youth and foster parents, provided insightful testimony. The main recommendation was to implement the provisions of the Chafee Foster Care Independence Act, including:

- Extend Medicaid in Texas for youth 18 to 21 years of age who have left foster care.

- Change the Texas rule to increase the asset resource limit to $10,000 for foster care.

- Use new funds for room and board assistance, and provide transitional housing opportunities for young adults.

- Provide realistic lifeskills training for youth, as well as specialized training for foster care providers.

- Lower the age for federal funding of the PAL program to 14.

Texas plans to use a portion of the allowable funding for transitional room and board for youth ages 18 to 21 who have left foster care. The state agency is working with the Texas Department of Health and the Health and Human Services Commission to identify the cost of providing extended Medicaid coverage to youth ages 18 to 21 who have left foster care. The agency plans to meet with the Texas Department of Human Services to discuss a referral process for the extension of Medicaid. In coordination with community partners, Texas plans to expand its current independent-living program across systems and to look at the possibility of engaging new constituencies.

Housing is a critical need for youth aging out of foster care. Texas will explore safe, affordable housing options for youth, such as host families and supportive landlords in local communities. Youth with disabilities who age out of the system have additional difficulty making the transition to adult living. In an effort to help these youth, Texas is proposing a rule change that would allow foster parents to be dually licensed to care for children and adults. Many youth with disabilities could then continue to live with their foster families as they transition into young adulthood. This policy modification would give foster parents and agencies extra time to help certain youth prepare for independent living. Staff and community partners will examine the possibility of developing scattered-site apartment placements for youth. The scattered-site apartment model provides youth with flexibility of location, as well as mainstreaming with tenants who are not all former foster care youth. Portions of the new room and board funds will be used to assist youth with time-limited rent payments, utilities, and food. Texas projects spending approximately 25% of the new independent-living funds on room and board to assist youth ages 18 to 21 years old who have left foster care. Texas has developed provisional guidelines for aftercare room and board. Allowable expenditures are rent and utility deposits and payments, as well as groceries. Generally, the amount of assistance per young adult is based on financial need. It typically does not exceed $500 per month. The total amount of assistance a young adult may receive is $3,000. Staff are exploring the possibility of developing host homes and supportive landlords. Supportive landlords are persons willing to provide discounted rent to youth who were formerly in foster care.

The state agency is working with the Texas Department of Housing and Community Affairs to develop a formal partnership agreement to help youth access housing. This action is expected to expand statewide opportunities for youth in need of affordable housing.

Also, the state agency has linked with the Texas Workforce Commission to streamline referrals of young adults for certain Welfare-to-Work funds. Youth ages 18 to 25 years old who have aged out of foster care are categorically eligible for Welfare-to-Work services. PAL program staff are meeting with the local workforce boards to discuss a direct referral process for former foster care youth. Young adults will be able to obtain assistance in on-the-job training, job placement services, child care, emergency or short-term housing, and certain transportation needs. The goal of this assistance is to help young adults successfully transition into gainful employment.

There is much work yet to be done. However, Texas has taken a number of important steps toward developing an opportunity structure designed to help foster young people become productive and self-sufficient citizens.

chapter 14

Independent-Living Housing Issues

MARK KRONER

Importance of Transitional Housing

An increasing number of communities are giving youth direct experience in living independently, before they age out of the state placement system. Many communities are creating situations in which a youth is able to take over the living arrangement in which he or she lived while in care, eliminating the need to move again at discharge.

The passage of the Foster Care Independence Act of 1999 has increased awareness of the role housing plays in the transition of foster youth to adult living situations. Although some housing-based independent and transitional living programs have been up and running in many communities for years, many states still have little to offer youth in this vital area. As a result of recent legislation, a new option for states is to use up to 30% of money allocated for housing as authorized by the Foster Care Independence Act. Two separate funding sources, the John H. Chafee Foster Care Independence Program and the Federal Runaway and Homeless Act, have exerted major influence on the development of services for older youth and young adults.

This chapter discusses several issues that states, counties, and agencies will face as they develop housing options for older foster youth who emancipate from placement, as well as programs that serve these youth.

It should be noted that the terms *independent living* (IL) and *transitional living* (TL) are often used interchangeably to describe services provided to older youth and young adults, but they have different meanings to practitioners around the country. Some communities use *TL* to mean a supervised living arrangement for youth in custody before they go into a less-supervised setting such as a scattered-site apartment.

Housing Options: Definitions

A typical inventory of IL housing options (taken from Kroner [1999]) includes the following:

- **Community-Based Group Home.** A house of 6 to 12 youth in the community, which uses existing community services but provides some treatment around-the-clock by trained staff.

- **Specialized Family Foster Homes.** An arrangement in which a youth is placed with a community family specially licensed to provide care and sometimes specifically trained to provide independent-living services.

- **Shelters.** A facility whose purpose is to provide short-term emergency housing to teens in crisis.

- **Live-in Roommates.** A situation in which a youth shares an apartment with an adult or student who serves as a mentor or role model. The apartment can be rented or owned by either the adult or the agency.

- **Host Homes.** A situation in which a youth rents a room in a family or single adult's home, sharing basic facilities and agreeing to basic rules while being largely responsible for his or her own life.

- **Boarding Homes.** A facility that provides individual rooms for youth or young adults, often with shared facilities and minimal supervisory expectations.

- **Shared Houses.** A minimally supervised house shared by several young adults who take full responsibility for the house and personal affairs.

- **Semisupervised Apartments (Scattered-Site Apartments).** A privately owned apartment rented by an agency or youth, in which a youth functions independently with financial support, training, and some monitoring.

- **Single-Room Occupancy.** A room for rent, often near a city center.

- **Specialized Group Homes.** Sometimes also referred to as semi-IL or -TL programs, these homes are usually staffed as a group home but house older teens and focus on developing self-sufficiency skills.

- **Subsidized Housing.** Government-supported low-income housing.

Licensing Issues

Most states have a few housing-based IL programs (ILPs) in operation or are starting them. States taking initiative in this area will need to review licensing codes and regulations to make certain they are not overly restrictive or prevent youth from living in less-restrictive settings, such as individual apartments or host homes. Small group settings such as shared homes or supervised congregate apartments, with 6 to 10 youth living in the same complex, need to be free from rules such as posting menus, requiring 24-hour or double coverage, or establishing inflexible curfews for all residents.

A goal of IL services is to gradually pass responsibility to the youth, not to have the youth make an adjustment to a living arrangement that will not be part of his or her future plans. The process of "letting go" is different from the traditional goals of child welfare programming. Licensing can keep this from happening. States that have not developed licensing standards specific to IL housing options can draw on the experiences of states that have tackled this issue (e.g., Connecticut, New York, Iowa, Arizona, Ohio).

There is risk involved in permitting youth to have more freedom and choices, but it is a risk that many programs have learned to manage with planning, a mix of supervisory and monitoring strategies, a continuum of living arrangement options, and ongoing training of staff and youth.

Funding

Housing-based IL services are funded in several ways. Lighthouse Youth Services in Cincinnati has a purchase of services contract with the local county children's services board and receives a per diem for each youth referred to its program. The per diem covers about 80% of actual costs, with the difference being made up through grants, donations, and client contributions. Youth Continuum in New Haven, Connecticut, receives a daily state rate for each youth in care. Both of these agencies are non-profit. Franklin County Children's Services in Columbus, Ohio, a public, county-based agency, operates its own IL housing program. It has shifted funds from traditional services, such as foster care and residential treatment, to support scattered-site apartments for older youth. Other programs, such as the Kenosha Human Development Organization in Kenosha, Wisconsin, have obtained a combination of Housing and Urban Development grants, federal TL funds, and local support.

Foundation grants, private donations, United Way funds, youth contributions, state discretionary grants, and income from training and consulting services often contribute to the cost of operating these programs.

Public Versus Private

Most housing-based ILPs around the country are operated by nonprofit organizations. Public agencies usually are not able or willing to enter into lease agreements with private landlords due to liability issues. However, public agencies like Franklin County Children's Services in Columbus, Ohio, have found landlords willing to permit 17- and 18-year-olds to act as their own lease signers. Other ILPs sign the leases to maintain control of the apartment and be able to move a youth out on short notice if necessary.

It appears that most of the housing-based IL programs have been started and operated by nonprofit groups. Starting such programs takes a level of risk taking, flexibility, and creativity that is not always encouraged in the public sector.

Supervised Versus Semisupervised Living Arrangements

Communities and organizations are often hesitant to place youth in settings without 24-hour supervision. In most cases, youth remain in supervised settings until discharged from care and then for the first time are assisted in finding new living arrangements, often without ongoing adult availability or financial support. But many programs are realizing that it is actually easier to supervise youth living independently in sites scattered throughout a community than it is to keep an eye on a houseful of teens with similar issues with nervous neighbors next door. Experienced agencies have found that problems common to group-living situations, such as fights, thefts, unwanted sexual contact, and property damage, are typically less frequent among youth living alone in property owned by someone not associated with the system.

The success of congregate living arrangements often depends on the mix of youth or the charisma and leadership style of the adults involved with the site. One or two irresponsible but popular youth can negatively dominate the activities and tone of a group-living situation. The departure of a competent resident manager can disrupt a group's cohesiveness for months. If an agency-owned group-living situation experiences a major problem, neighbors might take action to close the site, leaving the agency with a piece of property, the need to find new living arrangements for the residents, and no source of income to support the property. In scattered-site settings, the agency can work out arrangements with landlords whereby a lease can be cancelled if things do not work out to either party's expectations.

This is not to say that the scattered-site model does not have its own set of problems. Youth living alone can often be magnets for other youth or family members looking for a place to hang out without adult supervision, including youth from a tenant's previous group home or residential treatment facility. Problems can develop at a site that are not discovered until weeks after they occur. Communities might not have apartments that are affordable or landlords willing to rent to older teens or young adults. Rural areas often lack apartment resources. Conversely, in urban centers such as New York City, Seattle, and San Francisco, vacancy rates are as low as 1%. Rent for a studio apartment (in a relatively safe neighborhood) can exceed $1,000 a month. Some programs are creating roommate situations to cut costs. Others use small, shared homes housing three to four youth and a live-in staff person. Shared homes usually do not have to be licensed as group homes.

Host homes and adult roommate arrangements, such as those created by Spectrum Youth Services in Burlington, Vermont, offer another option for agencies. Both involve having a youth share a house or an apartment with an adult or couple. The site can be owned by the adult or rented by the agency. This option might be necessary in rural areas where apartments are scarce or in urban areas with high-end rents. This option can be used for high-risk youth who are pregnant, have disabilities, have criminal records, have mental health issues, or are chemically dependent, depressed, or medically fragile. Agencies have to develop effective screening processes, do police and reference checks on potential adult housemates, and have regular training and supervision time in place.

Issues for Consideration

Agencies that decide to develop group-living situations need to be aware of community zoning requirements, neighborhood resistance, school district boundaries, and the time it will take before the arrangement is ready for residents. Required safety upgrades for group-living settings, such as fire escapes or sprinkler systems, can tax a budget. When choosing the location of a group-living site, organizations should consider safety and accessibility issues, distance to public transportation, grocery stores, and employment opportunities. If these group sites are funded by per diem, agencies must have assurance that this site will be used to capacity to cover staffing costs. Conversely, such programs will only be able to grow to the size of the beds available, whereas a scattered-site program can take in as many youth as there are available apartments in a community.

Communities and states have different rules for group homes, some of them quite demanding. Group homes are usually defined by specifying a certain number of nonrelated people who can live together. Programs might be able to get around group home regulations by limiting the number of youth to the number below the group home limit. Lighthouse Services operates two shared homes with three beds for youth and one room for a live-in resident manager. They share a kitchen and living room.

A goal of many ILPs is to have youth exit the system where he or she will continue living. Agencies using group-living arrangements need to be able to assure that there will be housing for a youth when he or she leaves the group setting, whether or not he or she is still in custody. Moreover, subsidized housing alternatives are opening up for youth older than 18 who cannot afford to pay the full cost of rent in a privately owned apartment. Waits for these arrangements, however, can be lengthy.

Supervision and Monitoring

Creating a system of monitoring and supervision based on the needs of individual clients demands flexibility in staffing and recognizes that although some youth need almost daily contact, others are so busy with productive activities that it is hard to find time to see them. Programs usually combine a combination of site visits, office visits, and regular phone contacts that can be adjusted depending on the maturity and level of functioning of individual youth. A teen who has had six months of predictable progress can suddenly require daily support due to a significant change in his or her life. A youth with a medical condition like diabetes might need increased contact during certain periods.

Unannounced visits can uncover suspected problems such as a relative who has moved in or the harboring of friends on the run from the youth's previous group home. Electronic monitoring bracelets or intensive surveillance/tracking strategies can be used to monitor an 8 P.M. curfew on a recently released sex offender or otherwise high-risk youth. Giving resident managers, landlords, and even neighbors staff pager numbers can help manage potentially volatile situations such as parties, fights, or illegal activities. Most programs allowing youth to live alone have enough staff on board to be able to meet with each youth weekly and maintain a 24-hour on-call system.

Crisis Management

Needless to say, youth living without constant supervision for the first time will create or find themselves in situations that necessitate outside intervention. Not unlike a college dorm resident manager, IL staff will face an number of problematic situations. Staff need to be aware of potential problems and know the steps necessary to manage problems and crises as they occur. A sample of situations common to ILPs is listed below. This can be used as a training tool for new program staff.

- A landlord calls the IL office wanting a youth out of his property by the weekend due to the continuous traffic of noisy teens.

- A female participant who has been in her own apartment for six months becomes pregnant, and no other program in the community will accept pregnant girls.

- A youth runs away from his fully furnished apartment, with all of his bills covered, a week after he is moved from his foster home.

- A landlord tells an IL social worker that his other tenants are all going to move because they are intimidated with the friends of the IL client who lives in his complex.

- At the request of a referring agency caseworker, the ILP rents an apartment outside of the city and the newly installed youth decides he or she wants to live in the city center.

- A client pages on-call staff on a wintry Saturday afternoon saying her apartment has no heat.

- A resident manager tells a social worker checking on a client at the apartment complex that he thinks the client's mother has moved in.

- Police close a supervised apartment building due to continuous neighborhood complaints about the residents' behavior when the resident manager is away.

- A resident manager says that an IL program participant's waterbed (which violates program rules) leaked into the manager's apartment below.

- A client who has been doing well living independently for six months overdoses on cold medicine a week after breaking up with her boyfriend.

- At a dependency review hearing, a juvenile court judge cannot believe a particular youth is living alone without 24-hour supervision, even though the youth is being terminated in two months.

- A visiting social worker discovers her new, 17-year-old client has a brand new $2,000 entertainment system from Rent-a-Center.

- A youth pages the on-call person at 2 A.M. complaining of serious stomach pains.

- A youth moves into a complex with five other older youth and begins supplying them with drugs.

- The ILP receives a $600 phone bill from a youth living independently who found a way around the phone blocks and likes to call various hotlines.

- The neighbors of a small transitional home with four participants calls the IL office threatening to call city hall if "those wild kids" are not removed from the neighborhood.

- A youth calls the office at 4:59 P.M. on Friday and states he is out of food.

- A youth calls stating that his living allowance money was stolen right after he cashed the check.

The child welfare field is accustomed to managing chronic crises in whatever setting they occur. The difference in the IL component is that ILP staff should step back and give youth major responsibility to resolve the crisis, with staff acting in a backup, supportive, or consulting role.

A Living Arrangement Options Continuum

Programs that have been operating for some time have found that it helps to have multiple living arrangement options in place. Some youth can handle the freedom and responsibility of living alone better than others.

Some responsible youth have friends who cause them to be evicted from an apartment. Others have mental health issues that require them to live with an adult roommate or with other youth in a shared-home setting.

The ability to remove a youth on short notice, placing them temporarily in a shelter, boarding home, group home, or host home, can buy time to come up with alternative living arrangements. Youth often learn valuable lessons from an eviction or a return to a more supervised setting. A second chance for young adults who are evicted due to rowdy friends might be just what is needed in averting future problems.

A few case examples show how this can work:

George enters a group home at age 16 after spending a week in a runaway center. After he turns 17, he is placed in his own apartment. He is evicted after five months and is placed back in the runaway shelter until an opening comes up in his old group home. Once back at his group home, he agrees to follow a three-month contract to earn his way back into his own apartment. George fulfills his contract and is placed in another individual apartment. After he receives his general equivalency diploma, he is given 30 days until discharge from the system. Because he has a job, he is able to keep his apartment, the security deposit, and all of the program-purchased supplies.

Al is 17 and has been in residential treatment since he was 14. Al has made significant progress in all areas of his life. However, Al's family is unstable and has limited ability to support Al in the near future. His caseworker does not feel that Al is ready to live on his own. The caseworker knows a former foster mother who raised 20 foster youth and 3 of her own sons and is now living alone. The foster mother is asked to take Al in until he graduates from high school in eight months. Al moves in with his host and agrees to respect her house rules and property. The host mother agrees to have regular contact with the IL program that will work with Al to report any concerns. Al knows that his host is not in a parental role and comes and goes as he would if he lived alone. He also knows that his host will always find time to talk about his day or just listen to his thoughts about his life. When Al graduates, he gets assistance in finding his own apartment down the road from his home.

Hillary is referred to an ILP at age 17 and is doing well in all life areas. She is placed in her own apartment, but the landlord asks her to leave when she becomes involved with a known drug dealer. Her care providers feel it would be counterproductive to place her at the group home, which is occupied mainly by 13- to 15-year-olds. Instead, she is placed in a shared-living home with three other females and a live-in student. Hillary agrees to follow a strict two-month contract to earn another chance in her own apartment.

Youth who seem ready to live alone often have a hard time with the sudden freedom and multiple choices of how to manage one's time, money, friends, and so forth. Youth who at first need regular supervision can often do well on their own later. Youth who act out in group-living situations might not do so when in their own space. Agencies need options to accommodate these realities. A continuum of living arrangement options allows an agency and youth a chance to find the right fit.

Risk Management

Is placing a youth alone in an apartment really more risky than housing 6 to 12 teens in one house? Will youth left alone at night get into more trouble than youth in residential treatment centers? If a youth living alone commits a crime while in the community, is it any different than a youth who commits a crime while on the run from a group home, residential treatment center, or foster home? Each community will have to decide the level of risk and control it needs to have in place before committing to less-restrictive living arrangements. But a gradual lessening of control to permit the normal development of self-reliance calls for less supervision and increased freedom.

Agencies can lessen the chance for litigation and negative publicity by being proactive in managing risk. The author recommends the following procedures as cardinal principles in managing risk associated with apartment options and IL:

- Documentation of all contacts with youth (phone, face-to-face visits, comments from neighbors, etc.), problems perceived, and action taken is essential to avoid questions about neglect.

- Workers must be able to respond to a crisis around the clock. Having an on-call system in place that is easily accessible to youth, shared-living staff, resident managers, and landlords is essential to controlling crises.

- Short-term, back-up housing plans for out-of-control youth such as a shelter, group home, respite foster home, or boarding home helps prevent things from getting worse on somebody else's property.

- Hiring trained staff with experience in working with youth— people who know normal and abnormal adolescent behavior as well as mental health, chemical dependency, neighborhood, and cultural issues—is vital.

- Workers must have increased contact with high-risk youth and youth who are severely depressed, in a medical crisis, have experienced a personal loss, or are involved in illegal activities.

- There should be regular contact between ILP and referring agency staff (if different) about the progress of each youth.

- Liability insurance must be sufficient to cover major damages or personal injury. Some agencies back this up with rental insurance on each unit.

- Agencies must train staff who visit youth in community-based settings on safety issues.

- The agency must have signed documents stating the local court's approval of a living arrangement.

Staff Issues

Professionals trained to intervene and actively be involved in the decisionmaking process for youth assigned to their caseload must develop a different stance when assisting a youth aging out of care. Increasing a youth's ability to plan and make choices is a necessary developmental step that does not always lead to immediate positive outcomes. IL workers must learn "how not to be helpful," so that youth can learn to take responsibility for their actions. IL workers wrestle with the reality that decisions made by youth are not always the most efficient ones to meet service goals. Juvenile court personnel must support care provider efforts to shift responsibilities to the youth and accept that this might mean that original goals take longer to accomplish.

Policies for Youth

As agencies begin to place youth in living arrangements without 24-hour supervision, youth will inherit the responsibility for self-monitoring. Programs need to develop policies that help youth adjust to adult expectations. Policies need to reflect safety issues for youth, liability issues for agencies, and practical guidelines that help youth understand community, landlord, and property protection.

A youth placed on house restriction for damage done at a group home needs to understand that when living in a privately owned apartment, such actions can lead to angry outbursts from resident managers, payments to landlords, eviction, a criminal record, and court costs. Youth need to understand their responsibility for rent, phones, utilities, transportation, laundry, and other costs of daily living. Also, policies about driving cars, having visitors or pets, harboring runaways, using drugs and alcohol, buying things on credit, borrowing and lending money, decorating apartments, and playing loud music need to be established.

Programs will also have to decide how strict to make grounds for early termination from a program. Youth in ILPs will make many of the same choices college students and young adults living at home make. Discharging a youth in the child welfare system who breaks program rules is a much harsher sentence than suspending a student from college or cutting off Internet access at home. Again, each community has to reach a system consensus on dealing with serious rules infractions.

Screening and Intake Issues

Many factors enter the picture as agencies decide which type of living arrangement is most appropriate for an individual youth. Not all youth can handle the freedom and responsibility of living alone. Some never will. Some youth cannot handle living in group situations but do well on their own, and others need to start in a semisupervised setting before making the leap to apartments. Other youth who want to remain dependent and have others provide for them might have to be coerced into moving into an apartment as they get closer to a discharge date.

It is safe to assume that many youth in this situation are not usually ready developmentally for such a move. Most youth are not totally financially independent of their parents until their mid-20s. This happens primarily because the child welfare system is unable to financially support youth until they are fully prepared and mature. Waiting until a youth is developmentally ready can result in a system actually avoiding the necessary but difficult work of transition planning while the youth is in care.

Below are some of the factors to be taken into consideration when deciding on the most appropriate living arrangement.

- **Age.** Level of maturity is a better indicator of success than age. Many program allow youth as young as 16 to live in their own apartments.

- **Level of Functioning.** Can the youth really handle living in a specific site without causing serious harm to himself or herself or others?

- **Educational Situation.** Can the youth continue his or her current education program when moved to this site?

- **Employment Experience.** Will this youth be able to go to school and work part-time while living without 24-hour supervision?

- **Behavior at Previous Placement.** Was this youth responsible and cooperative in his or her previous living arrangement? Did he or she exhibit any violent or destructive behavior?

- **Emotional Support.** Does this youth have enough support in the community to be able to live alone?

- **Time Left in Custody.** Does the ILP have enough time to work with the referred youth?

- **Mental Health Issues.** Is a youth with a history of suicide attempts or other mental health issues able to live without 24-hour supervision?

- **Court Record.** Can a program assume the liability of placing a youth with a history of felony offenses in his or her own apartment?

- **Attitude.** Does this youth want to become self-sufficient? Does he or she want to live alone? Will he or she run away from a group-living situation?

- **Medical Issues.** Does the youth have chronic medical issues that require close supervision? Can he or she self-medicate if necessary? Does he or she have the ability to follow a strict diet if required or make medical appointments on her own if pregnant?

- **High-Risk Factors.** Are there other factors that would jeopardize the neighbors, tenants, program, or agency in any way? Is the youth a sex offender or an arsonist?

It Takes a System

Care providers who operate housing programs understand that the transition process needs to start early and should not be left to a couple of people during the last few months a youth is in custody. Youth who have spent a lot of time in group or institutional settings need real-life experience in functioning independently while still in the care of competent adults. Youth often comment that they were not allowed to enter a kitchen in a foster or group home or use laundry facilities. Not only are many youth not learning skills most people learn from their parents, they are being kept from learning them. If current providers cannot allow youth the chance to practice daily living skills, they need to connect their older youth with people who can do this. Guidelines for a comprehensive transition system are as follows:

- Start lifeskills training early and practice often.

- Change licensing rules to allow for less-restrictive living arrangements.

- Build in real-life activities in all placement settings, such as cooking, budgeting, using public transportation, and making appointments, into weekly routines.

- Train foster parents and group home staff on how they can help youth develop self-sufficiency skills.

- Educate court system personnel about the realities of youth leaving care.

- Educate board members of agencies willing to try placing youth in less-restrictive settings about the risks and potential rewards of developing such a service.

- Develop a mix of living arrangements that fit the needs of youth and the realities of the local housing situation.

- Involve current and former youth in ILPs in program development, system advocacy, fundraising, and program evaluation.

A system that focuses on protective and custodial care must begin to let go of these tasks in an extremely short period of time. What happens developmentally to youth from "normal" households does not have a chance to happen in the current child welfare system time frame. Much of the research about youth who have been discharged from the child welfare system has been done with a population that did not have an opportunity to live independently while in care. Increasingly, practice experience from ILPs around the country indicates that many youth can function independently and are able to leave the system with potentially stable living arrangements in place.

The process of taking on adult responsibilities happens at a different pace for youth from traditional families. Foster youth need to accelerate this process if they are to make it as responsible adult community members. Adding the real-life experience created by using new living arrangements will give foster youth a chance to develop the skills needed to live on their own.

Reference

Kroner, M. J. (1999). *Housing options for independent living programs*. Washington, DC: CWLA Press.

Community College Opportunities for Older Foster Youth: The California Profile

Michael Olenick

The California Profile

California has engaged the community college system as a partner in providing independent-living activities directed toward older foster youth. Community colleges provide lifeskills training and financial aid workshops and assistance, and generally help foster youth make a connection to postsecondary education.

The Community College Foundation (CCF) provides a critical link between the California Department of Social Services (CDSS), the 58 California counties, and 60 of California's 107 community colleges. Currently, CCF contracts with Los Angeles County and San Francisco County to provide enhanced programming and outreach to foster youth. Every year, it provides services to more than 7,000 foster youth ages 14 to 21.

There is a historical connection between independent-living programs and community colleges in California. California community colleges have been involved in the child welfare field since the early 1970s, when a small group of schools received federal grants to provide educational opportunities to foster parents. In 1984, the state legislature created funding to establish a statewide foster parent education program conducted through the community college system. When independent living legislation became a reality in the mid 1980s, an infrastructure was already in place so that independent-living programming for foster parents and foster youth could be quickly implemented.

Why Community Colleges?

There are several explanations for the involvement of community college systems and CCF in preparing foster wards for self-sufficiency.

Economics

According to U.S. Department of Labor statistics, the average wage difference between a non–high school graduate's earnings and the earnings of high school graduates is more than $7,000 per year. The difference between a high school diploma and an associates of arts degree adds an extra $6,000 in yearly wages. A bachelor's degree increases economic return by an additional $9,000. A pragmatic self-sufficiency plan may encourage youth to graduate from high school and go to college. Community colleges provide an experience that can motivate youth to stay in school and create a sense of familiarity with a setting that is not too overwhelming. Because a high percentage of all college students in California attend community colleges, providing opportunities at the community college level increases the likelihood of motivating foster youth to seek additional education. The tuition cost of attending a California community college is low, just $11 per unit, or $176 to take a 16-unit full-time load. There are opportunities to enroll in certificate programs as well as matriculation programs to four-year universities.

Social Capital

Foster wards frequently say they were unaware of the resources available to them. When they come to CCF, workers try to involve them in the California Youth Connection, a foster youth advocacy organization. CCF also convenes youth advisory committees made up of youth from a variety of college programs to give feedback on the program. CCF hires current and former foster youth to act as peer counselors, so that youth can talk to more experienced young adults about issues. Also, CCF has been fortunate in recruiting several former foster youth for professional positions once they have completed a bachelor's degree.

Exposure

First-hand exposure to a community college permits foster youth to experience a world that is alien to much of the foster care system. It provides former wards with opportunities to be successful in a postsecondary curriculum, which often is their first success anywhere. It also allows foster young people to become aware of the variety of opportunities available to them, such as dual enrollment in high school and college, which is a way to add to the acquisition of high school credits, making graduation more attainable. Some community colleges make it possible to earn credit for lifeskills training classes while youth are preparing for emancipation.

Program Description

There are several programs directed toward foster youth by California's community colleges and CCF. CCF has received funding from CDSS since 1987. Since 1988, Los Angeles County has contracted with CCF for an independent-living program at 18 campuses in Los Angeles County, and since 1996, has contracted with CCF to conduct the newly initiated Early Start to Emancipation Program, a program for 14- and 15-year-old foster youth. In 1999, San Francisco County also contracted with CCF to conduct tutoring, mentoring, and lifeskills, vocational, college preparatory, and computer classes.

Initially, the state-funded program was directed toward caregivers, foster parents, group home staff, and foster family agencies. More recently, California has shifted focus so that more than half of the offerings are directed toward foster youth. Now, 50 community colleges provide workshops on lifeskills-related topics, college tours, computer instruction, and financial aid. In addition, 15 other counties contract directly with a local community college.

Los Angeles County and CCF created a relationship between 18 community colleges to conduct two major activities. Primarily, they created an outreach staff, which was hired from communities where youth lived. Outreach advisors interview youth, attempt to persuade them to attend lifeskills classes, arrange for transportation to classes, accompany youth while they are transported to classes, and sometimes attend class with youth. They become mentors and confidants. Outreach advisors enable youth to make connections with college resources as well as with adults and peers, which they might not otherwise make.

Program Parameters

Over the years, the program has discovered considerable variation in the offerings by colleges. It also discovered that there was no way to know whether there was any training effect on youths' knowledge, skills, or attitudes regarding independent living. Although CCF encourages local creativity, it needed some level of comparability across programs. Several years ago, CCF workers developed a pretest and posttest instrument that could be used by programs to determine whether youths' knowledge, skills, and attitudes change as a result of training received. The researchers discovered that they had to redefine expectations for target programs. Working in concert with the Department of Social Services, the researchers developed a set of five competencies (which they later expanded to seven) that they believe foster youth should acquire before leaving care. These include employment, daily living skills, survival skills, education, and computer skills. For each skill area, they developed a set of competency standards.

The researchers analyzed questionnaires from 1,300 youth. Results indicate that foster youth have improved in their knowledge, skills, and attitudes about employment, lifeskills, and survival skills. However, results regarding choices, consequences, and interpersonal skills have been less clear. Students demonstrate knowledge about the negative consequences of alcohol and other drug use, including tobacco, but not in their attitudes about the possible consequences of using these substances.

Over the past several years, Los Angeles County has developed a program for younger foster youth, the Early Start to Emancipation Program (ESTEP). This program is unique in creating a model for foster youth that qualifies for federal independent-living funds.

ESTEP is the result of several separate initiatives. CCF developed Early Start, an intervention program for middle school students who show potential to go to college but also are at risk for dropping out of high school. The program was a series of workshops during the school year that provides support for youth as they progress through high school. Supported by private foundation funds, ESTEP programs appear successful in maintaining more than 80% of youth through high school, which is a higher graduation rate than attained by nonfoster youth in comparable geographic locations.

Moreover, the Los Angeles County Superior Court convened a task force based on a grand jury finding that the county was not preparing foster youth adequately for emancipation. The task force made a number of recommendations, which included quarterly assessments for foster youth who were starting to make the transition from middle school to high school. The director for the Los Angeles Department of Children and Family Services approached CCF to conduct the initial assessment. The assessment suggested that components of Early Start and ESTEP be used.

ESTEP consists of an assessment of youth and a one-day motivational event, which informs youth of the issues they need to prepare for in the next few years. There are also monthly workshops that help foster youth adjust to the transition to high school. For those youth who need reading and math skills, tutoring help is available. The researchers discovered that 35% of the youth assessed were more than two years below grade level in reading ability, 40% were one or two years below grade level, and only one in four were at or above grade level. When the researchers presented this information to the Los Angeles Commission on Children and Families, they were informed that this breakdown was similar to that found throughout the Los Angeles school area. Researchers also discovered that most youth in high school were not receiving adequate counseling on the appropriate classes to take, primarily because of unfavorable ratios of more than 1,000 students per counselor in many high schools. Foster youth were even less likely to receive expert counseling, and many were not taking the right classes to be eligible to enter a four-year university.

Foster youth tutored in the program have shown varying results in math and reading scores. Although the program is limited in tutoring resources, when workers provide 50 hours of in-home tutoring, they see progress that is measurable on standardized tests. The program also uses a tutoring program that is self-reporting, so one can see progress by the materials being used. The researchers interviewed caregivers to determine their perception of progress. Caregivers reported that foster youth are more motivated to attend school and are making greater efforts to do well in school.

Challenges

There are several challenges in developing these programs. Scholarship requests show 75% of the youth say they want to attend college. Unfortunately, CCF lacks resources sufficient to develop a tracking system that can identify foster youth who are attending California's community colleges. Although CCF can identify some youth if they attend a program on the same campus at which they enroll, it cannot identify a youth who, for example, attended an independent-living program at San Francisco City College and then enrolled across the bay at Merritt College. Youth do not always disclose that they were a ward of the court, and once a case is closed, it is difficult to identify them.

CCF keeps in touch with quite a few youth who enroll at community colleges and has found that there are barriers they must overcome to be successful. Often, he or she is the first person in his or her family to attend college. It often happens that with first generation college attendees, there is very little familial understanding of the demands of college; hence, most receive little support. Also, many foster youth have to deal with issues of regulating their own lives after having been in highly regimented living situations. They have to cope with working and securing stable housing. Because they often do not have a stable support system to draw strength from, when they encounter a college crisis, they often become overwhelmed and drop out of school. It is apparent that college-level peer support programs are beneficial. Currently, the author is aware of two such programs, both at state colleges that provide mentors and peer supports.

The author, however, receives numerous reports from foster wards, who attest to the benefits that accrue from postsecondary education. The following vignettes are drawn from them.

Effects on Life Circumstances

Berisha, Age 21

I am an emancipated foster youth; I entered the system at the age of 2 with my sister, who was 3. My sister and I moved around, constantly living in different foster homes. I attended a total of 11 different schools by the time I graduated from high school. My grades were poor. I had a 1.5 overall grade point average. I had no hopes or plans to attend college. I attended the Pasadena Community College's independent-living program upon emancipation at 18. I had no clue what the program had to offer. I was amazed about the many resources that were unknown to me. I took a lot of notes in the class. I got to know the outreach advisors and trainers very well. I was now aware of transitional housing, financial resources, and medical assistance. College seemed possible. I learned how to network, and my fears of asking for help ceased. After emancipation, I was on my way to being homeless, like many foster youth, but I remembered hearing about transitional housing in class. I was able to get into a housing program. I started to attend community college. My life was coming together. I also was introduced to the California Youth Connection, which is an organization of current and former foster youth that advocate on behalf of foster youth rights. The independent-living program was like a light in a dark tunnel, and the staff were angels. Without this program, I am certain that I would have been another statistic. I am currently going into my senior year at California State Uni-

versity in Los Angeles and I am on the dean's honor roll with a 3.6 overall grade point average. My major is social work, and I plan to give back and help others.

Christian, Age 25

I was in the system for 18 years, from ages 3 to 21. The foster care system, in my eyes, has two sides—a rough side and smooth side. Throughout the time I was in the system, I was placed in four different homes, each being very different than the previous. The hardest thing to deal with was adapting to different living situations.

I was in my first placement for 10 years. It never crossed my mind that by venting my frustrations to a teacher about the physical and sexual abuse I was enduring within my home life, it would turn everything upside down. That evening, in a flash, I lost everything, my school, my friends, and my so-called home. I was moved from South Gate to Pasadena, clear across town. To me, it seemed I was being moved to the other side of the world. Leaving behind everything that was familiar to me. To live in a group home with 11 others, attend a predominantly Caucasian school, and make new friends was a tough situation to face. That was only the beginning. Little did I know I would be repeating this process two times thereafter. The rewarding part was the relationships I developed along the way. Relationships with staff, teachers, family, and friends that I hold close to my heart even today.

Being in the system helped me become a strong and open-minded individual. It makes me see life through different eyes and appreciate all that I encounter within it, the good and the not-so-good. It helps me appreciate some of the things that others take for granted, such as "family."

I can honestly say 1994 was a year that brought forth much opportunity for me. I was chosen to participate in the community college's independent-living program, where I connected with a group of wonderful adults who helped me grow in many ways. The skills that I was taught within the program were valuable survival skills—skills that I would come to depend on as I grew older and would very much need after I would no longer be under system supervision.

I always believed there would be a time where I would have the chance to "give back." That time came in 1994 when I was introduced to a foster youth advocacy organization known as the California Youth Connection. CYC (as it is also known) is a nonprofit organization that was formed by a group of foster youth that felt the need to voice their concerns. The organization was developed by and for foster youth, past and present. I've been an active member for six years. Participating not only on a local level, but on a statewide level as well. I have participated as a liaison between chapters, as a youth advisory member, and as a board member. Being a part of CYC helped lift my self-esteem tremendously. It gave me hope when I was in the system by helping me realize I wasn't alone. There were others who had treaded waters in similar ways as myself and had not drowned.

I was also given a second opportunity to "give back" when I was hired to become a part-time peer counselor with the CCF. I work hands-on with youth presently in care as they participate in the independent-living program, at a college campus site, as I had once done.

Working with youth is rewarding in itself, I guess because I saw a little of myself within each one of them. I choose to stay involved in the system because it gives me great satisfaction knowing that I am giving back my knowledge and personal experiences to those who follow in my footsteps.

Although I no longer work as a peer counselor, but rather as a full-time clerk for…ESTEP, which serves 14- and 15-year-old foster youth, I still believe that my participation in ILP [the independent-living program] taught me discipline and how to take responsibility for myself and my actions. CYC taught me how to be a team player and stand up for what I believe in. All of these combined have made me a more levelheaded person.

Sonya, Age 27

The independent-living program has been an important factor in my life. I learned that I would eventually be responsible for myself. The program stressed the importance of doing things on my own. In addition, it provided me with adult support and a variety of options that would allow me to accomplish those goals.

Through the independent-living program, I was presented with the facts about what it meant to emancipate. Prior to this program, I had no idea what was expected of me once I turned 18. It was explained to me that once a foster youth turns 18, they are no longer the responsibility of the county. Instead, foster youth are on their own, meaning where they lived, what foods they ate, their clothes, everything that would keep them from starving or being homeless was now their responsibility. Learning this information was a scary thing because I had no idea what I wanted to do with my life after high school.

Going to college was the "adult" thing to do, but I didn't know the first thing about getting into college. What I did know was that college required money, and although I had a part-time job, I knew I didn't make enough to live on my own and there definitely wasn't enough money to pay for college.

Through the ILP, I learned about financial aid, and because I was a foster youth, I would qualify for money that would pay for college and the dorms. As long as I stayed in school, I would continue to get that money.

The fact that my education would be paid for wasn't important to me at that time. What struck my interest about going to college were the dorms. I saw the dorms as my ticket to independence. At this time I didn't care about school, I just wanted a safe place to live, and once I learned that the dorms provided that as well as three meals a day, all I wanted to know then was what do I have to do to get into the dorms. I was told that I had to make good grades to get into college first. So that's exactly what I did. I brought all my grades up to As and Bs, and two days after I graduated from high school, I moved into my own dorm room.

I knew that in order for me to remain in the dorms, I had to continue making good grades. Eventually, I realized that education was important; having a college education would afford me opportunities that I would not have had without a degree.

Not only did the ILP provide me with resources, but I also developed friends and mentors through my outreach advisor. My outreach advisor was available on a consistent basis. He informed me of different resources available on and off campus. He also encouraged me to get involved in different foster youth activities. Through those activities, I was able to meet other adults, who also became friends/mentors.

The great thing about having this type of support was that I was able to call on them for any reason. Whether it was just to talk about what was going on in my life, or just someone to confide in. I am thankful for the ILP because I learned the importance of being self-reliant. I became aware of different options that would prepare me for emancipation. Through the ILP, I was able to meet people who made a significant difference in my life. Many of my personal achievements were possible because I had an opportunity to go through this program.

The California CCF

The mission of CCF is to facilitate connections between education and business. An important foundation goal is to advance the case for education as a critical strategy in improving the lives and well-being of all citizens. Community colleges in California have served more than 150,000 youth and adults in programs directed toward preparation for independent living. With respect to foster care, in fiscal year 1998 to 1999, educational training reached 16,519 foster youth and adult-care providers. Of this number, 11,883 were foster youth. Overall, the California CCF has a major stake in the well-being of all foster wards. The programs and policies discussed here can be of value to other states, jurisdictions, and organizations.

Chapter 16

Personal Responsibility: A Goal for Adolescents in Foster Care

BETSY KREBS AND
PAUL PITCOFF

> *It's like that commercial where the lady gets*
> *into the cockpit and they just give her the plane to fly.*
>
> —*Leonard, age 24, when asked what it is like to be discharged from foster care*
>
> *Regardless of where you live—kinship, foster home, or group home—*
> *you are going to be responsible for yourself when you leave the system.*
> *No one told me that when I was in care.*
>
> —*Samantha, age 23*

Barriers to Learning Personal Responsibility in the Present Foster Care System

The 1999 Foster Care Independence Act (the Chafee Act) provides states with funding to "assure that participants recognize and accept their personal responsibility for preparing for and then making the transition from adolescence to adulthood." Most people would agree that you cannot teach teenagers to swim without access to a pool, lake, or ocean. Nor can you teach them cooking if you never let them near a kitchen. You would not blame a teenager who could not swim or cook in these circumstances. Yet many people criticize teenagers in foster care for not being responsible, although the teens are being raised in an environment that is antithetical to taking on personal responsibility. For example:

> *Diana*, *a 19-year-old, lives in a group home. She attends college and, through someone she met at a part-time job, is offered a position in the accounting department of a prestigious law firm. Because of Diana's busy schedule, she is not in the group home very much, leaving early in the morning and returning in the evening. The group home supervisor*

231

> marks her absent without leave (AWOL) each time she
> misses a house meeting, where the residents are encouraged
> to air their complaints, typically about stealing each others'
> clothing. The supervisor marks her AWOL when she arrives
> in the evening, missing dinner. No one saves her a plate of
> food. Finally, the supervisor tells Diana that she must quit
> her job because it interferes with her life in the group home.
> Diana refuses, and one evening soon after, she returns from
> work to the group home to find her belongings shoved into
> garbage bags. The group home supervisor tells her from now
> on she is "on restriction" and must stay in the house in her
> pajamas, getting dressed only with staff permission. Diana
> leaves the group home, although she has nowhere to go.

Diana was taking responsibility for her life by working at a law firm to learn more about a profession she was interested in and to earn money to support herself. Her decisions may not have been suitable for the needs of her group home, but they were reasonable, considering her long-term goals. The agency's punitive actions were an obvious deterrent to Diana taking on personal responsibility.

In the authors' work with more than a thousand foster care children and teens, first as attorneys and then as program developers, they have found that foster care teens are eager and able to take on personal responsibility, in the right circumstances. First, workers must expect that individual teens can and should be preparing for a future as participating citizens. Second, workers must connect that future with present expectations that the teen can and will assume responsibility for reaching his or her individual goals. Third, it should be recognized that for a teen to accept responsibility, workers must first give them responsibility and provide role models and positive recognition for them.

The problem is not with teens shirking responsibility, but with a system that actively works against young people succeeding in life. If policymakers and practitioners want teens to accept personal responsibility, they must first understand why the existing environment often defeats their purpose.

A Small Futures Perspective

> Just because you're in foster care doesn't mean that you have
> to limit where you want to go. Just because I'm in foster
> care doesn't mean that when I grow up I have to be a
> McDonald's person. (Jessica, age 17)

Most foster care environments, whether foster homes, group homes, or residential centers, do not convey the expectation that teens will achieve anything significant in the future. No one identifies the teenager with his or her goals for the future, and there is rarely positive discussion about the future for the teenager. Instead, the focus is on day-to-day management of teens. In short, the foster care system has a "small futures" mentality for youth in placement.

Self-sufficiency is the goal of most independent-living programs. At best, many hope that former foster care youth will avoid jail and homeless shelters. The goal of self-sufficiency is disconnected with the teen's interests, aspirations, or values. Instead, it focuses on simply keeping the teen from being a further drain on taxpayers. The system fails to meet this goal in many cases, such as when graduates do become homeless, incarcerated, or dependent on welfare. Even the system's success stories often depict young people who are barely surviving—living in temporary housing, holding cashier jobs at fast food restaurants, constantly worrying about how to stay afloat.

Some of the system's low expectations are explicit: New York City policy is that young people aging out of foster care (who may be as old as 21) must have only an 8th-grade competency in reading and math. Others are more insidious, such as when a group home worker asks a teen, "Why are you bothering with high school when you could get a general equivalency diploma?"

Foster care practitioners create environments that do not require teens to act responsibly. This is evident in many independent-living programs at foster care agencies. Young people are not required or expected to attend independent-living workshops. For the teens who do attend, there is no requirement that they be on time, do homework, or learn anything. Teens wander in and out of workshops well after they have been scheduled to begin or just at the end, to pick up their stipends. Many foster care agencies pay teens a stipend even if they do not attend workshops.

Lack of System Accountability for Emancipated Youth

Foster care providers rarely suffer consequences if young people leaving their care fail. Local governments and contracting agencies turn out hundreds of young people each year who have no plan for the future, not to mention no home and no job. Yet those same agencies continue to be awarded contracts to take custody of young people.

The foster care system has only a short-term interest in teens. The need to manage teens' behavior is viewed as more important than teaching them personal responsibility, which is a longer term strategy, and one that requires an investment in the teens' futures.

Crises Take Precedence

> There were other kids in the group home who were louder, who fought more, and who got in more trouble, and those were the ones that got most of the attention. If you were quiet, people really didn't pay attention to you. (Leonard, age 20)

Controlling teens' behavior is given priority over understanding their goals for the future and helping them take responsibility for achieving those goals. With no big picture for teens' futures in mind, the system focuses on the parts of a teen's life that are mainly out of their control—the pathology of their family of origin, the crises caused by continual changes in placement, inadequate caring environments, loss of school time, and so forth. Professionals in the system are forced to focus on crises and immediate problems, putting long-term planning essential for assuming personal responsibility on the back burner.

Social work and casework staff will often interrupt independent-living workshops, seeing them as an opportunity to pull teens out of the workshop to talk to them about problems in their cases. Social work and casework staff rarely seem interested or respectful of teens' activities, in or after school.

Lack of Role Models and Supports for Personal Responsibilities

> My foster mother never told me, this is what you have to do to run a household. It was just like she got her money and gave me $100. Even if she would have taken me with her to buy groceries, that would have helped. Instead it was like, I got the check today and here's your cut. (Malika, age 22)

The foster care system fails to recognize that "accepting personal responsibility" implies a transaction of giving and taking. Many people in the foster care system are reluctant to give significant responsibility to teens, perhaps afraid it will be too much trouble. Most parents, educators, and employers understand that handing over responsibility takes time. For parents, the final transfer of responsibility comes when the young person is truly independent, usually well beyond the chronological age of emancipation imposed by the system.

*At the group home it was really easy for me not to do any-
thing [to prepare for the future]. No one was really on my
back to do anything. Then reality hit and I had to start paying my own bills and doing everything on my own all of a
sudden. It was like a set-up. (Leonard, age 20)*

Learning requires making mistakes and failing. Yet, when it comes to
important skills like budgeting money or time, for example, the system
gives teens very little opportunity to try and fail. Most youth learn after
foster care, when they get eviction notices, their phones are turned off,
and they have no money in the bank. For these young adults, facing such
setbacks for the first time can be disastrous. Some foster care workers
discourage teens from enrolling in challenging programs because they fear
the teens might not succeed and might be overcome by failure. Although
this might seem benevolent, it backfires when the teen has to then experience failure for the first time as a young adult.

The placement system suffers from a serious lack of role models. Foster care fails to model personal responsibility for teens. Teens in care have
daily contact with caseworkers, foster parents, and lawyers who are regularly late to appointments, break commitments, or fail to return calls. Intimate relationships and bonds are created with teens in care but often
are broken. Cases are confused and homogenized. Confidentiality is repeatedly broken, along with the accompanying expectation of trust.

Group home workers should, but often do not model personal responsibility for teens. Instead, they often exhibit resentment and lack of empow-
erment. They are frequently in competition with the teens. They often feel
that the teen is getting off too easy, whereas the worker is underpaid and
disrespected. Some workers take this out in anger and scapegoat their clients. Others confide in the teen and explain how life really doesn't offer
many opportunities. Their philosophy is that resentment and lack of em-
powerment is all one can look forward to as an adult. It is not enough for
teens in care to see role models on television. When teens actually meet
and get to talk with role models, the teens' aspirations and sense of confidence will rise.

System Fails to Support Teens Who Do Assume
Personal Responsibility

Many teens need help with things the foster care system does not provide.
The teen's school might be unsuitable for them or their foster home unsafe. Perhaps they need a green card or driver's license so they can work.

Maybe their own child needs medical attention. The system is not working for them, so they take matters into their own hands and resolve the problem. Instead of rewarding or recognizing these efforts, the system criticizes and sometimes punishes the teens for taking on some responsibility.

Teens in foster care will take on responsibility if the process is relevant to their needs and interests. If workers help the teen identify his or her own goals, they have a better chance of teaching the teen personal responsibility. Every teenager in foster care has some goal or ambition for the future. Their goals or ambitions are not to avoid contracting sexually transmitted diseases or becoming homeless. Rather, they aspire to be nurses, designers, chefs, lawyers, or journalists. They hope to become parents, to live in safe neighborhoods, to be part of a community. To teach personal responsibility, the system must build on these goals. If the foster care system wants teenagers to take on more responsibility, it needs to convey the expectation that each teen in care is a future participating citizen. This expectation recognizes the teen's individual worth and potential to contribute to society. The expectation of participating citizenship in the future underlies most transactions in which adults try to get young people to accept responsibility. In families, schools, apprenticeships, job training programs, and the military, efforts to get a teen to accept personal responsibility are long-term. Part of the motivation to teach personal responsibility in these situations is self-serving. For example, parents normally do not want their grown children to rely on them for money and a place to live when the child is 30 years old. An employer does not want to have to provide constant supervision to a worker. The long-term goal provides the adult with the incentive to allow teens room to fail as they learn the skills of taking on responsibility.

Teaching Self-Advocacy

Instead of conceiving the problem as young people needing to accept personal responsibility, Youth Advocacy Center (YAC) has defined the need for young people to take control of their lives. *Taking control* envelops the notion of personal responsibility but focuses on the potential for autonomy, planning, decisionmaking, and reaching future goals.

The authors founded YAC to teach teens in foster care to advocate for themselves and take control of their lives. It is dismaying that young people are told to rely on child welfare caseworkers, social workers, lawyers, and judges to make decisions about their lives, and too many former foster care youth end up homeless, uneducated, unable to sustain employment, in jail, or facing grave health risks.

Self-advocacy is a process to plan and act to reach one's goals. Self-advocacy is focused on the future and requires taking action. Skill in self-advocacy means one has the ability to plan and execute a strategy for winning a case, using a dynamic range of intellectual, analytical, and communication skills. Self-advocacy includes the following components: setting short- and long-term goals, researching relevant information, understanding the goals of "the other side," connecting personal goals with others' goals, identifying allies, critically analyzing situations, identifying one's strengths and weaknesses, planning strategy as well as written and oral presentations, dealing with setbacks and rejection, and building on successes.

Self-advocacy is useful in a number of situations: a person getting a good job, a businessperson closing a deal, a student protesting an unfair grade, an employee getting a promotion, a community organizer lobbying for social change, a tenant negotiating to get back a security deposit, a dissatisfied consumer returning a purchase.

YAC teaches young people in foster care the concepts and skills of self-advocacy in an after-school seminar. The class is conducted much like a college seminar, with a group of about eight students and one teacher. Students use two texts that YAC has developed, the Self-Advocacy Casebook and the Goal Plan Workbook. The casebook is a collection of cases or stories of individuals (many in foster care) who are struggling to resolve a problem or to reach a goal. The casebook provides material for individual written assignments and group discussions. During the course of the seminar, students must identify their own long-term career and education goals. They apply the skills and concepts they are learning and set objectives to be achieved in the near future. The workbook is filled out during the second part of the seminar, when the young person focuses on his or her goals and plans.

Seminar participants also attend periodic meetings with outside professionals. First, students may meet as a group with guest advocates, leaders in journalism, entertainment, finance, and government, who discuss how they reached their own goals and offer information to students. These meetings provide role models, expose teens to the world outside of foster care, and broaden their knowledge of possible career choices. Second, students can go on informational interviews, individual meetings in which they follow an agenda to make a presentation and solicit information from a professional in the field in which the student is interested.

- After meeting with a vice president of JP Morgan, Janice, a 17-year-old veteran of the foster care system, commented that she was now going to seriously pursue her math homework. "He told me it was like medicine. It might not taste good but the results would help me reach my goals. I think of him every time I'm doing my math homework. What an office!"

- Samuel was 18 and reported that he was often in trouble regarding fights. After meeting with a columnist at *The New York Times*, he was awestruck. The interviewer asked him why. Samuel thought a moment and then responded, "Now I know I can talk with an important grown-up." Sam just completed his first year at college.

- Jenny was 19 and had been in 17 different placements since she was 6 years old. When we met her, she presented herself as a "bad person." After meeting a prominent, New York restaurant pastry chef, Jenny was ecstatic. "He started out like me. Had nothing. Now he makes desserts that everyone loves! They cost 10 dollars!" Jenny now has a stronger direction in the culinary field and is diligently exploring training opportunities.

YAC holds students to high standards of accomplishment. Students are required to attend every class and to be on time, complete homework assignments, develop written and oral presentation skills, and participate in a wide variety of cooperative group exercises. For many of them, this is the first time that they have experienced such rigor and the demand to achieve at a high level.

Teenagers want someone to care enough to tell them their actions have consequences. Believing enough in them to hold them to standards demonstrates a genuine respect for their ability to be personally responsible. Presenting challenges to teens and allowing them to fail helps them to learn about accepting responsibility.

> *Jasmine, a 17-year-old, had been increasingly disruptive during the sessions of a self-advocacy seminar. The teachers attempted to work with her and failed. Her disruptions were making it impossible to keep the seminar on track. After explaining the problem, the teachers asked her to leave, effectively kicking her out of the class. She was extremely upset with this decision. The teachers reviewed their policy that students who failed to meet attendance or behavior stan-*

dards are dropped from class. They explained to Jasmine that this was not punishment, and that she would be accepted into a new semester if she thought she could control her behavior and wanted to learn the skills being taught. It would be totally in her control.

Several months later Jasmine wrote an article for a foster care agency newsletter about her experience at YAC. We were hesitant to read it! Yet in her article, she gave the program glowing praise, and said how lucky any foster youth would be to complete the program. She was treated as personally responsible for her actions. By removing her from the seminar she learned that actions have consequences. At the same time, she was provided a limited security net that she would not likely find in the world after she left foster care. She understood that we respected her and it was only her willingness to control her behavior that would matter if she reapplied. Jasmine's positive report about the seminar indicated that she reflected on the importance of personal responsibility.

If states want teens to accept personal responsibility, they need to support teens working toward long-term goals post–foster care. Foster care agencies with custody of teens must focus primarily on preparing teens for a future in which they are participating citizens.

Toward a Future-Oriented Program Model

The following program model can prepare teens for participating citizenship. It is based on 12 years of work with hundreds of teens in care and dozens of foster care agencies. To succeed, this program requires a genuine commitment by an agency.

Agencies with custody of young people age 16 and older should be required to provide support for each teen to develop a year-by-year career goal plan, looking toward age 25, which will be called the "Y25 plan." The Y25 plan must be based on the individual teen's aspirations and goals.

Building relationships with adults is a key feature of the Y25 plan. As part of the Y25 plan, the young person must go into the community and meet individuals who can be helpful to him or her now and in the future. In addition, families and other adults identified by teens should be involved in developing and supporting Y25 plans.

A key and consistent adult (the Y25 coordinator) in the life of the teenager takes responsibility for helping the teen execute the plan. The Y25 coordinator formally reviews the plan semiannually to identify ways of achieving the teen's stated goals. The Y25 coordinator meets with the teen once a month. The only issues to be discussed relate to the teenager's desired profession and/or occupation and the Y25 plan. Discussion about other issues or concerns related to the teenager's placement is disallowed. The Y25 coordinator makes suggestions for following through on work necessary to complete or update the plan. The Y25 coordinator also helps the teenager implement elements of the short-term goal plan, such as arranging informational interviews and professional internships, getting information on financial assistance for college, and so forth. The Y25 goal plan should be reviewed annually. Areas in the plan that require modification, additional support, or new resources can be identified.

The agency should offer periodic Y25 goal plan training to teenagers for the purpose of developing skills necessary to complete the Y25 goal plan. The training could be led by someone on the staff or by an outside agency. The leader should be able to facilitate teen groups, be willing and able to hold teens to high standards, and be able to focus completely on career planning and self-advocacy issues to the exclusion of all other placement-related issues for the time of the session. Ideally, the leader also would have work experience in the private sector.

General orientation meetings should be offered for staff and foster parents of teenagers and preteens, explaining the purpose of the Y25 goal plan process and ways parents can encourage their teenager to complete this process. Every adult at the agency who interacts with teens should be made aware of the teen's Y25 plan. This means that other concerns about problems and crises may be given less priority, because all would recognize that planning for the teen's future is of top importance.

The Y25 goal plan should be available to all staff working with the teenager, as well as to the foster and/or birthparents. All adults interacting with the teen are encouraged to acknowledge the teenager's intended career goal. Caseworkers, counselors, medical professionals, lawyers, and judges can raise the questions, "What does this young person want to do with his or her future?" "How far along is he or she?" "What can I do to help?"

The process of developing a Y25 plan can teach and enhance many traditional independent-living skills, as well as reinforce many aspects of self-advocacy. Included in a Y25 list might be:

- The ability to identify specific goals.

- The ability to relate personal goals to those of other individuals and organizations.

- The ability to identify allies and supporters.

- The ability to understand budgeting as a decisionmaking tool.

- The ability to make effective presentations.

- Each teen must demonstrate a competence in advocacy skills. This must be demonstrated both in writing and orally. For example:

  - Getting an appointment to meet with a professional to obtain information and career advice.

  - Gaining admittance to an educational or training program.

  - Getting an interview with a human resources professional at a large company or organization.

- Each teen in care would have to complete several informational interviews with professionals in the fields of interest for that teenager. Each teen would have to write a letter introducing themselves and request assistance for achieving some substantial goal. The teen would also have to write a report identifying information gained from the interview, such as recommended education or training, important internships, or job experiences.

- Each teen must be able to document their respective strengths and assets in writing and in an oral presentation.

- Each teen must explore the possibility of getting a degree from a four-year college.

  - Meeting with a professor at a college to explore educational paths.

  - Completing the college and financial aid application process.

- Each teen must demonstrate mastery of the majority of independent-living skills, including but not be limited to:

  - Budgeting/financial planning,

  - Health care,

  - Meal preparation,

  - Negotiating home rental and maintenance, and

  - Researching one's environment.

For any program to successfully teach teens in care personal responsibility and prepare them to be participating citizens, child care staff and foster parents must be supported in their respective roles. These individuals can have a lasting effect, for better or worse, on the future of teens in care. Adults in direct contact with teens must elevate their expectations for teens and be confident in expressing these expectations to the teens. Caregivers must find out what individual teens want for themselves and encourage them to see themselves as contributing to society in the future. Caregivers should support teens' aspirations and not rush to judge them as unsuitable or unrealistic. The teen's aspirations are a means to engage the teen in assuming responsibility.

Caregivers of foster care teens must permit teens to experience the consequences of their actions, including failure. Common issues for teens in care are: clothing allowances, savings accounts, curfews, commitments, and personal care. These are good areas in which to teach personal responsibility. If the system wants teens to learn how to manage and budget money, teens must have experience with money. Let teens have bank accounts and give them free access to those. When and if they fail, help them try to figure out ways to make up for their mistakes. Foster parents and child care staff should be prepared for teens to fail as they struggle to adopt new areas of personal responsibility. They should learn how to communicate feedback about that failure without communicating that the teen is a failure.

Overall, it is essential to hold teens to high standards. If teens are enrolled in an independent-living class, they should be expected to attend all sessions, demonstrate they learned something, and receive a stipend only after satisfying requirements. Moreover, all staff and foster parents who have contact with teens must be conscious of their own behavior in terms of personal responsibility. They need to honor their own commitments because teens learn about responsibility from observing them.

In conclusion, foster care environments for teens must allow opportunities to learn personal responsibility. Foster care policymakers and practitioners should shift focus to include postemancipation services for older teens. It is important to develop policies and programs that convey the belief that teens in foster care can become participating citizens. Caregivers of teens must learn new ways of interacting with teens that give them more responsibility and control in planning for their own futures.

Reference

Foster Care Independence Act, P.L. 106-169 (H.R. 3443), 113 Stat. 1822 (1999).

Chapter 17

Wraparound Services: Facilitating the Transition from Foster Care to Young Adulthood

DAGMAR MORAVEC AND
HEWITT B. "RUSTY" CLARK

Perspective on Wraparound

This chapter illustrates the application of the wraparound process with youth in the foster care system in their transition to early adulthood. The two vignettes involve the most challenging of youth in the foster care system—those with emotional/behavioral difficulties—and highlight the roles that the wraparound process can play in supporting, teaching, advocating, and guiding youth from the foster care system as they transition to adulthood.

The wraparound process is a strengths-based, family-centered, team approach for creating individually tailored supports and services to meet the unique needs of children with difficulties and those of their families in two or more life domains. The process is driven by the family's "voice" and strengths. It is mediated through the guidance of a team of the parents, the child, and selected relatives, friends, and providers who care about the family's well-being. A resource coordinator assesses the child's and family's strengths and needs. The coordinator also facilitates the team's creation and implementation of a support plan. The plan assists the child and family in achieving their goals and improving their quality of life within the natural settings of home, school, and community (Clark & Hieneman, 1999, p. 184).

In both stories, many of the essential elements of the wraparound process are illustrated, such as: (a) Strengths, interests, and voice of the child and family drive the process; (b) team members provide an unconditional commitment; (c) strategies to help the child and family are individually tailored, culturally competent, and built on strengths; and (d) ownership of the process focuses everyone on the achievement of the child's and family's goals (VanDenBerg & Grealish, 1996). Every effort is made to involve birthparents as primary team members in the wraparound process. Unfortunately, at times, they are not willing to play a significant role on the team. Also, when older youth have a wraparound team, their voices become even more essential to the expression of their hopes, dreams, and goals for the future.

Jessica's Story: Wrapping for Support, Teaching, and Guidance

Jessica was 14 when wraparound entered her life. She had been in foster care for several months and was having a hard time. She was self-mutilating, depressed, and angry. Structured situations that involved following family rules and attending school caused constant friction, frustration, and ultimately led to dangerous activities including drug use and disappearing for days with possibly promiscuous activities occurring.

Jessica was one of six Caucasian siblings, the first daughter after two sons. Three more daughters followed. One of the girls died at age 3 from complications of cerebral palsy when Jessica was 5. The parents divorced when Jessica was 8. Her father left the family and had limited contact, usually only around holidays. Her mother continued to live in the family home and raise the five children. Jessica's mother was employed at a school for handicapped children as a paraprofessional. She worked hard to raise her family "right." However, she was prone to bouts of depression and fierce anger, which affected her child-rearing techniques and personal choices. The family was deeply religious and found comfort and support within the spiritual teachings and community of the church family. The children attended a private, church-sponsored school.

When she was 10, her relatively new stepfather began sexually abusing Jessica. She told her mother, who confronted the perpetrator, and told her pastor. They were counseled, and the perpetrator promised to not repeat the abuse. The abuse was not reported again until three years later. At that time, it was determined that the abuse had continued over the period. Jessica was told, even then, by the pastor that she must forgive and forget. Her mother and stepfather divorced when she was 13. Jessica had started questioning religion, hanging out with new friends, smoking and drinking, skipping school, and not following household expectations. She and her mother got into verbal and physical confrontations. Finally, child protective services intervened after a particularly volatile situation, deciding that it was not safe for Jessica to continue to live at home. She was placed in the care of a family friend, a licensed foster placement with the state, far removed from other family and friends. After a month or so, the placement started to fracture. Jessica attempted suicide and was hospitalized. She became aggressive toward younger children in the home. She cut her body with knives and other sharp objects, expressing exhilaration and delight and experiencing a peaceful high after the cutting.

Wraparound linked Jessica with her foster care worker, her foster family, a therapist, school personnel, several loyal friends, and the wraparound resource coordinator, creating a support team for her. During the next eight months, life began to level out for Jessica, with her team focusing on strengths and building plans of support around her goals regarding school and home. She attended school, sometimes with team support and sometimes alone. She participated in therapy, both individual and group. She had respite at structured and natural sites. Sometimes she still disappeared to her old life, but her visits there were shorter and less dangerous, with her rarely hurting herself. The team met time and again to revisit the methods that worked and to innovate when ideas failed. The resource coordinator and other team members and personnel from the school assisted Jessica by guiding and teaching her study skills, ways to make friends who had interests similar to hers, how to overcome test anxiety, how to accept criticism without reacting in anger or self-harm, appropriate dating behaviors, and the options of abstinence and condom use for safe sex practices. The team recognized Jessica's talent in art and created opportunities for her to attend concerts and art museums and to join school and church choirs. Over the course of time, Jessica's art teacher became an active mentor for her. During team meetings, there were celebrations of strengths and successes and crisis plan management when Jessica expressed her former destructive behaviors. The team continued to be there for Jessica, believing in and standing by her, no matter what transpired. Jessica began to trust the process and, with guidance, became the lead team player.

When her foster placement dissolved, she was ready for the challenge of returning to her old town, which was not far away. She lived in two additional foster placements, each for approximately one year. She enjoyed being part of a family. She bonded with her foster families and continues contact with each. Jessica also reconnected with her birthfamily in structured settings and with ground rules for Jessica. She spends time with her two younger sisters, playing games, doing their hair, helping with homework, and shopping. She has come to a certain understanding that she and her mother do not see eye to eye, and will not live in the same house, but that they can still love one another.

During the many transitions, her team followed, forming and re-forming, as Jessica's needs and supports changed. She learned to make and lead her own team "family," as she called it. During the past year, she, with the guidance, teaching, and support of her resource coordinator and other team members, moved on to independent living, finished her general equivalency diploma, held a steady job, and enrolled at the local community college. She is a strong, independent young woman. She is still prone to making impulsive decisions regarding men, but has become smart about keeping long-term goals in front of her, thereby avoiding pregnancy and abusive habits. She learned how to access resources, work with and in a team, get her voice heard and her needs met, and be a real mentor for other foster care teens. She now is part of others' wrap teams, and knows that her team circle will always surround her.

Devin's Story: Dreams from the Sideline of a Wraparound Playbook

Devin was a coach's dream. Selected to the city league all-conference and the all-area football dream team, he had a shoebox filled with letters from colleges that had expressed interest in him, starting when he was barely a sophomore. A slick young man with charm and tremendous athletic drive, he had achieved awe-inspiring football recognition that his team of supporters hoped would lead him past his troubled past and self-destructive ways.

Turbulence was part of Devin's history. He came to the attention of state juvenile workers because of a series of attention-seeking and personal survival crimes. Haunted by the death of his infant brother, Devin seemed to never find peace. As an 8-year-old, Devin, had been left in charge of his 4-month-old brother while his mother was at work and his father was drinking. Heavy drinking and domestic violence were part of the family interplay. That evening, Devin's father passed out after drinking, and Devin took care of the baby, feeding him and putting him in bed with their father, then falling asleep alongside them. When his mother returned home from work, she found the infant dead between Devin and his dad. Medical authorities ruled that the baby had died of sudden infant death syndrome, but Devin felt responsible and believed the family blamed him for the death.

Devin, an African American, had always looked older than his years and now started hanging out with older teens. He experimented with smoking and alcohol. He shoplifted if there was not enough food at home or because he was simply hungry or thirsty. He was involved in an unarmed robbery and indecent exposure charge after mooning a city bus. Even as his continued involvement with the court escalated, workers favored him and gave him additional chances. He was full of potential, intelligence, and charm. He wrote poetry and discussed philosophy. He was a leader, as well as a true team player. His diverse interests and abilities grew, both positive and negative.

Devin's mother gave up when he was 13 and his out-of-control behaviors continued. Their relationship was filled with anger, ambivalence, and little respect. Devin's father had left home and was involved with crack cocaine and offered no stability or ability to parent this needy boy. The court and state needed new options. The wraparound team had been working together for more than a year to maintain Devin in the community. The resource coordinator who facilitated the team was from a collaboration formed by local county and state public service agencies. She initially met with Devin and his family to identify natural and professional supports to form the team. The family identified a family member, a church friend, two social workers from court and state social services, two school personnel, and a psychologist for the initial team. Four members from that initial team are still part of Devin's team, more than six years later.

The team started by responding to a series of identified needs. They helped Devin's mom obtain a job, located child care for a sibling, and assisted with the purchase of a telephone for regular and emergency contact. The family was connected to therapy and recreational options. The minister and schoolteacher created summer employment to provide structure and supervision for Devin. This job encouraged responsibility, good work habits, and a chance for Devin to be a role model for younger children, in addition to the paycheck. Local sports personnel and peers took to Devin and invited him to work out and practice with them, adding to his support network and opportunities for positive activities. Devin also made a connection with a substance abuse counselor and started working with him on the streets and in the community, teaching about drug use and gang involvement. When school resumed, the team worked actively with the school to ensure Devin's attendance and involvement in educational and athletic activities. Tutoring was another component of Devin's plan during the school year, ensuring his continued success and growth in academic as well as sport avenues. The team often had visitors from these activities, always grouping and regrouping as Devin's team, assuming the roles of formal and informal cheerleaders and coaches. The team met weekly, then biweekly, and finally monthly unless a crisis occurred to prompt more frequent gatherings. The team met in the family's home, at court, at school, at a community or juvenile center, or at a community restaurant. Despite all the efforts and hard work of Devin's wraparound team, the unraveling of the family with the pain of unresolved loss and self-destructive behavior led to residential and foster placement for Devin for the next five years. It should be noted that throughout the multiple transitions and upheavals, the wraparound team never stopped visiting or supporting Devin.

From the start, Devin's athletic ability enticed other people into his circle. It was his chance to escape his cycle. Time and again, it provided stability and security. Foster care was never easy for Devin. The intimacy, structure, and relationships that a family system needs to function were overwhelming demands for Devin. Trust and closeness were too much to ask from a child who had not dealt with, much less resolved, the complicated issues Devin had survived in his young life. Time after time, he tested the limits, until yet another foster home broke down and sent him away to a group setting, in which he was much more comfortable and successful. In addition, he could not deal with the tremendous depression that he experienced each fall at the anniversary of his brother's death. He turned to drugs, alcohol, and indiscriminate relationships to numb the pain. Yet denial was the ultimate constant. He would get close in therapy, and then he would disappear into the community to soothe the pain and reemerge in denial, momentarily healed.

Devin lived in two residential facilities and four foster homes before he reached adulthood. He still focused on the future through the promise football offered, with the constant support of his wraparound team. The team members never wavered. They went to games and school conferences, travelling to different parts of the state where Devin was placed. They advocated for him and taught Devin to advocate and speak up for himself. They worked with him on budgeting, personal hygiene, dealing with authority figures, anger management, dressing for work, completion of work tasks, study skills, appropriate dating skills, and independent living skills. To learn some of these independent living skills, Devin attended classes set up for foster care and state wards, but his team members connected the skills to real life applications. One member accompanied Devin on numerous shopping trips. They started by making a list of wants and a list of needs and then prioritized the list. For once, Devin did not purchase on first impulse, but was guided by his list as they went to different stores. They dealt with suspicious store managers, keeping anger and the desire to shoplift at bay. During this and other such ventures, many daily living tasks and personal relationship issues were discussed, processed, and even resolved.

Almost every team took Devin into their personal and work lives, modeling and coaching relationships and appropriate behavior. The team members challenged him when he was soft and lazy and then nurtured him when he hid behind a protective shell. The team continued to vacillate, examining the benefits of keeping Devin close and supervised versus giving him lots of room to make decisions. The team often functioned as a family. All the dynamics of raising a teenager, struggling with the need to be independent yet held close, were present. The same emotional reactions also occurred. Devin would be angry, silent, and closed off, and then would disappear. Often, this was followed by Devin's hesitant asking for something, usually unrelated to the initial subject, to break the ice and return to the safety of the team. The team members had some of the same struggles. They wanted the best for their "son," but frustration and embarrassment were often matched by the need to try to nurture and protect him. They experienced sadness tinged with the realization that all this back and forth work was necessary for Devin to grow up and find his own way, whether or not it was the team's ideal way. The team always included his mother in planning and visits with the hope that she would continue the bond that Devin so yearned for in his life. The team brought new foster parents, teachers, and coaches into his support circle. They celebrated Devin's successes and cried over his challenges or defeats. Devin had nicknames for all the team members and the roles they had played for him.

When he was 18, Devin had a sexual contact with a 14-year-old girl and was accused of criminal sexual conduct. Because he was an adult, the wraparound team could do little except talk to the judge about all the potential this young man had. He had football scholarship offers to major schools, but as allegations surfaced, the offers faded. Depression hit, and Devin went to jail. His team stayed near him. They believed in him, sometimes more than Devin did. They told him he could still play football and use his intelligence. The team cheered him on, but Devin was done with that dream. However, he still wanted and sought out his wraparound team. He hung out with his mom, and with her and a team member, he secured a job. He started reintegrating into the community, reestablishing ties with his siblings and other family. He called his team asking for support, advice, and occasionally for a free lunch! Devin is still hungry for success, for being part of a team/family, for a different life. As a young adult, he is maintaining employment, living with his mother, exploring college options, staying clean and out of trouble, connecting with friends from work and from the police club gym, where he does well in boxing tournaments. Although Devin is still trying to formulate his future goals, he knows he has the defensive and offensive lines in his team to back him in achieving his goals.

Wrap-up Summary

The life of a young person is a process, as is wraparound, neither of them always yielding the ideal outcome, but always providing another opportunity to regroup and refocus. In both of these vignettes, there are points in the lives of the child and other family members at which healthier pathways with the possibility of more positive outcomes might have been achieved had a wraparound process been available earlier. Workers cannot wait until a youth has been in out-of-home placement for years or for a crisis to occur, particularly if these types of events can be avoided through the provision of a family-friendly, effective process of supports and services.

Parallel developments to the wraparound process encompass some of its support features and are even more focused on futures planning and on competency development of children, parents, teachers, and other key people. The alternative approaches of positive behavioral support (Koegel, Koegel, & Dunlap, 1996), transition to independent process system (Clark & Davis, 2000), and multisystemic therapy (Henggeler, Schoenwald, Borduin, Rowland, & Cunningham, 1998) continue to undergo program development, research, and dissemination efforts with encouraging findings (e.g., Clark & Davis, 2000; Clark, Lee, Prange, & McDonald, 1996; Clark, Unger, & Stewart, 1993; Henggeler et al., 1999; Kincaid, 1996; Vaughn, Dunlap, Fox, Clarke, & Bucy, 1997). More information about each of the approaches is available at: Transition to Independent Process: http://www.fmhi.usf.edu/cfs/policy/tip; Positive Behavioral Support: http://www.fmhi.usf.edu/cfs/dares/flpbs/statement.html; Multisystemic Therapy: http://www.mstservices.com; Wraparound: http://www.air.org/cecp/wraparound

Each of these approaches, particularly transition to independent process, has been applied to transition-age young people with emotional and/or behavioral difficulties, some of whom are from the foster care system.

References

Clark, H. B., & Davis, M. (Eds.). (2000). *Transition to adulthood: A resource for assisting young people with emotional or behavioral difficulties.* Baltimore: Paul Brookes.

Clark, H. B., & Hieneman, M. (1999, Summer). Comparing the wraparound process to positive behavioral support. *Journal of Positive Behavior Intervention, 1,* 183–186.

Clark, H. B., Lee, B., Prange, M. E., & McDonald, B. A. (1996). Children lost within the foster care system: Can wraparound service strategies improve placement outcomes? *Journal of Child and Family Studies, 5,* 39–54.

Clark, H. B., Unger, K. V., & Stewart, E. S. (1993). Transition of youth and young adults with emotional/behavioral difficulties into employment, education, and independent living. *Community Alternatives: International Journal of Family Care, 5*(2), 19–46.

Henggeler, S. W., Schoenwald, S. K., Borduin, C. M., Rowland, M. D., & Cunningham, P. B. (1998). *Multi-systemic treatment of antisocial behavior in children and adolescents.* New York: Guilford Press.

Henggeler, S. W., Rowland, M. D., Randall, J., Ward, D. M., Pickrel, S. G., Cunningham, P. B., et al. (1999). Home-based multi-systemic therapy as an alternative to the hospitalization of youths in psychiatric crisis: Clinical outcomes. *Journal of the American Academy of Child and Adolescent Psychiatry, 38,* 1331–1339.

Kincaid, D. (1996). Person-centered planning. In L. K., Koegel, R. L. Koegel, & G. Dunlap (Eds.), *Positive behavioral support: Including people with difficult behavior in the community* (pp. 439–465). Baltimore: Paul Brookes.

Koegel, L. K., Koegel, R. L., & Dunlap, G. (1996). *Positive behavioral support: Including people with difficult behavior in the community.* Baltimore: Paul Brookes.

VanDenBerg, J. E., & Grealish, E. M. (1996). Individualized services and supports through the wraparound process: Philosophy and procedures. *Journal of Child and Family Studies, 5,* 7–21.

Vaughn, B. J., Dunlap, G., Fox, L., Clarke, S., & Bucy, M. (1997). Parent-professional partnership in behavioral support: A case study of community-based intervention. *Journal of the Association for Persons with Severe Handicaps, 22*(4), 186–197.

Chapter 18

Assessment:
An Interpretive Summary

EDMUND V. MECH

Investment in human capital is a worldwide phenomenon, with average levels of education rising in all developed countries....In the United States, between one-half and three-quarters of all new jobs will require some college training because of the demands of modern technology.

—*Crawford (1991, p. 32)*

The Foster Care Independence Act will enable teens who are aging-out of the foster care system to succeed in that difficult transition to adulthood...it's a sensible investment of resources.

—*U.S. Representative Nancy Johnson (2001, pp. 1–2)*

Roots and Wings: A Dual Challenge for Service Delivery

Independent-living services for youth living in foster care are an important element of child welfare systems in the United States and other countries. Children need many supports to grow and develop. Supports that are indispensable to preparing for independence are parental commitment, continuity of care, family stability, and a sense of permanence. This chapter refers to the various aspects of family environment as *roots*. Most families play a major role in preparing their children for independence and economic self-sufficiency. This chapter refers to the ability to break away from continued dependence on one's family to independence as *wings*. Families can transmit roots and wings to their children. The root systems of foster wards are likely to be insufficient, as the wards come, in large part, from dysfunctional families and unstable households. Once placement occurs and the substitute care system takes over, high percentages of state wards have difficulty preparing to achieve independence and self-sufficiency. Young people are usually placed in foster care through no fault of their own. The emergence of systems of independent-living services represents a positive effort by society to correct, modify, or otherwise compensate youth in placement for family deficiencies, as well as for imperfections in the foster care system itself. Although state programs must strive to build first-class opportunity structures for older foster wards, the ultimate responsibility rests with youth themselves to take advantage of opportunities and use them as bridges to independence and self-sufficiency.

Advocates for Foster Youth

Numerous organizations and youth-serving agencies advocate for the improvement of independent-living services. The list encompasses national, state, and local institutions, and includes leadership from the White House and Congress as well as the efforts of hundreds of child welfare practitioners across the nation. Advocacy groups have spoken; legislators have listened and acted. The 1999 Chafee Foster Care Independence Act is an example of legislative responsiveness. The Foster Care Independence Act represents landmark legislation that recognizes the need to extend assistance to foster youth until age 21. Organizations that provide continuing leadership to the foster youth independent-living movement include the U.S. Children's Bureau, the Child Welfare League of America, the Annie E. Casey Foundation, the National Resource Center for Youth Services at the University of Oklahoma, and the National Independent Living Association. Conferences, institutes, workshops, and seminars on independent-living services are convened regularly. High-visibility training programs are sponsored by the National Resource Center for Youth Services, the Annie E. Casey Foundation, the Child Welfare League of America, and the Daniel Memorial Institute. Research-oriented studies appear in journals such as *Child Welfare, The Children and Youth Services Review, Child and Adolescent Work*, and *Social Work*. With respect to opportunities for research on independent living, the possibilities for expanding the knowledge base and affecting program improvement are numerous. This field must continue to move toward building a strong, factual-theoretical foundation as a basis for service delivery. Program issues that rank high on the priority lists of independent-living advocates are: educational achievement, improved employment and career preparation, and social, personal, and emotional conditions that pose barriers to independence. In addition, there is the ongoing challenge of responding to placement system problems. This refers to deficiencies in state agency practices that must be rectified if foster wards are to progress toward independence. A series of placement issues that must be addressed are described in a monograph published by the Institute for Child and Family

Policy at the Edmund S. Muskie School of Public Service, University of Southern Maine. Issues identified are based on a conference organized by the National Resource Center for Youth Services, University of Oklahoma, and funded by the Annie E. Casey Foundation ("Improving Economic Opportunities," 1998).

With respect to preparation for employment and improving economic opportunities for foster young people, the conference outlined a series of recommendations. The following passages are quoted from that conference report ("Improving Economic Opportunities," 1998, pp. 8–9):

1. Begin teaching social skills when youth enter placement. Connect youth to community citizens for possible long-term contact.

2. Connect foster youth with the world-of-work. Foster youth need to acquire technological skills and should be provided with opportunities to utilize and apply these skills.

3. Foster wards need opportunities to participate in realistic work experience situations. Establishing relationships with the business community is a vital element in building work and career opportunities.

4. In teaching world-of-work skills, emphasis should be directed toward job retention, job responsibility, and punctuality in meeting work schedules, as well as the importance of a positive attitude toward supervision.

5. Connect foster youth to events such as job fairs and visits to technical institutes, colleges, and universities.

Developing a comprehensive foster youth opportunity structure requires many talents, cooperation across subsystems, and a knowledgeable core leadership group. Elements that should be included are:

- Training foster parents who focus on preparing wards for independent living.

- Creating cooperative partnerships between youth-serving agencies and education systems is vital but has been slow to unfold.

- Developing a network of postemancipation services for foster wards who require assistance after leaving placement.

- Developing a coalition of education advocates for foster wards, whose task is to help youth access postsecondary education and achieve success in educational endeavors.

- Advocating and assisting youth who are preparing for independence in locating affordable community housing.

Overall, the ingredients considered vital in developing opportunity structures for independence and self-sufficiency are: partnerships with schools, participatory involvement of business and industry, housing resources, and active participation by adult mentors and citizen advocates, as well as families who are willing to provide foster homes that focus on preparing youth for adulthood.

Increasingly, foster youth are serving as their own advocates. The placement system is beginning to accept suggestions for improvement from youth themselves. Appendix 4 summarizes trends in the development of state youth advisory boards. Appendix 5 is a foster youth survivors script that highlights the experiences of young people in placement.

In other countries, opportunity structure legislation, recommendations, and proposals are emerging at a rapid rate. In Australia, the *Summary Report from the Prime Minister's Youth Pathways Action Plan Taskforce* (2001) contained 24 recommendations. Heading the list is education with stipulations that young people are given an opportunity "to complete 12 years of schooling or its vocational equivalent" (p. 9) and that "young people living without adequate support are linked to a local service network with an individual worker or agency assigned a support responsibility (p. 15)."

In the United Kingdom, the Children (Leaving Care) Act, 2000, amends the historic Children Act 1989 and extends the responsibility of local authorities to youth who leave care. Included in the amended version are such elements as that local authorities must arrange for each eligible youth to be assigned a personal adviser until youth reach age 21. Local authority organizations keep in touch with all youth who leave care, including those ages 18 to 21. The "pathway plan" continues until at least age 21 and covers education, training, employment/career plans, and housing arrangements.

In Northern Ireland, provisions in the Children (Leaving Care) Bill are similar to the amended Children (Leaving Care) Act in England and Wales. Stipulated in the Northern Ireland version are pathway plans and personal advisers.

In Canada, the National Youth in Care Network (2000) has expressed continuing concern about the educational needs of youth in placement. One of their conclusions is that "most of the time success in life and success in school go hand in hand" (p. 3).

Overall, in the United States as in the other countries surveyed, education stands out as one of the key elements in the path to independence.

Toward Achieving Economic Self-Sufficiency

Factors that shift the odds in favor of achieving economic stability are: education; career preparation; mentors and wraparound services; transitional apartments; subsidy assistance, including a favorable tuition-waiver policy; and personal and shared responsibility.

These elements are the building blocks necessary to achieve economic stability. This multifactor framework is the essence of an effective opportunity structure. Opportunity structures are not abstractions. The extent to which opportunity structures exist within programs and jurisdictions can be assessed. Opportunity structures can be identified, described, and measured. Independent-living programs should inventory their social capital resources and describe the opportunities that are available. A critical sixth factor comes into play—namely, foster youth themselves. Variability exists in motivation, goal setting, commitment to reach goals, and a willingness to take advantage of opportunities that are available. Independent-living programs should be responsible for generating opportunity structures for foster wards. There is, however, little reason to hold state agencies and service delivery personnel responsible for the postemancipation status of youth who fail to capitalize on opportunities open to them.

Short-circuiting education, failing to complete a postsecondary program and/or specialized training, settling for employment in minimum wage jobs with no benefits, and early parenting are pitfalls to be avoided. It is likely that youth advocates, child welfare workers, foster parents, mentors, teachers, and other citizens support the message that the centerpiece of self-sufficiency is education, education, and more education. Foster youth themselves must choose the road to be traveled. Will it be a road that uses a series of shortcuts and dead-ends in continued dependence on society, family members, or friends? Or will it be a more prudent, disciplined route? The high road, so to speak, which features educational achievement, career preparation, and accomplishment? To foster young people, we must say loud and clear, "Society can help; it can provide resources, but your future is in your hands."

By the same token, state child welfare programs must accept the challenge of building state-of-the-art opportunity structures for foster wards. Evidence-based aspects of independent-living research suggest the following elements are essential in an effective opportunity system:

Education/Career Preparation. Establish expectations for upgrading the literacy levels of wards to include reading, writing, and comprehension. Progress should be monitored using age and grade-level norms. Assessment tools need to document educational, social, and employment competencies. Periodic checks should be conducted on the preparation levels of foster wards in hard and soft skills. Emphasize the importance of educational achievement as a pivotal factor in promoting successful transitions to independence. Without exception, birthfamilies, caregivers, relatives, foster families, and congregate and residential facilities should be expected to reinforce the value of education not only on paper, but also in deed. Although high school graduation is generally viewed as a minimal standard for attaining economic self-sufficiency, a high school diploma or a general equivalency diploma are probably insufficient preparation for competing in the 21st-century workplace. A high percentage of young people now aging out of placement are prime candidates for joining an ever-widening foster care underclass. Postsecondary education is imperative. It is particularly suited to foster wards who have the motivation, ability, resources, and support to move beyond the outmoded standard that high school alone is good enough. The Early Start to Emancipation Program in California is making postsecondary education possible for hundreds of foster wards. Also, the career academy model has support in California and is growing in other states. In addition to academic curricula, vocational, technical, and occupational apprenticeships are necessary to accommodate non–college bound youth.

Living Arrangements/Transitional Apartments. Evidence exists that placement instability, mobility, and insertion into restrictive environments is detrimental to the acquisition of independent-living skills. Youth who experience group and residential care, psychiatric hospitalization, and so forth are not as well-prepared for independent living as are youth who experience less restrictive living environments (i.e., kinship care or a regular foster home). Transitional apartment experience is one of the living arrangements that can facilitate acquisition of independence. One option that can be highly beneficial is to offer youth an apartment-based practice living experience starting at age 17, or at least nine months prior to emancipation. If a practice apartment experience is not working, wards can always return to a former placement and try again when their readiness level is more firmly established. Anecdotal reports from the field suggest that once youth experience a supervised practice apartment arrangement, there is usually little inclination to return to a traditional placement.

Mentoring/Wraparound Services. Mentoring has emerged as a feasible intervention. Mentors are widely used as resources in preparing foster wards for independence. Foster wards should be afforded opportunities to connect with a mentor at least one year prior to emancipation. Optimal benefits accrue if mentor and mentee are able to maintain an active, positive relationship for a minimum of one year after emancipation. Most programs ask too little of mentors with respect to duration of commitment. The average commitment is nine months. More time is needed. A two-year commitment is recommended.

Just as adult mentors are an important element in the process of easing young wards into community living, wraparound services are a valuable asset. The wraparound model uses natural-systems citizens to assist newly emancipated youth in adjusting to community life and meeting the obligations associated with responsible citizenship. In theory, "pure" wraparound team membership involves parents, relatives, teachers, ministers, and citizen volunteers from business and a range of occupational endeavors. Most specialists recommend against using placement system workers as facilitators for a wrap team.

Subsidy Assistance. Governments use subsidies to accomplish goals that are beneficial to society. Subsidy assistance in various forms is vital in facilitating the transitions of foster young people to self-sufficiency. A subsidy is a contract between donors (i.e., society, taxpayers, state independent-living programs) and donees (foster youth who are striving to become self-sufficient). Subsidies are tangible resources—cash as well as noncash—that enhance progress toward self-sufficiency. A reasonable subsidy structure should include the following resources: food stamps; housing vouchers; medical coverage (Medicaid); financial assistance to help pay for basic household start-up costs, such as rent and utility deposits, bedding, and kitchen utensils; as well as monthly cash allotments to assist in the transitional process. Tuition waivers are gaining support as a resource to give foster wards access to postsecondary education and training programs.

Overall, safety net services and means-tested programs are vital, especially in the early stages of aiding youth in the transition process. An indispensable resource in the transition process is the independent-living subsidy (ILS). The ILS model typically includes: (a) a plan for self-sufficiency that is achievable with a reasonable time period (18-24 months), (b) the requirement that the youth is employed and capable of contributing a specified amount each month to his or her financial support, and (c) the requirement that the youth has the basic skills needed for implementing an independent-living plan and is willing to work with a responsible adult volunteer, who serves as a resource until independence is achieved.

Shared Responsibility. It is desirable to work toward establishing mutual responsibility expectations between a program and youth. The main task in independent-living systems is to design an opportunity structure that responds to the needs of target youth. It is difficult for young wards to succeed unless the opportunities offered are recognized and optimized. With respect to current practice, there is a dilemma. Mentors cannot mentor unless mentees are active participants in the match. Apartments cannot work unless youth do their part in demonstrating responsible behavior. Pregnancy and early parenting pose barriers and lengthen the odds against achieving self-sufficiency. Numerous examples can be given that document the necessity of young wards to take responsibility for their actions and respective futures. Holding the child welfare system as the sole agent responsible for turning out "successful" young adults is shortsighted. A one-sided approach overlooks the importance of placing responsibility on youth for their own futures. Studies of adolescents and young adults who are high achievers suggest the presence of potent mediating variables such as internal locus of control, achievement motivation, and level of aspiration. Psychological variables such as these are very real, but unfortunately, they are not under the direct control of the child welfare system.

Expanding the Knowledge Base

It is important to conduct studies that are likely to inform practice. A favorite type of study on independent living is the retrospective follow-up design. The retrospective approach obtains information from foster youth a few years after they have been discharged from placement. "How are they doing" information is collected for education, employment, income, housing, and similar indicators. Retrospective procedures are useful in early stages of program development and can help identify deficiencies in the preparation of wards for independent living. A number of retrospective as well as short-term prospective studies have been completed, and beneficial information has been obtained. The field should shift focus, however, to include a more targeted, productive research agenda. Investigations undertaken in the following areas will contribute information that can inform and improve practice.

Area 1—Long-Term Outcomes. There is a need to shift emphasis from conducting retrospective studies and short-term prospective follow-ups to more definitive, longer-term, prospective investigations. Short-term studies that strive to assess outcomes 90 days, 180 days, or 1 year following discharge are unlikely to provide as accurate a picture of progress as are longer-term, follow-up studies. Short-term studies are likely to depict foster youth as doing poorly after discharge. Longer-term studies are in a better position to describe the developmental struggles of foster wards in striving for self-sufficiency and to document positive accomplishments and outcomes.

Area 2—Utilization of Community-Based Resources. Studies are needed of the extent to which foster youth use community resources following discharge from care. Which resources do youth find helpful, which resources are overlooked, and which resources are needed but not available? Child Welfare League of America standards emphasize the importance of youths' being able to locate and use community-based resources. Natural-systems resources such as churches, Boys and Girls Clubs, social organizations, and citizen mentors can play vital transitional roles. Child welfare workers and foster wards should work together to connect with community resources in advance of discharge from placement.

Area 3—Studies in Personal and/or Shared Responsibility for Successful Transitions. Congressional intent of Section 477 in the John H. Chafee Foster Care Independence Act is that state wards "recognize their personal responsibility to prepare for and make the transition to adulthood." In enacting legislation that provides extended services for foster wards until age 21, Congress placed an important obligation on youth to assume responsibility for their own futures. State independent-living programs can create first-class opportunity structures, supports, and resources as bridges to self-sufficiency, but it is the youth themselves who are critical to their own independence. One study within the personal responsibility domain would be to document best practices in how to develop and implement shared responsibility agreements with older foster wards.

Area 4—Status of African-American Males Following Discharge from Foster Care. The postemancipation self-sufficiency status of African American males deserves investigation. Nonwhite youth are over-represented in out-of-home placements relative to their presence in the general population. It is not unusual for nonwhite youth to comprise 35% or more of state foster care caseloads. Older, nonwhite young adults are likely to spend substantial time living in costly congregate placements prior to discharge. The paradox is that congregate/residential settings are also high in restrictiveness, which tends to work against quality preparation for independence and self-sufficiency.

Moreover, reports on the development of African American youth include repeated warnings about the hazards that face nonwhite adolescent males in terms of entry into adult society. Edelman and Ladner (1991) described the prospects for nonwhite males to attain a reasonable level of economic self-sufficiency as "out-of-the-question." A similar perspective espoused by Gibbs (1988) characterizes the black male as an "endangered species." Sum and Fogg (1991) concluded that nonwhite adolescents, especially black youth, experience poverty rates that are "three to five times that of white non-hispanic poverty rates" (p. 42). Yet, despite the writings of numerous racial-minority youth scholars and advocates, analytical studies on the independent-living preparation of African American males in placement are virtually nonexistent. With respect to school achievement, Irvine and Irvine (1995) challenged prevailing beliefs as to why black youth have difficulty in school. The argument that black youth have "come to view intellectual activity and achievement as the domain of whites" (Irvine & Irvine, 1995, p. 130) is rejected. Their recommended solution calls for teachers, instructional techniques, and curricula that are culturally responsive. Other black youth advocates emphasize internal variables such as "motivation" and "positive mental attitude" (Kunjufu, 1986) or the Afrocentricity model espoused by Perkins (1986). Perkins pointed out that youth cannot teach themselves to become responsible adults. He stated, "Community elders have a responsibility for helping to train youths to become responsible adults" (Perkins, 1986, p. 198). Glasgow (1981), in his volume, *The Black Underclass*, leaned toward an opportunity structure approach. Glasgow stated, "If this nation is to break underclassness and its accompanying social ills, it must provide opportunities for young

Blacks to become attached to a sound system of income and mobility" (p. 184). Glasgow is against using a public welfare strategy as a solution. He stated, "Public assistance must never be accepted as the primary source of income by Black work-capable citizens" (Glasgow, 1981, p. 184). A congressional hearing on "Barriers and Opportunities for America's Young Black Men" was convened in 1989, under the jurisdiction of the House Committee on Children, Youth, and Families. The prevailing emphasis in testimony was on confirming the myriad of problems faced by black youth on succeeding in mainstream society (Sum, 1989). Solutions were proposed, but only in sketchy, broad-brush fashion. There was support for the community coalition model with roles for church and religious leaders, retired persons, blue-collar and white-collar workers, fraternal and civic groups, social groups, and so forth, with the assertion that "everyone can play an active role." The fact remains that despite periodic concerns about the well-being of nonwhite youth, there is a shortage of empirical evidence as to the status of emancipated foster wards. Follow-up information is very much needed on nonwhite males.

Area 5—Characteristics of Caregivers and Service Delivery Personnel. Little information has been collected on the characteristics of caregivers and service delivery personnel. The independent-living field lacks systematic information on the education backgrounds and work experiences of child welfare personnel. A similar gap exists with respect to the characteristics of foster parents who serve older adolescents. Overall, it is important to document the extent to which child welfare independent-living workers and foster parents are connected to the values and beliefs embodied in education and in striving for self-sufficiency. What are the value and belief systems of child welfare workers and caregivers who interact on a regular basis with foster wards?

Area 6—Status of Independent-Living Services for American Indian Youth. The Chafee independent-living legislation provides opportunities for tribes to consult and collaborate with states to obtain community-based services for Indian youth. The task of transitioning to adulthood and eventual self-sufficiency poses special difficulties for Indian youth. One of the obstacles is the dual expectation that "Indian youth need to learn living skills that are...applicable in their tribal communities as well as in mainstream America" (Clemens, 2000, p. 4). Moreover, Indian youth experience high rates of alcohol and substance abuse. Coupled with excessive school dropout rates, these factors pose severe barriers to employability, job retention, and access to career preparation opportunities.

It is disturbing to learn that school dropout rates range from 45% to 85% and that the majority of Indian youths leave school by Grade 9. Another facet of the Indian youth profile is a high out-of-home placement rate, which is nearly double the rate reported for other children. The placement rate reported by Clemens is 12.5 per 1,000 Indian children versus 6.9 per 1,000 for non-Indian children. If the 12.5 per 1,000 estimate is accurate, then the out-of-home placement rate for Indian children has risen nearly 50% since the 1980 children and youth in placement census report by the Office for Civil Rights (Mech, 1983).

Analyses of independent-living programs that serve Indian communities are needed. Questions that deserve answers include: What is meant by independent-living services for Indian communities? What is considered a successful transition for Indian youth? What is the organizational structure and design of independent-living programs for Indian youth? Despite variability across reservations, tribes, and states, information is needed on self-sufficiency preparation for Indian youth.

Area 7—Skills Acquisition: Measurement and Assessment Issues. Long overdue are analyses of assessment procedures, instruments, and psychometric devices for gauging the preparation of foster wards for self-sufficiency. With respect to measuring readiness for independent living, the Daniel Memorial Inventory and the Ansell-Casey test are the instruments that are known best. The Daniel Memorial material has been in use for many years, and the organization is a pioneer in the assessment area. Little field research has been conducted with respect to testing the psychometric properties of assessment devices or the extent to which instruments now in use are predictive of outcomes.

Overall, the field is deficient in collecting empirical information on skills acquisition among foster wards. An article by Hahn (1995) takes note of the limited role that measurement and assessment plays in foster care. Hahn reported on a field test of several assessment devices that was conducted in New York City. Four instruments were administered to foster youth ages 16 to 17. The devices were: (a) the Test of Basic Education, (b) the Test for Everyday Living, (c) the Daniel Memorial Independent Living Assessment for Life Skills, and (d) the Effective Social Skills Test. Hahn's report is instructive. The results cited by Hahn provided the New York's child/youth welfare administrators with differential information as to which youth lacked the skills required for successful transition to independence. With respect to reading comprehension, one of the skills considered as basic for attaining self-sufficiency, foster youth surveyed were on average reading four years below their grade level. A four-year average deficit in reading comprehension poses a serious challenge for schools and for the foster care system. The New York City results represent but one example of what is likely a widespread condition. Despite the availability of standardized measures that offer normative information against which to compare individual or group profiles, at this juncture, independent-living networks appear unwilling or unable to document, certify, or otherwise gauge the skill level of foster wards. School systems collect information in a variety of areas, including subject matter grades, cumulative records, and standardized test scores. To what extent are child welfare workers retrieving school-related data for state wards and using this information in formulating transitional plans for independence?

The educational status of wards deserves attention, as does the question of criterion measures in judging the usefulness of assessment procedures. Practitioners as well as research investigators have shown limited interest in the extent to which numerical scores, rating scales, and other assessment devices are predictive of subsequent performance.

As part of the University of Illinois Foster Youth Project, an effort was made to test the predictive value of an assessment device, the Life-Skills Inventory. The inventory was administered as part of a battery of instruments intended to assess readiness for independent living. Youth ($N = 534$) in a variety of placement settings were tested individually on or about age 18, but prior to emancipation. A 50-item, multiple-choice inventory was used. Each item was weighted four points, and the maximum score possible was 200 points. The point distribution was as follows: The highest score was 196 points, the lowest was 52 points, and the mean score was 128 points. At the age 21 follow-up, five outcome measures were used: education level, employment, income, public aid use, and orientation toward self-sufficiency.

Table 18.1 summarizes the correlation matrix between lifeskills scores at age 18 and five outcome measures (education level, employment, income, public aid cost, and orientation toward self-sufficiency) obtained at age 21.

Of the 30 coefficients, 20, or 67%, reached statistical significance at the 5% level of confidence. The highest coefficients were between life-skills scores and education level. The overall education coefficient of .377

Table 18.1

Correlations Between Life-Skills Inventory Scores at Age 18 and Selected Outcome Indicators at Age 21

Race/Ethnicity	n	Education Level	Employment	Income	Public Aid Cost	ORSS	Overall
White Male	90	.466*	.245*	.290*	.034	.179	.337*
Nonwhite Male	55	.441*	.208	.019	.139	.105	.314*
White Female	161	.309*	.096	.091	.241*	.422*	.346*
Nonwhite Female	104	.362*	.092	.224*	.232*	.359*	.377*
Overall	410	.377*	.158*	.177*	.186*	.291*	.355*

Note: ORSS = orientation toward self-sufficiency.

Source: Age 21 follow-up; Foster Youth-in-Transition Project, University of Illinois at Urbana-Champaign.

*Denotes statistical significance at .05 or less.

suggests a link, but is too low for practical use. This draws attention to the importance of testing the predictive value of assessment devices against a criterion. Assessments can produce numerical information, but numbers unrelated to subsequent behaviors, consequences, or outcomes are difficult to interpret. Much remains to be accomplished in assessing independent-living services and in measuring the effects of services on preparing foster wards for independence.

A Look to the Future

Independent-living services are recognized as a worthwhile way to help foster youth prepare for self-sufficiency. There is public support for such programs. Legislators are in favor of self-sufficiency services. Youth advocates, social agencies, and child welfare practitioners have labored long and hard for federal legislation to assist foster wards to achieve independence. The field has now achieved its goal. The Foster Care Independence Act provides authorization, a clear mandate, financial support, and latitude for innovativeness in program development. The essential provisions of the act are summarized in Appendix 1. The highlights are: (a) a $140 million entitlement, increased from $70 million; (b) an increase in the age of eligibility of foster youth who can be served to age 21; (c) equal benefits to Indian children; (d) a set percentage of program funds to be used for room and board; and (e) the states' option to extend Medicaid coverage to foster youth ages 18 to 21.

The field has legislative support and increased financial resources. The goals of independence and economic self-sufficiency are compatible with traditional American values. Standards to guide independent-living services have been updated by the Child Welfare League of America. It remains for states to create new and improved opportunity structures and to demonstrate that the Chafee legislation works. Legislation is a means to an end. Legislation provides mechanisms and resources for accomplishing goals. Too often, once legislation is enacted, program operation becomes an end in itself, often taking on the characteristics of an industrial assembly line. Accomplishment, outcomes, and performance are set aside. The field must take steps to protect itself from being diverted from its mission, which is "to identify children who are likely to remain in foster care until 18 years of age and to help these children make the transition to self-sufficiency" (Section 466, SSA, Subtitle A, Section 101).

Keeping the mission of preparing youth for self-sufficiency is the very least that society owes these young people. The noted philosopher, George Santayana (1905), cautioned that, "Those who cannot remember the past are condemned to repeat it" (p. 284). In many ways, independent living as a field of practice may be at the crossroads. The challenge in moving ahead is to improve opportunity structures for youth, to use every shred of evidence possible to improve practice, and to advocate for excellence in service delivery. Appendix 2 contains an inventory of program resources related to helping practitioners keep abreast of trends in independent-living services.

The next phase in the development of independent-living services is implementation of the Chafee legislation. In the process, the field will continue to encounter efforts to label foster youth as "problems," as "failures," as "castoffs," and "second-class citizens." When reporting on foster care issues, media coverage tends to reflect a negative perspective. Articles in *The New York Times*, the *Los Angeles Times*, the *Washington Post*, and the *Chicago Tribune* are examples of how older foster wards are depicted as victims. Sengupta (2000), in a *New York Times* article, concluded, "Homelessness is a common fate; at the Covenant House Teen Shelter in Manhattan, 80% of the roughly 400 teenagers who stay there nightly are former foster children, many come directly from the jails on Rikers Island" (p. B6).

The *Los Angeles Times* tracked the postemancipation status of three foster wards over an approximate 12-month period. Two of the youth are described as follows:

> *Janea and Sam skip between homeless shelters and seedy hotels…some nights they double-up with other homeless families stuffing ten people into a motel room….Janea and Sam dabbled in petty crimes mainly as a matter of survival. Janea wrote hundreds of dollars worth of bad checks to buy clothes, blankets, food…when stores started rejecting the worthless paper…the couple began shoplifting. (Willon, 2001, p. A43)*

The article concluded, "Those who work with foster children see only inevitability to their lives, an intractable cycle of addiction, abuse, and indifference that is tough to break, regardless of government programs." The *Los Angeles Times* report may apply to the three or four youth cited, but a steady barrage of negative coverage does not give a balanced picture of the postemancipation status of foster wards. Journalistic interests tend to reflect foster youth who are in difficulty or headed for a poor outcome. Case selectivity leads to one-sided reporting and conclusions that may be erroneous and/or premature. If repeated often enough, the "poor outcomes syndrome" will become a permanent label for emancipated foster youth. The newly developed federal-state National Youth in Transition Database is expected to provide substantive information on independent-living services and outcomes. Appendix 3 summarizes key elements in this data information system.

A balanced perspective on the postdischarge status of foster youth that includes their progress, achievements, and accomplishments is needed. There is little merit in limiting follow-up efforts to short-term studies. Ninety-day, 6-month, 12-month, or 24-month postdischarge follow-ups usually show that significant numbers of foster youth have difficulty transitioning to independence. Short-term follow-ups are useful in helping to identify service delivery needs and program gaps, but the results should not be construed as conclusive. One interpretation of the Chafee legislation is that extending services to age 21 along with additional resources will help prepare foster wards for *eventual* self-sufficiency.

Most observers are aware that the odds are against large numbers of foster youth becoming economically self-sufficient by age 21. Emancipation from dependence requires that all youth, foster as well as nonfoster, undergo periods of experiential reality as the price of independence and responsible adulthood. Developmental maturity has its own timetable. Age 21 is a convenient marker, but is probably outmoded as a milestone in today's culture of extended dependency. Hence, if more accurate information is desired about foster youth transitions to adulthood, longer-term follow-ups are needed. Emphasis should be placed on collecting transition data well beyond age 21. A follow-up standard of age 25 and beyond is not unreasonable. The oft-cited Wisconsin follow-up project uses a short-term longitudinal design. Not unexpectedly, 12 to 18 months after leaving care, the results indicate the transition to independence is difficult for youth leaving the placement system (Courtney, Piliavin, Grogan-Kaylor, & Nesmith, 2001). The Wisconsin project has potential for extending the follow-up period and assessing how youth fare at age 25 and beyond. Longer-range outcome information is very much needed.

Extended-age follow-up efforts require financial resources as well as collaborative partnerships with key agencies and organizations. Follow-up coalitions may include federal agency and/or private foundation support, state child welfare cooperation, technical expertise from academic investigators, as well as leadership from organizations such as the Child Welfare League of America and the Annie E. Casey Foundation. Emphasis should be on identifying the unrealized potential and talent that exists in graduates of the foster care system, as well as on providing a balanced analysis of their progress, accomplishments and prospects for the future. In the final analysis, a solid database derived from tracking the postemancipation progress of former wards is the best foundation from which to build effective independent-living programs and services.

To do less would be a disservice to the thousands of foster wards who look to the placement system to point them in the right direction and help prepare them for adult living.

References

Children (Leaving Care) Act, 2000. Available from http://www.hmso.gov.uk/acts/acts2000/20000035.htm

Children (Leaving Care) Bill, Northern Ireland Assembly. Available from http://www.ni-assembly.gov.uk/legislation/primary/2001/niabill5_01.htm

Clemens, N. (2000). *Improving access to independent living services for tribes and American Indian youths* (pp. 24). Seattle, WA: Casey Family Programs, and Portland, OR: National Indian Child Welfare Association. Available from http://www.welfareinfo.org/ruralchildwelfare.asp

Courtney, M., Piliavin, I., Grogan-Kaylor, A., & Nesmith, A. (2001). Foster youth transitions to adulthood: A longitudinal view of youth leaving care. *Child Welfare, 80*, 685–717.

Crawford, R. (1991). In *the era of human capital: The emergence of talent, intelligence, and knowledge as the worldwide economic force and what it means to managers and investors*. New York: HarperCollins.

Edelman, P., & Ladner, J. (1991). *Adolescence and poverty. Challenge for the 1990's*. Lanham, MD: University Press of America.

Gibbs, J. T. (1988). *Young, black, and male in America*. Dover, MA: Auburn House.

Glasgow, D. (1981). *The black underclass*. San Francisco: Jossey-Bass.

Hahn, A. (1995). The strategic use of assessment to reform independent living policies in states. In E. Mech & J. Rycraft (Eds.), *Preparing foster youth for adult living* (pp. 73–77). Washington, DC: Child Welfare League of America.

Improving Economic Opportunities for Young People Served by the Foster Care System, Phase 3, Conference Proceedings. (1998). Portland, ME: University of Southern Maine, Edmund S. Muskie School of Public Service.

Irvine, J., & Irvine R. (1995). Black youth in school: Individual achievement and institutional/cultural perspectives. In R. Taylor (Ed.), *African-American youth* (pp. 129–142). Westport, CT: Praeger.

Johnson, N. (2001, November) *Common ground newspaper of the New England Association of Child Welfare Commissioner's and Directors, 1.*

Kunjufu, J. (1986). *Motivating and preparing black youth to work*. Chicago: African American Images.

Mech, E. V. (1983, December). Out-of-home placement rates. *Social Service Review, 57*, 659-667.

National Youth in Care Network. (2000) *About the national youth in care network*. Retrieved from http://www.youthincare.ca/about/index.html

Perkins, U. (1986). *Harvesting new generations*. Chicago: Third World Press.

Santayana, G. (1905). *Life of reason, Reason in common sense*. New York: C. Scribner's Sons.

Sengupta, S. (2000, March 28). Pushed out of foster care, thousands lack life skills. *The New York Times*, pp. A1, B6.

Sum, A. (1989). *Testimony before the Select Committee on Children, Youth, and Families. Barriers and opportunities for America's young black men* (pp. 8–44). Washington, DC: U.S. Government Printing Office.

Sum, A., & Fogg, N. (1991). The adolescent poor and the transition to early adulthood. In P. Edelman & J. Ladner (Eds.), *Adolescence and poverty* (pp. 37–109). Lanham, MD: University Press of America.

Summary report from the Prime Minister's Youth Pathways Action Plan Taskforce. (2001). *Footprints to the future*. Available from http://www.youthpathways.gov.au/report.htm

Willon, P. (2001, December 2). Ready or not; Crashing hard into adulthood. *Los Angeles Times*, pp. A1, A40–A43.

Foster Care Independence Act of 1999

(P.L. 106-169, 106TH CONGRESS)

Purpose of the John H. Chafee Foster Care Independence Program

Part E, Title IV, Section 477 of the Social Security Act reads:

PURPOSE—the purpose of this section is to provide States with flexible funding that will enable programs to be designed and conducted—

(1) to identify children who are likely to remain in foster care until 18 years of age and to help these children make the transition to self-sufficiency by providing services such as assistance in obtaining a high school diploma, career exploration, vocational training, job placement and retention, training in daily living skills, training in budgeting and financial management skills, substance abuse prevention, and preventive health activities (including smoking avoidance, nutrition education, and pregnancy prevention);

(2) to help children who are likely to remain in foster care until 18 years of age receive the education, training, and services necessary to obtain employment;

(3) to help children who are likely to remain in foster care until 18 years of age prepare for and enter postsecondary training and education institutions;

(4) to provide personal and emotional support to children aging out of foster care, through mentors and the promotion of interactions with dedicated adults; and

(5) to provide financial, housing, counseling, employment, education, and other appropriate support and services to former foster care recipients between 18 and 21 years of age to complement their own efforts to achieve self-sufficiency and to assure that program participants recognize and accept their personal responsibility for preparing for and then making the transition from adolescence to adulthood.

Highlights of the John H. Chafee Foster Care Independence Program

AMOUNT—$140 million capped entitlement.

STATE MATCH—20% state match required on total allocation.

ALLOCATION FORMULA—Based on the proportion of children in both Title IV-E–funded and state-funded foster care in the state for the most recent fiscal year; no state shall receive less than $500,000 or its 1998 allotment, whichever is greater.

SET-ASIDE—1.5% of authorized program funds set aside for evaluation, technical assistance, performance measurement, and data collection.

ELIGIBLE YOUTH—Those up to age 21 who are likely to remain in foster care until age 18 and those who have aged-out of foster care, without regard to their eligibility to Title IV-E–funded foster care. A portion of funds must be used to serve eligible youth ages 18 to 21 who left foster care because they reached age 18.

BENEFITS TO INDIAN CHILDREN—State must make benefits and services available to American Indian children in the state on the same basis as other children.

PARTICIPATION BY YOUTH—Young people must participate directly in designing their program activities and accept personal responsibility for achieving independence.

FUNDING FOR SERVICES TO YOUTH AGES 18 TO 21—States must use a portion of their funds for assistance and services for youth ages 18 to 21 who left foster care because they reached age 18.

USE OF FUNDS FOR ROOM AND BOARD—States may use up to 30% of their program funds for room or board for youth ages 18 to 21 who have left foster care because they reached age 18, but not age 21.

EMPHASIS ON PERMANENCE—Clarification that independent-living activities should not be seen as alternatives to permanence for children and can be provided concurrently with adoption and other permanency activities.

HEALTH CARE—States are given the option to extend Medicaid coverage to youth ages 18 to 21 who were in foster care on their 18th birthday, or some subset of this group, and encourages such coverage.

ASSET LIMIT—Asset limit changed to allow young people to have $10,000 (rather than $1,000) in assets and remain eligible for Title IV-E–funded foster care.

TRAINING FOR STAFF AND PARENTS—States must certify that Title IV-E funds will be used to provide training to help adoptive and foster parents, workers in group homes, and case managers address the issues confronting adolescents preparing for independent living.

COORDINATION—State must certify in its plan that:

- State has consulted with public and private organizations in implementing the new program;

- State will coordinate the new program with other federal and state programs for young people; and

- State will consult and coordinate with each American Indian tribe in the state.

OUTCOME MEASURES—The Department of Health and Human Services (DHHS), in consultation with federal, state, and local officials, advocates, youth service providers, and researchers, is required to develop outcome measures to assess state performance and the effectiveness of independent-living services.

EVALUATION—The DHHS Secretary must develop outcome measures and data elements to track state performance on outcomes and penalties for states that do not report; 1.5% of authorized program funds is set aside for evaluation, technical assistance, performance measurement, and data collection.

Minimum Components of the Five-Year Plan for the John H. Chafee Foster Care Independence Program

Description of how a state will:

- Administer, supervise, or oversee the programs carried out under the plan.

- Design and deliver independent-living services consistent with the purposes of the Chafee Independence Program.

- Ensure statewide, although not necessarily uniform, coverage by the program.

- Serve children at various ages and stages of development.

- Involve both the public and private sectors in service delivery.

- Use objective criteria for determining eligibility for the program and ensuring equitable treatment under the program.

- Cooperate in national evaluations of the effectiveness of the services in achieving the purposes of the Chafee Independence Program.

Certifications by the Chief Executive Officer of a state that the state will:

- Provide assistance and services to children who have left foster care because they have attained age 18, but not age 21.

- Spend no more than 30% of its annual allotment for room or board for children who have left foster care because they have attained age 18, but not 21, and none of it for room or board for children younger than age 18.

- Use its training funds authorized under Title IV-E of the Social Security Act to help foster and adoptive parents, workers in group homes, and case managers understand and address the issues confronting adolescents preparing for independent living and, where possible, coordinate such training with independent-living programs.

- Have consulted widely with public and private organizations in developing the plan and given all interested members of the public at least 30 days to submit comments.

- Make every effort to coordinate Chafee Independence Program–funded activities with other federal and state programs for youth (especially programs funded under the federal Transitional Living Grant Program). These include abstinence education programs, local housing programs, programs for disabled youth (especially sheltered workshops), and school-to-work programs offered by high schools or local workforce agencies.

- Consult with each American Indian tribe in the state about the activities to be carried out under the plan, coordinate the programs with such tribes, and make the programs' benefits and services available to American Indian children in the state on the same basis as other children.

- Ensure that adolescents participate directly in designing their own independent living activities and accept responsibility for living up to their part of the program.

- Have established and will enforce standards and procedures to prevent fraud and abuse in the programs carried out under the plan.

Transition to Adulthood: A Foster Youth Resource Inventory

National Organizations

Child Welfare League of America (CWLA)
http://www.cwla.org/

CWLA is an association of more than 1,100 public and private non-profit agencies that assist more than 3.5 million abused and neglected children and their families each year. CWLA offers publications, training, consultation, and programs to inform and educate families and professionals.

National Resource Center for Youth Services (NRCYS)
http://www.nrcys.ou.edu/

NRCYS enhances the quality of life of at-risk youth and their families by providing human services professionals with timely information, training, technical assistance, conferences, books, and curricula. *Daily Living*, a quarterly newsletter, provides up-to-date information on programs and activities that prepare youth for adulthood.

Casey Family Programs
http://www.casey.org/

Casey Family Programs is committed to helping youth in foster care make a successful transition to adulthood. Casey services also include adoption, guardianship, kinship care, and family reunification.

National Foster Care Coalition
http://www.nfcap.org/

The National Foster Care Coalition is a unique affiliation of national organizations and foster care alumni, which coordinates advocacy efforts and diverse alliances that strengthen foster care and community supports to ensure children, youth, and families reach their full potential.

National Indian Child Welfare Association (NICWA)
http://www.nicwa.org/

NICWA is dedicated to providing access for every American Indian child to community-based, culturally appropriate social services. They provide permanency technical assistance in the form of training and a manual, the *IV-E Technical Assistance Resource Manual*.

Orphan Foundation of America
http://www.orphan.org/

The Orphan Foundation of America helps parentless teens make the difficult transition from foster care into independent adulthood and believes that education, be it a college degree or a vocational training certificate, is the foundation for success.

Jim Casey Youth Opportunities Initiative
http://www.jimcaseyyouth.org/

The Jim Casey Youth Opportunities Initiative brings together the people and resources needed to help youth make the connections they need to education, employment, health care, housing, and supportive personal and community relationships.

National Independent Living Association (NILA)
http://www.nilausa.org/

NILA is a national network of public and private organizations, individuals, youth, and foster parents representing all 50 states. It is committed to the enhancement of independent living and transitional living services for older, at-risk youth and their families.

Government Organizations

U.S. Department of Health and Human Services, Administration of Children and Families (ACF)
http://www.acf.dhhs.gov/

ACF is a federal agency funding state, local, and tribal organizations to provide family assistance (welfare), child support, child care, Head Start, child welfare, and other programs relating to children and families. The ACF website also provides links to foster care program information, the Children's Bureau, and the Adoption and Foster Care Analysis and Reporting System.

State Programs

New York
Independent Living Resource Center
http://www.hunter.cuny.edu/socwork/ilrc/

The Independent Living Resource Center at the Hunter College School of Social Work provides training that supports independent living, self-sufficiency, and transitional services that promote positive youth development in child welfare agencies in New York City.

Youth Advocacy Center (YAC)
http://www.youthadvocacycenter.org/

YAC's mission is to teach young people in foster care to advocate for themselves and take control of their lives. YAC believes in the aspirations and potential of teenagers in foster care.

California
California Youth Connection (CYC)
http://www.calyouthconn.org/

CYC is an advocacy and youth leadership organization for current and former foster youth. CYC is composed of young people who, because of their experiences with the child welfare system, now work to improve foster care, educate the public and policymakers about the unique needs of children in foster care, and change the negative stereotypes many people have of youth in care.

Oregon
Northwest Human Services
HOST Youth and Family Program
http://www.northwesthumanservices.org/host.htm

HOST provides services in Marion County that include temporary shelter, crisis intervention, case management, family lifeskills, and transition programs.

Northwest Media, Inc.
http://www.northwestmedia.com/

Northwest Media offers videos for lifeskills, independent living, foster and adoptive care, and sex and health education.

Alaska
Division of Family and Youth Services
http://health.hss.state.ak.us/dfys/IndependentLiving/default.htm

This extensive website has state-specific and national links to helpful information. This program is aimed toward increasing the skills young people in foster care need for self-sufficiency in adulthood and increasing the educational, vocational, and housing opportunities for youth who age-out of foster care.

International Organizations

Canada
National Youth in Care Network (NYICN)
http://www.youthincare.ca/

NYICN is a national charitable organization completely driven by youth in care (14-24 years of age) across Canada. NYICN exists to nourish the development of Youth in Care Networks across Canada, while helping its members find their voices and regain control over their lives through support, skill building, and healing opportunities.

England
National Children's Bureau (NCB)
http://www.ncb.org.uk/

NCB promotes the interests and well-being of all children and young people across every aspect of their lives. It advocates for the participation of children and young people in all matters affecting them and challenges disadvantage in childhood.

Australia
Association of Children's Welfare Agencies
http://www.acwa.asn.au/acwa/info/acwa/About_ACWA.html

The primary object of this association is the improvement of the quality of care available to at-risk, dependent children and young people who need substitute care in the state of New South Wales and the

Australian Capital Territory. The association provides a variety of services, including consultation, training, research, publications, and supportive community programs.

The Source
http://www.thesource.gov.au/

The Source is the Commonwealth government's website for young people. The site provides information on youth fights, learning, money, lifestyles, and careers.

Norway
http://www.ettervern.org/asp/lesartikkel.asp?nyhetsID=6

This is the English short version of the Norwegian website on Aftercare, leaving care, and independent living. The site has been constructed and is owned by the Norwegian Leaving Care Project of Grepperød Youth Residential Home. It answers questions for those in Norway and provides a global perspective. The website has many useful links.

Other Resources

The National Research Library
http://www.cyfc.umn.edu/NRL/

Useful collection of literature on many topics involving youth, independent living, school to work, transitional living and more.

Publication

Loman, L. A., & Siegal, G. L. (2000). *A review of literature on independent living of youths in foster and residential care*. Available from http://www.iarstl.org/papers/IndLivLit.pdf

Appendix 3

National Youth-in-Transition Database

Legislative Framework for a National Youth-in-Transition Database (NYTD)

The Chafee Foster Care Independence Act of 1999 (P.L. 106-169) requires an assessment of outcomes experienced by youth when they leave care. The prospect of a national-level database for foster youth independent-living programs is a welcome development. Section 477 (f)(i) of the Chafee legislation directs the U.S. Department of Health and Human Services (USDHHS) to develop outcome measures that can be used to document the performance of states operating independent-living programs. Outcome measures are to include:

- Educational attainment (with a high school diploma as a minimum standard),

- Employment and labor force participation, and

- Avoidance of dependency on public assistance programs, nonmarital childbirth, homelessness, and contact with the correctional system and/or incarceration (USDHHS, 2001).

A report by the Office of the Inspector General (OIG; 1994) gave impetus to the framework for a national database to track the performance of independent-living programs.

The essence of the OIG (1994) report was that:

- Program reporting by states has been inconsistent,

- State reports failed to target program performance or to document outcomes, and

- Variability and gaps in state program information systems made it difficult for the Administration for Children and Families to gain an accurate national level profile of independent-living program services or outcomes.

OIG proposed a series of corrective measures. Included in its statement on options for improvement are the following:

- Require states to establish measurable goals and to report on their progress;

- In state reports, maintain a clear focus on information related to independent-living services that are provided to youth and document youths' progress toward economic self-sufficiency;

- Establish a basic (minimum) dataset requirement for state independent-living programs that includes reporting on demographics, services, and outcomes; and

- Focus on the status of youth at discharge. Encourage electronic reporting, specifically for tracking independent-living outcomes.

Data Elements: Outcomes and Measures Specified in the Chafee Foster Care Independence Act of 1999

The emerging NYTD is intended to consolidate information about services delivered and outcomes attained into a data system that provides states with a standard as to what is to be accomplished in their independent-living program. The essential aim of NYTD is to document the extent to which state child welfare systems provide foster wards with the skills, services, and supports to allow them to transition into adulthood.

The Chafee legislation specifies expected outcomes in four areas (see Table A3.1), as follows:

- Attain economic self-sufficiency, that is, be employed and avoid public assistance.

- Have a safe and stable place to live.

- Attain academic or vocational educational goals, that is, receive a high school diploma.

- Postpone parenthood (avoid nonmarital birth and high-risk, illegal activity).

The four outcome areas encompass 12 measures and require information on 19 data elements. The requisite outcome measures and data elements are listed in Table A3.1.

Implementation: Data Collection Procedures

NYTD proposes two separate tracks for outcome data collection. Track 1 is a discharge interview, which will be administered to all exiting youth age 16 and older. Track 2 is a postdischarge survey that uses a sampling approach. Data collection is directed at outcomes experienced by former wards after leaving foster. Track 2 proposes to use a system of youth identifiers to be collected in both outcome tracks so that postdischarge information for individual youth can be linked with their discharge interviews. The decision to use a Track 1 model, that is, to interview all exiting youth age 16 and older, stems from an earlier federal requirement that states have to report on "results achieved 90 days after participants completed the program" (OIG, 1994, p. 16). The 90-day stipulation created a series of data inconsistencies, in which some states provided data on youth 90 days after discharge from state custody and other states reported on youth 90 days after completion of a particular independent-living program or service while still in state custody.

Moreover, many states reported difficulty in contacting representative numbers of youth 90 days after discharge. To generate consistency in state reports, OIG (1994) report recommended that states focus on the status of youth at the point of discharge (p. 16). With respect to Track 2, the postdischarge survey of samples of foster wards who leave care, the U.S. Children's Bureau plans to use a technology-based data collection procedure. Youth will self-report outcome information through a website or automated telephone system. The objective of the website and automated telephone survey methodology is to minimize in-person interviewing, as generally youth will enter their own information, and maximize the response rate. States will monitor survey returns and follow up with youth who are scheduled to participate in the survey but do not. The outcome data will be entered directly into a database maintained by the U.S. Children's Bureau, eliminating the need for states to enter, hold, and report the data (USDHHS, 2002).

TABLE A3.1

Outcome Indicators for the National Youth-in-Transition Database

OUTCOME	MEASURE	DATA ELEMENT
1. Increase the Number of Youth Who Have Resources to Meet Their Living Expenses	1.1 Of all youth discharged from foster care or receiving independent-living services (ILS) during the reporting period, what percentage were employed full-time and part-time during the reporting period?	Full-time employment; Part-time employment
	1.2. Of all youth discharged from foster care or receiving ILS during the reporting period who were not employed full-time, what percentage were enrolled in school?	Current school enrollment
	1.3 Of all youth discharged from foster care or receiving ILS during the reporting period, what percentage held a job, apprenticeship, internship, and so forth, for at least three consecutive months during the reporting period?	Job experience; training experience
	1.4 Of all youth discharged from foster care or receiving ILS during the reporting period, what percentage had financial resources other than employment, such as Supplemental Security Income (SSI), scholarships, stipends, Temporary Aid to Needy Families, support from family or spouse, Chafee room and board, or other resources during the reporting period?	SSI; scholarship; stipends; Temporary Aid to Needy Families; support from family or spouse; other

TABLE A3.1

(continued)

OUTCOME	MEASURE	DATA ELEMENT
2. Increase the Number of Youth Who Have a Safe and Stable Place to Live	2.1 Of all youth receiving ILS during the reporting period, what percentage were homeless at some point during the reporting period?	Homelessness
	2.2 Of all youth who were homeless, what was the duration of homelessness (three or fewer nights, more than three nights but less than two weeks, two weeks to a month, or more than a month)?	Duration of homelessness
3. Increase the Number of Youth Who Attain Educational (Academic or Vocational) Goals	3.1 Of all youth discharged from care or receiving ILS during the reporting period, what percentage had a high school diploma, general equivalency diploma (GED), or associate or bachelor's of arts degree?	Degrees received
	3.2 Of all youth discharged from care or receiving ILS during the reporting period, what percentage had a vocational certificate or license?	Certifications received
	3.3 Of all youth discharged from care or receiving ILS during the reporting period, what percentage were enrolled in high school, GED classes, or post–high school vocational training or college during the reporting period?	School enrollment during reporting period

TABLE A3.1

(continued)

OUTCOME	MEASURE	DATA ELEMENT
4. Increase the Number of Youth Who Avoid Involvement with High-Risk Behaviors	4.1 Of all youth discharged from care or receiving ILS during the reporting period, what percentage were referred for substance abuse assessment or counseling during the reporting period?	Referral for substance abuse assessment or counseling
	4.2 Of all youth discharged from care or receiving ILS during the reporting period, what percentage had been incarcerated at some time during the reporting period?	Incarceration
	4.3 Of all youth discharged from care or receiving ILS during the reporting period, what percentage gave birth or fathered a child born during the reporting period?[a]	Children born

[a] This measure is analyzed in conjunction with the youth characteristic regarding marital status to determine out-of-wedlock births.

References

Office of the Inspector General. (1994). *Independent living programs for foster care youths, Strategies for improved ACF management and reporting*. Washington, DC: U.S. Department of Health and Human Services.

U.S. Department of Health and Human Services, Administration for Children, Children's Bureau. (2001). *Report to the Congress: Developing a system of program accountability under the John H. Chafee Foster Care Independence Program. The Department of Health and Human Services' plan for developing and implementing the National Youth in Transition Information System*. Washington, DC: Author. Retrieved from: http://www.acf.hhs.gov/programs/cb/programs/chafeereport.htm

U.S. Department of Health and Human Services, Administration for Children, Children's Bureau. (2002). *Proposed data collection, Chafee Foster Care Independence Program, National Youth in Transition Database*. Washington, DC: Author.

Foster Youth Speak Out

The voices of foster youth are vital to the planning, development, and assessment of independent-living services. A report issued by CWLA asserts that "current and former foster youth are essential participants in any reevaluation or changes, because no one can be...more articulate about how the foster care system has—or has not—worked" (Knipe & Warren, 1999, p. 1). The system has slowly begun to accept suggestions for improvement from youth themselves. Foster youth input is now a required element in the Foster Care Independence Act of 1999. The Chafee Independence Act stipulates that state agencies

> *will ensure that adolescents participating in the program, participate directly in designing their own program activities that prepare them for independent living. (P.L. 106-169, Section 477, Part 3(H) Certifications)*

For more than a decade, with respect to issues pertaining to preparation for independence, youth advocates and foster youth themselves have made efforts to communicate their experiences and needs to administrators, legislators, and policymakers. The California Youth Connection (CYC), for example represents a statewide organization of current and former foster youth. CYC was formed in 1988 in response to concerns that the opinions of foster youth were not valued or taken into account in planning or implementing services. Many of their concerns and suggestions have now been heard and acted on in legislation. Examples are: (a) provisions that foster care services be available to youth until age 21, (b) basic standards for counties to operate independent-living programs, (c) special training for foster caregivers in helping youth transition to independence, (d) creation of emancipation teams (the emancipation team concept reflects a version of wraparound philosophy), and (e) development of aftercare programs for emancipated youth.

In the United States, the trend is toward a youth advisory board structure. As of 2001, approximately 80% of states report having an active youth advisory board. The following are examples.

Arizona

Arizona's youth advisory board meets quarterly on a statewide basis. Meetings are facilitated by the state independent-living program (ILP) coordinator. Guest speakers are scheduled as needed. Arizona has six districts that are individually responsible for facilitating similar boards. Area boards are to meet with the area program manager quarterly.

Activities involving the youth boards include:

- Planning and participation in an annual youth conference,

- Quarterly statewide meetings to discuss issues related to out-of-home care and plan activities,

- Participation in Positive Youth Development efforts (Arizona is one of nine states that are grantees of the Positive Youth Development Grant),

- Foster parent training, and

- Legislative efforts to improve the program.

The statewide board is currently in the process of reexamining the structure and goals of the board and will be provided training over the coming year to improve the functionality of the board.

Connecticut

Connecticut has an active youth advisory board, whose members are 17 and older and are participating in the Community Housing Apartment Program. Two youth from each of the five regions of Connecticut gather for a statewide meeting three to four times per year. Each region meets monthly and elects two cochairs and a secretary each year.

Members of the regional boards are involved in the following activities:

- Contributing to and maintaining a regional newsletter,

- Facilitating regional meetings, and

- Brainstorming ideas and advocating for changes to state policy.

The statewide board meets with the agency commissioner to present issues that have been discussed by the regional boards. The regional boards have successfully advocated for additional services to parenting teens resulting in substantial policy changes. The boards have been key in the implementation of the following services to youth:

- Monthly stipend to parenting youth;

- Child care assistance for parenting youth;

- Financial assistance in obtaining start up items such as cribs, linens, and so forth; and

- A system of minigrants to program youth for various items that support self-sufficiency.

Florida

The Florida Youth Advisory Board is made up of representatives from the 15 local advisory boards and meets four times per year. Florida has assigned staff who work specifically with the board, separate from the IL state coordinator.

The statewide board is involved in a wide array of activities, including:

- Holding quarterly meetings to discuss and problem solve youth issues;

- Youth mentoring (ILP youth and adults in community);

- Legislating to improve quality of care and other youth issues;

- Public speaking, educating the public and judicial community, promoting teen adoption, and so forth;

- Performing foster home recruitment, including making public service announcements;

- Foster parent training; and

- Producing local newsletters.

The statewide board is currently involved in initiatives to allow for driver's licenses for youth, securing computers for youth, and producing a statewide newsletter for youth.

Kentucky

Kentucky's Youth Action Committee is made up of youth from the 16 regions of Kentucky. Two youth for each region participate in committee meetings, which occur quarterly.

The Youth Action Committee is involved in the following activities:

- Youth handbook,

- Program newsletter, and

- Youth panel presentations.

The youth panel presentations have occurred in conjunction with the annual Foster Parent Conference, which is attended by case managers as well as foster parents. The youth panel presentation at the 1999 conference was videotaped and is in the process of being edited for distribution as a training tool.

Missouri

Missouri is divided into seven areas, including St. Louis City and Kansas City. Each area has an area youth advisory board, which selects its representatives to the state youth advisory board. Each area is allowed three representatives on the state board. Other members of the state board include community members and alumni.

Area boards address:

- Issues directly related to youth in care,

- Peer counseling,

- Community projects, and

- Community involvement.

State board activities include:

- Issues for youth in care with input to state policy and procedures,

- Testimony before legislature on various issues,

- Annual conferences for area members, and

- Development of a state board handbook of terms and responsibilities.

This board has gotten state appropriations increased for such items as clothing allowances and is planning a conference strictly for children's services workers and foster parents to increase the awareness of ILP.

Similar youth participation movements exist in other countries. In Canada, a key organization is the National Youth-in-Care Network. A report titled *Transitions to Adulthood* (Martin & Palmer, 1997) issued by the Child Welfare League of Canada in conjunction with the Canadian Foster Family Association contains findings from a series of focus groups with youth in and out of care. The report proposed recommendations for change in several areas, including health, education, and employment. One of the areas targeted for change was that of "post-ward ship support." Youth surveyed pointed out that confusion exists with respect to the amount of financial support available and the rules governing eligibility for support.

In addition to the contributions of Festinger (1983) in the United States in drawing attention to the importance of paying heed to the voices of foster youth, and the creative young people's Speak Out series in Canada (Fay, 1989), the pioneering efforts of Stein (1990) and colleagues in the United Kingdom stand as a major achievement in facilitating a movement that encourages youth in care to come together and share their experiences. Initiated in Leeds, England, in the early 1970s, the mobilization of youth speak out groups "provided a national platform for the views of young people in care and led to the setting up of their own organization, the National Association of Young People in Care (NAYPIC), in June 1979." (Stein, 1990, p. 1)

Overall, issues pertaining to youth who are preparing to leave care, to age out, or to emancipate from placement transcend state, regional, or national boundaries. The themes of preparing youth for economic self-sufficiency, personal-social competence, and citizenship in a democratic society are transnational in nature, and extend to the international community. Items for future consideration should include a series of foster youth independent-living conferences that are international in scope, the development of cross-national data systems, and periodic "social outcome" reports on the adult status of former foster wards.

References

Fay, M. (Ed.). (1989). *Speak out: An anthology of stories by children in care*. Toronto, Canada: Pope Adolescent Resource Center.

Festinger, T. (1983). *No one ever asked us...A postscript to foster care.* New York: Columbia University Press.

Knipe, J., & Warren, J. (1999). *Foster youth share their ideas for change.* Washington, DC: CWLA Press.

Martin, F., & Palmer, T. (1997). *Transitions to adulthood. A youth perspective.* Ottawa, Canada: Child Welfare League of Canada.

Stein, M. (1990). *Living out of care.* Barkingside, UK: Barnardo's.

Appendix 5

Family Violence and Young Survivors: Life Before, During, and After Foster Care

"Family Violence and Young Survivors" was written by Elizabeth L. Leonard, MSW, Field Coordinator for the Foster Youth-in-Transition Project at the University of Illinois. The roles were acted out by the Oregon Street Players, graduate students in the School of Social Work at the University of Illinois. The players made their debut in "Family Violence and Young Survivors" in May 1997 before an audience of more than 100 social work administrators, supervisors, and practitioners who were connected with the field-internship program at the university.

The script centers on violence to children, how the child welfare system and the courts respond to child maltreatment, and the consequences for young victims. It is based on excerpts gleaned from more than 1,000 interviews with foster wards enrolled in the Youth-in-Transition project. Each speaker plays multiple parts; the names in parentheses indicate who is speaking, and the names in all capital letters indicate which part they are playing. The setting is the Monroe County Courthouse in Midwest City, USA. The seven survivors have now aged-out of the state placement system and are struggling to make it on their own. The Honorable Harry Callahan is the presiding judge. Judge Callahan wants to know how these young people are doing, and what his court can do to help improve the system. Here are their stories.

(Narrator): *Good afternoon. I am Edmund V. Mech, a faculty member in the child welfare specialization at the School of Social Work. Our topic is Family Violence and Young Survivors: Life Before, During, and After Foster Care.*

Family violence covers a range of unacceptable behavior that occurs within the privacy and intimacy of family relationships. Acts of violence may be directed at children, spouses, or other household members. Our presentation is about violence to children, the manner in which the child welfare system and the courts respond to child maltreatment and the consequences for young victims. The script is based on excerpts from interviews with foster youth in Ohio, Indiana, and Illinois. More than 500 former foster youth are enrolled in our project. The young survivors depicted in this presentation are now in their early 20s. Each has aged out of care and is in the process of trying to make it on their own. The theme is one of social justice, which is long overdue for young people who come into an impersonal system through no fault of their own.

This presentation revolves around seven survivors who return to Midwest City, USA, for a reunion. They take the opportunity to arrange a meeting with a local judge, the Honorable Harry Callahan. Judge Callahan is interested in knowing how they have been doing since leaving care. The vignetteers try to convey to him how maltreatment, separation from one's own home, and years in foster care has affected them. Before we check in on Judge Callahan's meeting with the young survivors, a few background comments are in order.

Currently, there is great debate and considerable difference of opinion as to how to make the child welfare system more responsive to children. A major child welfare reform package enacted in 1980 was intended to give us a state-of-the-art legislative superhighway to an effective child welfare system. Apparently, the system is not working well enough. Voices from all sectors are once again calling for reform. We seem to attribute magical properties to every piece of major legislation. Maybe we expect too much. I personally know of no legislation that can guarantee competence or trans-

form a violent or abusive family into a warm, nurturing household.

Current child welfare programs contain many creative positive elements. Some examples are preventive services for families with emphasis on family preservation, case plans, parental visitation, periodic case reviews, least restrictive placements, placements that are geographically appropriate, reunification planning, risk assessment, and subsidies to encourage special needs adoption. In addition, the placement resource continuum has been expanded to include kinship (relative) homes, specialized and therapeutic foster homes, and smaller, familial group home arrangements. Despite the reforms described, much dissatisfaction exists. Large numbers of foster parents are dropping out, replacements are hard to find, and much agitation is directed at the courts. Less than half of serious, substantiated child abuse cases are prosecuted. Less than 20% of convicted child abusers serve more than 12 months in jail, and nearly 40% serve no jail time at all.

Society has given abusers what amounts to a free ride, and at most, a slap on the wrist. Many perpetrators now feel entitled to an automatic pardon. When accused of wrongdoing, most minimize or deny it. Those few who acknowledge wrongdoing generally expect, and even demand to be forgiven. Most perpetrators prefer to skip over the pain, personal anguish, and self-doubt that their young victims feel. It is unlikely that a few brief counseling sessions will put these families back together. Also, we should not overlook the fact that child welfare work itself can be dangerous, particularly so for protective service workers who must remove a child from a home. Violence against protective Service workers is a matter of record. Some have been shot at and wounded, others spit at, hit, shoved, and pushed. One client fired a bullet through a worker's car windshield. Someone removed lug nuts from a worker's car hoping to cause an accident. Other forms of abuse heaped on protective service workers include screaming or cursing at workers, making death threats, filing lawsuits, and attempting to get a worker fired. Harassment of protective service workers causes many to seek less hazardous employment.

Family violence is emerging as a major societal battle-ground. Yet too little attention is paid to the probable consequences for its victims. In our project, most of the young survivors had an abnormal and precarious adolescence in foster care. From ages 12 to 18, they spent most of their time shuttling from one placement to another. Without real parents or families, they had to make do. They survived with adult strangers, many caseworkers, transitory friendships, and numerous changes of address. Sadly, many of our project youth keep most of what they own in a shoebox. Substitute homes, parent surrogates, and shoeboxes can never compensate for the absence of a solid home and unqualified love. Our young people who have been in foster placement have been victimized and denigrated. The hit and run relationships that develop in foster homes, group homes, institutions, and on the street are simply not enough. The young victims know it and we know it. One of the powerful issues that remains to be resolved is their need to account for what happened to them and why. This usually boils down to unfinished business between them and their families. I see that the meeting with Judge Callahan is about to begin. Kim, will you let the judge know that we are ready?

(Gavel)

(Narrator): *Ok, let's start the meeting.*

(Kim) VOICE: *Family violence…*

CHORUS: *…and young survivors. Life before, during, and after foster care.*

(Kim) VOICE: *Why, why was this child not protected?*

(All) CHORUS: *There is no safe place, no justice, no appeal.*

(Kim) VOICE: *Where is a foundation to stand on?*

(All) CHORUS: *There is no safe place, no justice, no appeal.*

(Kim) VOICE: *Why was I the one dying inside instead of my abuser?*

(All) CHORUS: *There is no safe place, no justice, no appeal. Why, why was this child not protected?*

(Gavel)

(Tony): Violence experienced by children today includes physical, sexual, and emotional abuse; neglect; abandonment; and exposure to domestic violence. The U.S. Advisory Board for Child Abuse and Neglect concluded that the safety of the nation's children cannot be ensured. Why?

(Gavel)

Part 1

(Kim) VOICE: Before foster care, listen to the voices of the children.

(Kim) VOICE: I knew...

(All) CHORUS: ...there had to be a better way to live.

(Curt) MARIO: I'm Mario. One day when I was 14, my dad broke a broom handle over my shoulder, fracturing my collarbone. He pinched me so hard in the chest that it left a big bruise, then bloodied my lip. He physically abused me, my mom, and my brothers for years. He hit our heads against the wall and called it disciplining us. I don't know why it took me so long to realize that my health and life were in danger. It was a case of survival. I knew there had to be a better way to live. So I took it upon myself to find it. I went to the Department of Public Welfare and told them I wasn't going back home under any conditions. They tried to reunite me with my family, but no way was I going back home.

(Gavel)

(Kim) VOICE: All I wanted...

(All) CHORUS: ...was a normal life.

(Laura) JENNIFER: I'm Jennifer. The physical abuse wasn't so bad when I was younger. It reached its peak at age 12 when my mother said, "Come in here!" She pulled my hand and broke two of my fingers. She made me promise not to tell anyone. It hurt so bad I couldn't hardly move my arm. When my dad came home, I had to lie about my hand. A couple of weeks later, she hit me over the head with a belt buckle. It hit my left eye and I couldn't see out of it for five

days. Then a cataract formed from the scar tissue, and I had to have six eye operations. Today I don't see too well out of my left eye.

Several times she hit me on the head with my brother's weights, a wooden spoon, a stick from a tree, and I can't remember the rest. I only know I was scared. Scared to death all my childhood. I didn't know if I would live to be an adult or if my body would be in one piece. All the time I was thinking, "I must survive." I was too scared to tell anyone, even my dad.

All I wanted was a normal life. I don't think I could have taken it much longer. I was mentally shutting down. Now that I think of it, I was slowly dying inside. I have to say, I'm lucky to be alive!

(Gavel)

(Kim) VOICE: *My mother…*

(All) CHORUS: *…threw me out a second-story window.*

(Letty) MARY: *I'm Mary. I knew it was the end for me. First a babysitter, then Mom's boyfriend, and now my adoptive father. I just didn't know where to go, or who to tell. I thought no one would believe me, especially my mother. I was right. When I told her, she threw me out a second-story window, and that's how I got put in a foster home.*

(Gavel)

(Kim) VOICE: *My mom…*

(All) CHORUS: *…wouldn't do nothing.*

(Carrie) ALISON: *I'm Alison. I remember being awakened in the middle of the night by some drunk man touching me, rubbing me. I used to pretend to be asleep and wouldn't roll over. He told me if I cooperated with him I would get new shoes, clothes, and toys, just because I deserved them. I was 12 years old. He seemed to feel that because I was only a stepdaughter, he had a right to do what he pleased with me. I'm sure my mom knew about it, but she did nothing.*

(Gavel)

(Kim) VOICE: I just couldn't stay there...

(All) CHORUS: *any longer.*

(Tony) TYRONE: I'm Tyrone. My parents ran a small store, and we kids had to help. I was doing my share, but my mom was always wanting me to do more. We were always arguing. One day when I was about 15, she picked up a large butcher knife and came after me and slashed my hand. I yelled at my sister to call 911 because I was sure my mom was going to kill me. After years of verbal and emotional abuse, I knew I couldn't stay there any longer.

(Gavel)

(Kim) VOICE: I never told no one...

(All) CHORUS: *...so this better be confidential.*

(Imelda) AMANDA: I'm Amanda. When I was 12, my grandfather raped me. I went to stay for Christmas. On Christmas Eve he took me for a ride in his truck into town. He bought me a soda. On the way back, he stopped a mile from home. He raped me. Then he took me back to the house. He told me if I told he would make sure that I never saw my mother again. So when I got to the house, I took a shower and went to my room, and I laid there and cried. I never told no one.

(Sabrina) AMANDA: Then when I was 16, my stepfather raped me. It was Valentine's Day. My mom got drunk and passed out in her room. My stepdad came home from the bar a half-hour later and sat down next to me. He was drunk and stoned. He grabbed me, pushed me back on the couch, and raped me. Somebody must have called protective services, and I told them it was a lie. So this better be confidential!

(Gavel)

(Kim) VOICE: I felt...

(All) CHORUS: *...like a dirty whore.*

(Carrie) CHRISTINE: I'm Christine. I was sexually abused by my own father when I was a baby, and again when I was 8. My stepfather, other relatives, and an adoptive father molested me over a period of 14 years. I was also physically abused by my mom's boyfriends. During this time, I was in and out of 45 different foster homes, and returned to mother in between. The abuse occurred whenever I went home. They let me stay with my mom for a whole year when I was 8. That's when it got real bad. I asked to be put back in foster care because I didn't want to go on feeling like a dirty whore.

(Gavel)

(Kim) VOICE: I only wanted my mom...

(All) CHORUS: ...to be my friend.

(Kim) SARAH: I'm Sarah. I was physically abused by my mother between ages 7 and 12, and also sexually abused by her boyfriend from 7 to 11. Both were alcoholics and drug abusers. My mother did tricks on me while he would watch. When Mom was at work, he would force me to have sex with him and perform sex acts on him. He said if anyone knew, I would be in real trouble because it was all my fault, 'cause I liked it and wanted it to happen. Besides, nobody would believe me. She found out when I was 11 and had me put in foster care. I only wanted my mom to be my friend.

(Gavel)

(Kim) VOICE: The only way I could handle it...

(All) CHORUS: ...was to join a gang.

(Tony) RICHARD: I'm Richard. I grew up in a very violent home. When I was young, my father pushed me against a sharp table. One day he ran over me with his car and left permanent scars on my body, and emotional scars. Once I watched him set my mother on fire. He went to prison for murdering his girlfriend's baby. The only way I could handle all this was to use drugs and join a gang. When I refused to go to school and threatened my mom with a knife, she

wouldn't let me return home. I spent time in jail for that, and then they put me in a group home.

(Gavel)

(Kim) VOICE: *What's wrong with…*

(All) CHORUS: *…me?*

(Sabrina) SABRINA: *I'm Sabrina. I was sexually abused at different points in my life. The first time I was 3 years old by my stepdad. The next time, my mom's boyfriend. That lasted for 4 years, from 7 to 11. I went through periods in my early teens when I became sexually active. When it happens to you all the time as a child, sex means nothing to you. Nothing at all. I feel like I have a sign on my back saying "Sexually abuse me." One day, I was in a laundromat, and a man looked at me and began jacking off right in front of me. Its things like that get me to thinking, "What's wrong with me?"*

(Gavel)

(Kim) VOICE: *I learned to pretend…*

(All) CHORUS: *…I was someplace else.*

(Carrie) SUZIE: *I'm Suzie. When our real mom committed suicide, I was 8, and that was when my father started sexually abusing me and all my sisters. It happened to me between 8 and 14 fairly often. He also turned us on to drugs. He used threats if I didn't do what he said, saying people would blame me and think I was really bad. I was confused, afraid, and angry. In the beginning, I didn't know it was wrong. Then, when I found out, I only wanted it to stop. I felt so guilty I couldn't tell anyone. I learned to pretend I was someplace else. I didn't want people to know about it. If they knew, it would be like wearing a scarlet letter. When I was placed in a foster home, I was so glad to get away from him.*

(Gavel)

(Kim) VOICE: *I don't remember…*

(All) CHORUS: *…who burned my hands.*

(Curt) MICHAEL: I'm Michael. At my hearing, I heard the judge say I had been abused since an infant. I will never forget his words:

*(Ed) JUDGE (**with great emphasis**):* This child has been severely physically and mentally abused for 11 years!

(Curt) MICHAEL: He was talking about me, you know. I heard my mom tell the judge she wanted nothing to do with me. I don't remember who burned my hands, but my dad says my mom did it. I know she hit me with an extension cord and held a gun to my head, but I can't remember who burned my hands. It could've been my dad.

(Gavel)

(Kim) VOICE: If I never told...

(All) CHORUS: ...I knew it would never stop.

(Sabrina) AMY: I'm Amy. It started after my mother's death. I was 13. My father turned to alcohol and began to abuse me sexually, but he never got as far as intercourse. This went on for three years, and then my brother started doing the same thing my father was doing. I had to tell some-one, because I knew if I didn't, it would never stop, and it was making me emotionally disturbed. I got put in foster care when I was 16.

(Gavel)

(Kim) VOICE: I just wish...

(All) CHORUS: ...it would never have happened.

(Laura) BRENDA: I'm Brenda. It was just crazy. My fa-ther molested me and my sisters, and we went to a children's home for three years, and he got to stay home. When I think about it, it kind of puts a halt on reality, so I try not to think about it. It all started when our mom died. It was just a big mess. I just wish it just wouldn't have happened. When he was done with me, he would tell me that if I told anybody, I would have to leave or he would throw me out. I just don't

know why he didn't go to jail because he should've, because that's wrong.

(Gavel)

(Kim) VOICE: *If anybody was nice to me, I wondered...*

(All) CHORUS: *...what do they want with me?*

(Imelda) CARMEN: *Me llama Carmen...*

(Ed) JUDGE: *Could you repeat that?*

(Imelda) CARMEN: *I'm Carmen. I should've just left home and never returned, but where would I go? I had to protect my little sister. I was sexually abused from 6 to 15 by different family members. At 15, I was raped by a gangster who turned himself in, but he was out in one month. So I don't trust nobody, you know? And when he got out, at any time, any member of the gang could just come up and kill me. If anybody was nice to me, I said to myself, you know, "What do they want with me?"*

(Gavel)

(Kim) VOICE: *The safety of the nation's children...*

(All) CHORUS: *...cannot be assured.*

(Gavel)

Part 2

(Kim) VOICE: *During foster care...*

(All) CHORUS: *Are we helping, or harming?*

(Imelda): *Children in out-of-home placement pay a heavy price. Placement in a foster home, group home, or institution may be as risky as staying at home. Too many children in foster care are victims of abuse.*

(Laura): *My foster father was sexually abusing all the girls in the home. He made us all shower in the basement where he could watch us and fondle us. Before dinner, we each had to kiss him. He would put his tongue in our mouths and grab* our butts. In the morning, each girl would have to go into his room. My foster mother would leave the room, and we would have to let him play around with us for about an hour. He had intercourse with a lot of them, but he hadn't gotten around to me before I decided to leave that home.

(Letty): Nobody had complained because this was supposed to be the best foster home we could get. But I didn't believe that. I told a former foster mom who reported it to a caseworker, but the caseworker said I was lying just to get out of the home. I called the police. My foster father asked me not to press charges, but I refused. He plea-bargained and only served two years in jail. Nobody in the system believed me because my foster father was "deep in the church," and "an outstanding man in the community."

(Carrie): When we finally did get counseling, it wasn't very helpful. We only had three sessions. Then it ended. They never asked us how we felt about the abuse. Never let us talk. Instead, they asked us, "Why did we think he would do something like that?" and "Did you let him know you wanted him to do this to you?"

(Kim) VOICE: Ninety percent of cases of child sexual abuse presented to prosecutors never go to trial. In more than half the cases up for prosecution, charges are dropped or diverted into treatment. Plea-bargaining is also used extensively, leaving the offender with a record not identifiable as sexual abuse.

(Imelda): If you are a teenager, your chances for a trial are slim.

(Ed) JUDGE: (to CHORUS) Have you ever received any type of counseling or treatment?

(Kim): I had private counseling for six years.

(Laura): I went to a teen sex abuse group.

(Curt): Group therapy.

(Imelda): Some counseling.

(Letty): I went to sessions in children's homes.

(Sabrina): I had a counselor at the group home I was in.

(Tony): Two sessions.

(Carrie): Just my caseworkers—no special counseling.

(Ed) JUDGE: (to CHORUS) How helpful was the treatment?

(Kim): It was the best thing I've ever done in my life.

(Laura): It helped me realize it wasn't my fault.

(Curt): It didn't help me at all. I never felt comfortable enough to open up.

(Imelda): They put me on a medication that keeps me from feeling much.

(Letty): The group home helped me. They taught me how to be a person, how to love myself and care for me. So if it happens again, I know more about the law now, so I know what to do. Talking in a group was good. Everybody was in there for something, so everybody was like "Well, what are you in here for?" It was embarrassing to say, "Well, my father molested me," but it's just an embarrassing stage.

(Sabrina): I had one counselor who wasn't at all sensitive. When I told her I still could not trust any man to get close to me, her suggestion was to drink a six-pack before I went out on a date.

(Tony): It didn't help very much. I only wanted to forget and not talk about it.

(Carrie): One of my counselors would just sit there and ask me if I enjoyed it or if I had worn anything that might have turned my abuser on. Jeez, I was only 10.

(Curt): Agencies are reluctant to be responsible for child sexual abuse cases and unwilling to make the commitment to train their staff properly and develop appropriate community resources.

(Ed) JUDGE: (to CHORUS) Is there anything else that you want to add, or think would be helpful for me to know?

(Kim): *I felt like I was being punished when I was taken out of my home and put in an institution while he was never put in jail.*

(Laura): *I didn't like the way the system separated children and placed them in different homes. They didn't give my sister any help.*

(Curt): *I think the foster care system is what you make it. If you want to cause trouble, you can. I thought it was generally pretty good.*

(Imelda): *I was in the same foster home for four years until I was placed in a group home because of my "disruptive behavior" after my mother's monthly visits. The group home wasn't the best place for me, though. I had trouble developing relationships. I don't understand why they had to move me.*

(Letty): *Mostly I think the foster care system was helpful. The caseworkers were hard to contact, and I had to remind them often about lot of things, but there were people there who cared about me and wanted me to achieve.*

(Sabrina): *After my father died, I was supposed to be receiving Social Security checks during the whole six years I was in foster care. I never got to see a dime. When I left, I had no money, no job, and no place to live.*

(Tony): *They said it was mandatory to reunite me with my family. But I refused to go. I didn't feel that the caseworkers were very helpful. I had a new one every week, and no one told me who they were or when they changed. I was given the runaround. They really screwed me up. So I went out and found my own foster family.*

(Carrie): *I think they forgot about me, I really do. I never caused any trouble over the 16 years I was in the institution, never stole anything, never ran away, never bothered anybody, just did what they said. Maybe because I didn't create any waves, they just forgot me. I entered care when I was 4 because of severe physical abuse, and my mom died.*

(Laura): *When I turned 20, they seemed surprised I was still there. They said I would be going to a foster home because I*

needed to have some job experience and learn to get along with people on the outside. I never did understand why they put me in a foster home in the country where there are no jobs and nobody around my age. So then they moved me to another foster home in a larger town near a bakery. They said I could learn how to decorate birthday cakes. Somewhere along the way, I still think they must have forgot about me.

(Kim) VOICE: *There is no safe place...*

(All) CHORUS: *...no justice, no appeal.*

(Gavel)

Part 3

(Kim) VOICE: *After foster care...*

(All) CHORUS: *...we're still out here, trying to survive.*

(Ed) JUDGE: *How are you doing? What is happening in your life?*

(Kim): *I don't trust men.*

(Laura): *I'm down on myself.*

(Curt): *I have bad dreams and flashbacks.*

(Imelda): *I have a hard time trusting anybody.*

(Letty): *I have nightmares of the abuse.*

(Sabrina): *I shy away from social activities. I'm afraid people won't like me.*

(Tony): *I'm terrified of sex—afraid to do anything with anyone.*

(Carrie): *When I get in a car, I grab the handle and won't talk.*

(Kim): *I lost a lot of faith.*

(Laura): *I'm afraid to let people know, because they might take advantage of me.*

(Curt): *I still worry my girlfriend will find out—and then blame me.*

(Imelda): I have a basic distrust of all men.

(Letty): I have learned never to depend on anyone but myself. I watch men closely and won't let them come near my child.

(Sabrina): I am warning my daughter never to trust a man.

(Tony): I still worry that people will find out.

(Carrie): I wear loose clothes so no one can notice my body.

(Kim): I have low self-esteem and am self-conscious.

(Laura): I've been conditioned to take abuse from people, and it's become a way of life. It's hard to be independent when you feel powerless.

(Curt): I feel bad about myself.

(Imelda): It's ruined my entire life and relationships with men. I can't seem to love anyone.

(Letty): I'm scared to have someone love me.

(Sabrina): My abuse has messed up my life.

(Tony): I try really hard not to let it affect me.

(Carrie): I have emotional problems. I can't understand why my dad did it and why my mom wouldn't believe me. I lost my spiritual life.

(Kim): I wake up in a cold sweat. I have nightmares that my dad is in my room.

(Laura): I'm still a mess. I totally block out sexually.

(Curt): I don't believe in God anymore.

(Imelda): Just that once it's over, you will never forget it.

(Letty): The hardest thing for me today is knowing my mom never believed me and we can't ever be friends.

(Sabrina): You'd better believe I'll protect my children.

(Tony): When I get touched in a certain way it brings back bad memories.

(Carrie): I'm beginning to think there is no God.

(Kim): I'm all messed up. I never knew right from wrong. All I knew was sex, sex, sex—since I was 3. I cry a lot. I'm on lithium for my depression.

(Laura): I turned to God because he's the only one who can help me.

(Curt): It's now affecting my marriage and family. If there is somebody who can keep in touch with me I would be grateful.

(Ed) JUDGE: How do you feel the system helped or didn't help you?

(Laura): I finally learned to use my therapy, but it takes time to let yourself feel the pain and go on with your life. It never goes away, but eventually it gets easier. Therapy helped me feel less insecure and less needy. Now I can look back, reflect on it, pity the men, and wonder why.

(Tony): I was sad that I split my family up, but I had a better life without my mom and dad with me. I didn't get hit or touched and I had food on the table.

(Sabrina): I'd like to see my stepfather fry. What he did to me when I was just a baby is worthy of a painful death, and the other men that abused me should get their just due. I fear for my children.

(Imelda): My mother and I never got reunited, even though we both wanted to. My caseworker lied to me and my mother, playing one against the other. Mom was an alcoholic and pretty messed up, but she straightened out. Now I think we both feel we missed the chance to have a relationship together.

(Curt): Years in hospitals and lots of counseling was very helpful. I'm upset that my dad didn't receive any counseling. I think he is very sick and I feel sorry for him. Sometimes I even miss him, but I have to think about myself.

(Letty): When you are abused at a young age by people who are supposed to be protecting you, it places a huge bar-

rier in your mind. It doesn't allow you to perform to the best of your ability because you don't want to take any chances. It's an overwhelming feeling of betrayal. The abuse by a babysitter, a friend of my mom's, and, most horrifying of all, my adoptive father, affected my judgment toward all men. I can't trust them. But I still feel I have become stronger overall and more loving and caring. And, I still live a perfectly normal life. No matter what you've been through, you still make the decisions in your life. It will always be your life, and you have to make it what you want it to be. I've tried to do that and I'm very proud of who I am now.

(Carrie): As far as the family members and boyfriends of my mother who abused me, I can only feel sorry for all of them and for the young girls they might do it to in the future. I do feel some anger, but not a lot. I have gotten past that through therapy. Every time I talk about it I think it helps me more.

(Gavel)

(Kim) VOICE: Why, why were these children not protected?

(All) CHORUS: There is no safe place, no justice, no appeal.

(Kim) VOICE: Where are the lines of right and wrong if our abusers had none?

(All) CHORUS: There is no safe place, no justice, no appeal.

(Kim) VOICE: Why were we punished while our abusers went free?

(All) CHORUS: There is no safe place, no justice, no appeal. Why, why were these children not protected?

(Gavel)

Epilogue

(Ed) JUDGE: I'm troubled, deeply troubled by what I've heard today. We've tried everything—we have laws, we have social workers—and nothing seems to work. We don't seem to be able to protect our children, either in their own homes or in placement. Now, I am asking you, what do you think we should do? What can we do?

(All) CHORUS: Nobody ever asked us what we think.

(Ed) JUDGE: Well, I am asking you now...

(Kim): I think the perpetrators should be the ones removed from the home, not always the child. Perpetrators are sexually dangerous to the health and safety of others. I say, if they have broken the law, they ought to be put in jail.

(Curt): I think counseling should be mandated for the perpetrators while in jail. Abusers who have broken the law need treatment while in jail and after they have been released; they should be put on probation with ongoing supervision.

(Laura): I agree. And then there should be counseling for the entire family.

(Letty): Plea-bargaining should not be allowed as a way to avoid punishment for child abuse. Too often they continue the abuse and refuse treatment, and get away with it too. For the victims, there is no appeal.

(Sabrina): Yeah, and what about justice when the offender serves no sentence and refuses treatment?

(Tony): What about me? I'm almost 25 and still having trouble handling what happened to me. We need ongoing help after we leave placement.

(Carrie): I would like to see some reaching out to us after we leave the system. Some of us are going to need more help than we've received so far. Don't wait for us to ask for help, reach out to us and let us know what resources are available.

(Imelda): Maybe counseling for victims like us would be more helpful if done by survivors. They know what it's like and can give us the benefit of how they are trying to straighten out their lives.

(Ed) JUDGE: These are all good suggestions. Does anybody have any further ideas?

(Tony): Yes. I do, your Honor. With all due respect, I would like to suggest that the court system is also a big part of the problem and therefore, should also be a part of the solution.

(Sabrina): Studies show that girls are more likely to be removed from the family home than boys. Since the final decision regarding removal from home is made by the court, I would like to know why girls are taken out of their home more often than boys?

(Imelda): Crimes committed against family members by family members are still crimes—in most cases, they are felonies. I don't think the court is tough enough on the perpetrators of child abuse crimes.

(Ed) JUDGE: I will pass your suggestions on at our annual judges' conference next month. Have you any further thoughts on family violence before we adjourn?

(Sabrina): Yes, your Honor. Before we can make a dent in solving the problems of family violence, we must look at two notions that persist in America today. One is that women and children are like property and owned by males who see themselves as lord and master of the home.

(Tony): The second is the right of a man to do anything he pleases in the privacy of his own home. This means that any act of violence committed in the home is a family matter and not the business of the state. As long as acts of violence are inflicted on family members by family members in the family home, family violence and child abuse will persist.

(Imelda): As long as these notions remain acceptable to society, there will never be a solution to child abuse.

(All) CHORUS: There will never be a safe place, justice, or appeal.

(Ed and All) JUDGE and CHORUS: *(turning to the audience, with emphasis)* What do you think?

(Ed) JUDGE: This meeting is adjourned!

(Gavel)

About the Author and Contributors

Author

Edmund V. Mech, PhD, Indiana University, MSW, Bryn Mawr, is Professor Emeritus, School of Social Work, University of Illinois at Urbana-Champaign; Director/Principal Investigator, Foster Youth-in-Transition Project; and Director, Evaluation Unit, National Adoption Awareness Training Project, National Council for Adoption. He has received research awards from Lilly Endowment, Inc., the William T. Grant Foundation, and the Children's Bureau, U.S. Department of Health and Human Services. Former appointments include: Guest Scholar, Brookings Institution; Guest Scholar, Institute of Politics, Harvard University; Visiting Scholar, London School of Economics; Member, Employment and Training Panel, National Academy of Sciences; and Member, National Commission on Foster Care, Child Welfare League of America. Formerly, he was Director of the Research Center, Social Work and Social Research, Bryn Mawr College; Director, Regional Research Institute, Youth Development & Delinquency Project, Portland State University; and Director, Arizona Welfare Study, sponsored by the Arizona State Legislature and conducted at Arizona State University.

Contributors

Hewitt B. "Rusty" Clark, PhD, has developed and researched various innovative programs over the course of his professional career. He is a Professor in the Department of Child and Family Studies at the University of South Florida. Dr. Clark has three books and more than 85 publications. Dr. Clark's current research interest is evaluating the effectiveness of individualized intervention processes for children with emotional and behavioral difficulties. He is studying the transition to independent living for youth and young adults with emotional and behavioral difficulties and positive behavioral support strategies for at-risk children in foster care and their families. Dr. Clark provides training and consultation related to positive behavioral supports, person-centered planning, and behaviorally based intervention strategies for facilitating the transition of youth and young adults into employment, educational opportunities, and independent living.

Carrie C. Fung, MSW, JD, is currently serving as Assistant Public Guardian at the Cook County Office of the Public Guardian. She represents abused and neglected children involved with the child welfare system as their attorney and guardian ad litem. She received a JD from Loyola University of Chicago School of Law, with certification in child and family law through the ChildLaw Program. She received an MSW at the University of Illinois at Urbana-Champaign with a concentration in administration and child welfare. While at the University of Illinois, Ms. Fung was appointed as a Lois and Samuel Silberman scholar in child welfare and worked as a research associate on the Foster Youth Project at the University of Illinois at Urbana-Champaign.

Betsy Krebs, JD, is cofounder and Executive Director of Youth Advocacy Center, Inc., in New York, NY, which teaches teens in foster care to advocate for themselves and take control of their lives. Ms. Krebs is an Individual Project Fellow of the Open Society Institute. She graduated from Harvard Law School. She worked as an attorney representing foster care children in Manhattan Family Court. She has authored articles and publications about self-advocacy and for and about teenagers in foster care.

Mark Kroner, MSW, is Director of the Division of Self-Sufficiency Services for Lighthouse Youth Services, Cincinnati, OH. Mr. Kroner serves on the National Independent Living Standards Committee of the Child

Welfare League of America and the Ohio State Independent Living Task Force. He is a licensed social worker and has worked in the field as a social worker, group home director, group trainer, and consultant. Mark received a BA in psychology in 1973 and an MSW in June 1997. Mr. Kroner received the National Independent Living Association's Founder's Award in 2000.

Elizabeth L. Leonard, MSW, University of Minnesota, is Research Associate/Follow-up Coordinator, Foster Youth-in-Transition Project, University of Illinois; Coinvestigator, Mentors for Adolescents-in-Placement; author of Friendly Rebel: E. C. Lindeman, Social Philosopher, Adamant Press; and Field Coordinator, Evaluation Unit, National Adoption Awareness Training Project, National Council for Adoption.

Janet Legler Luft, LMSW-AP, is Preparation for Adult Living State Program Coordinator for the Texas Department of Protective and Regulatory Services in Austin, TX. She has a BS in education from the University of Texas at Austin. She has provided state and national workshops on independent living issues, and she serves on the Board of the National Independent Living Association.

Dagmar Moravec, MSC, has been coordinating the Ingham County Wraparound Initiative in Lansing, MI, since 1994. She also teaches criminal justice courses on juveniles and their families at Lansing Community College. Ms. Moravec has a master's degree in counseling from the University of Scranton, PA.

Michael Olenick, PhD, is Division Chief for Emancipation Services at the Los Angeles County Department of Children and Family Services. He was Senior Vice President for the Community College Foundation from 1987 until February 2002. During those 15 years, he created the independent living program and the Early Start to Emancipation Program, which connected Los Angeles Department of Children and Family Services–supervised foster youth with community colleges.

Paul Pitcoff, JD, is cofounder and Director of Education at the Youth Advocacy Center, New York, NY. Prior to receiving his law degree from Cardozo School of Law, Mr. Pitcoff was Founding Chair of the Department of Communications at Adelphi University. For more than 20 years, he guided the development of the academic program from its inception to its establishment as a department in the College of Arts and Sciences.

Mr. Pitcoff was an active filmmaker, producing and directing more than 25 award-winning documentaries for various national and local organizations.

Lora Schmid-Dolan, MSW, is a Prevention Specialist at the Daggett Middle School, Fort Worth, TX, Independent School District. She has worked as a family violence counselor for developmentally disabled and mentally ill adults and as a research coordinator. While at the University of Illinois at Urbana-Champaign, Ms. Schmid-Dolan worked with the Foster Youth Project and conducted the 10-year follow-up interviews with former foster youth.